Turkey's Integration into the European Union

Turkey's Integration into the European Union

Legal Dimension

Edited by Belgin Akçay and Şebnem Akipek

LEXINGTON BOOKS
Lanham • Boulder • New York • Toronto • Plymouth, UK

Published by Lexington Books
A wholly owned subsidiary of The Rowman & Littlefield Publishing Group, Inc.
4501 Forbes Boulevard, Suite 200, Lanham, Maryland 20706
www.rowman.com

10 Thornbury Road, Plymouth PL6 7PP, United Kingdom

British Library Cataloguing in Publication Information Available

Library of Congress Cataloging-in-Publication Data

Library of Congress Cataloging-in-Publication Data Available

ISBN 978-0-7391-8174-4 (cloth : alk. paper) -- ISBN 978-0-7391-8175-1 (electronic)

∞™ The paper used in this publication meets the minimum requirements of American National Standard for Information Sciences Permanence of Paper for Printed Library Materials, ANSI/NISO Z39.48-1992.

Printed in the United States of America

Table of Contents

Introduction

Relations of Turkey with the European Union have a very long history. It is nearly a fifty-year story. Officially it started with the famous Ankara Agreement. The exact meaning of Ankara Agreement is the Agreement Creating an Association between the Republic of Turkey and the European Economic Community. It was signed in 1963; following the signing of this Agreement there have been many steps in the relations. In the doctrine some authors compare these relations to a turbulent marriage. Though there are many different problems in this relation, it may be regarded as an ongoing relation and both parties manage to stay together.

As it is believed by most of the scholars, Turkey presents both a huge challenge on one side and also a great opportunity on the other side for the EU. But at the same time from the Turkish perspective the EU also constitutes a dilemma. Turkey is a huge country and has a growing population. The cultural and religious character is also quite unique considering the other member states. Being a member will help Turkey to ensure the democratization process. But especially when the current economic situation of the EU is considered and the Eurozone is taken into account, being a member may not be beneficial both for Turkey and the EU. On the other hand there are contrary views stating that now it is more crucial for both sides to become a member.

For becoming a member of the EU there are certain requirements and these requirements to become a member have been extended hugely, especially in the last decade. Therefore Turkey has to fulfilll these requirements if she wants to be a full member. The accession negotiations with Turkey started on October 3, 2005. Though there have been certain domestic and external problems these negotiations still continue. To accede to the EU, Turkey should first of all complete the negotiations with the European Commission on thirty-five chapters of the acquis communautaire. In other words the total body of EU law should be harmonized.

As the legal harmonization is the initial step to become a member, the aim of this book is to give a general view about Turkish Law and to compare certain fields of law with EU Law. In order to reach this aim first of all an overview of Turkey-EU relations will be given. Following that, Turkey's ability to assume the obligations of EU membership in the economic, political, and legal spheres shall be discussed. Two important fields of law, namely consumer protection law and competition law shall be considered, and also the new developments in these fields and their relation to EU Law shall be examined. One of the most important fears of EU is most probably the population of Turkey and the workers who work in EU countries and how this number may be increased with Turkey's accession. The principle of non-discrimination on grounds of nationality with regard to Turkish workers is an important discussion topic and again in this book this topic shall be discussed in detail. The role and the competence of the European Court of Justice will also be another subject taken into consideration.

As the authors of this book we aim to draw a framework regarding Turkish Law and enable the readers to learn about Turkish Law. It could easily be stated that though there are certain points to be completed, most aspects of Turkish Law are in harmony with EU Law. Turkey has taken many important steps in the past fifty-year history with the EU and especially from the legal perspective has fulfilled most of the important goals. We hope that after reading the articles in this book our readers will also have a vision of this development and Turkish Law as well.

Şebnem Akipek
Ankara, December 15, 2012

Chapter One

Changing Dynamics of Turkey-EU Relations

Belgin Akçay and Derya Büyüktanır

INTRODUCTION

Although the date of Turkey's application to European Economic Community (EEC) for association goes back to 1959, the establishment of relations with the Western countries is much older. The process of Turkish society opening up to the West began at the last phase of the Ottoman Empire[1] and continued until after the establishment of the new Turkish State in 1923 following the dispersion of the Ottoman Empire.

Turkey has always desired to be counted among the western countries, and has shaped its policies according to this aim. This modernization and westernization movement has attracted attention, particularly in the fields of foreign policy and the economy. Turkey's desire to westernize, and to join western institutions has arisen as a result of these efforts. Westernization has been understood not only as reaching the western countries' level of development in respect to the economy, science, and technology, but also creating a secular and democratic political order.[2] As a matter of fact, the demand to participate in the European Union (previously European Economic Community, then European Community) was perceived as a continuation of this line, and Turkey applied for associate membership of the EEC before many European countries.

On the other hand, it appears that even though economic and cultural reasons constituted the basis of the relations between Turkey and the European Union (EU) that began at the end of the 1950s, during that period, security problems and political issues were the most important factors. Russia's quest to control the Turkish Straits to reach the warm seas via the Black

Sea, has continued since the eighteenth century, and resulted in permanent pressure on Turkey. The Soviet Union's quests posed an important threat for Turkey, which resulted in Turkey deciding to align itself with the Western countries, including the USA, during the Cold War period.

Turkey is in a different position than the other candidate countries due to its significantly higher population, the majority of which is Muslim; its geographical position; its foreign policy; and its security perception. These differences have affected greatly, and continue to affect, the development of relations between Turkey and the EU. As a country always aimed at adopting European cultural and political values, Turkey may provide Europe with a new vision, and therefore should not be left out of the integration process.

This section of the book briefly analyzes the development of the relations between the Republic of Turkey and the EU. The historical development of Turkey-EU relations will be explained by taking into consideration the internal and external dynamics of Turkey and the EU, and the framework of basic documents, such as the Ankara Agreement, the Additional Protocol, Decision No 1/95 of the EC-Turkey Association Council and the Accession Partnership and Copenhagen Criteria. In this context, the relations between Turkey and the EU are analyzed in three different periods. The first period begins with the application for association and ends with the application for full membership (1959-1987); the second period begins with the application for full membership and ends with the customs union (1987 and 1996); and the third one explains the period after the Customs Union.

FROM APPLICATION FOR ASSOCIATION TO THE APPLICATION FOR FULL MEMBERSHIP (1959–1987)

Turkey applied to the European Economic Community (EEC) on July 31, 1959 according to the articles of the Treaty of Rome, to create a relation of association. At the end of 1950s, this application was made primarily because of security problems. Liberal Western democracies have created some organizational formations due, first, to the efforts to rebuild Europe, which was destroyed during the World War II, and, second, as a deterrent to the "Soviet threat" that arose after the war. Turkey has participated in all of these organizations. Turkey is one of the founding members of the Organization for European Economic Co-operation (OEEC)[3] founded in the context of the Marshall Plan. The Council of Europe was founded in 1949, and Turkey became its member after two months. Turkey became a member of NATO after a very short time of its foundation. Indeed, the EEC is an organization founded to bring forth the economic integration against the Soviet threat as well as presenting as a project which would provide peace and security among Western European countries. The difference of the EEC from the other organizations was that it was created by an institutional formation that was very well planned and which paved the way for transferring some economic authorities of member countries to supranational institutions. Turkey had preferred to take part in the Western Block in that period and regarded the EEC in the same context with other organizations founded in Europe.

Moreover, Greece was also an important factor for Turkey in the application for the associate membership of the EEC. The conflicts began after mid 1950s between the two countries and resulted in Turkey's deliberate policy against Greece. Thus, Turkey has decided to take part in the Western Block at the same time as Greece so as to prevent Greece from producing policies against Turkey. Turkey applied the same year for association immediately after Greece applied to the EEC on May 15, 1959.

Turkey applied to become a member of the EEC due to economical and political reasons. In the first half of the 1950s, the foreign aid and foreign capital investments were increased. Yet, in the second half of the same decade, the foreign trade balance was disrupted and a shortage in foreign currency started in Turkey due to a decrease in the prices of agricultural products in the international markets, since a majority of its exports were agricultural products. Increase in public expenditures resulted in budget deficits, high inflation, a foreign trade deficit, and a high level of government debt at the end of the 1950s in Turkey. These were difficult years for the country and these problems have resulted in returning to import substitution policies.

Developing economic relations with European countries, particularly with the founding members of the EEC, accounting for a large portion of Turkey's foreign trade was crucial at the end of the 1950s. Geographic proximity was also a factor that made trade with these countries attractive. Moreover, Turkey wanted this partnership with the hope that the EEC would provide foreign credit, and regarded the EEC countries as a source of new credit lines, especially after relations with the USA became strained.

The "Agreement Creating an Association between the Republic of Turkey and the European Economic Community (Ankara Agreement)"[4] was signed on September 12, 1963, and this agreement came into force on December 1, 1964 as a result of negotiations after Turkey's application in 1959.[5] This agreement was based on the establishment of a customs union between Turkey and the EEC. Turkey viewed the Athens Agreement as an example at the beginning of the negotiations for Turkey's association agreement to the EEC. The Athens Agreement was signed between Greece and the EEC in 1961 and its focus was economic integration based on the customs union between Greece and the EEC. Article 28 of the Ankara Agreement[6] states that: "The process of the Agreement clarifies that Turkey may undertake all the obligations stemming from the Agreement Creating the Community, and contracting parties analyze the possibility of Turkey's accession to the Community."

These expressions demonstrate that the Agreement's final aim was Turkey's full membership. Although both sides are obliged to assess the possibility of accession if the association proves to be successful, this article cannot be interpreted as an automatic transmission on the completion of the time-table lay down by the Ankara Agreement or a guarantee of admission for membership even if the fulfilllment of the conditions becomes evident. On the other hand, this Agreement aimed to prepare Turkey, as a partner country, for full membership through gradual economic integration, and it is important to note that this feature differs from the other agreements of association.[7] The aim of the Agreement was given as "Ensuring a continuous improvement in living conditions in Turkey and in the European Economic Community through accelerated economic progress, the harmonious expansion of trade, and to reduce the disparity between the Turkish economy and the economies of the Member States of the Community." The establishment of the customs union was envisaged at three stages: preparation, transition, and the final stage.[8]

During the preparation period of five years, Turkey would strengthen its economic structure with the aid of the Community in order to carry out its obligations that it undertook in the transition and final stages.[9] Turkey did not undertake an obligation in the preparation period. The "Transition Period," which spanned twelve years (excluding some exceptional reservations), began with the enforcement of the Additional Protocol that consists of 64 articles. Primarily, the schedule of the transition period was prepared according to the articles of the Additional Protocol. Turkey removed internal obstacles and the parties gradually established a customs union, with respect to the principle of bilateral and balanced obligations.[10] Turkey, according to the obligations it undertook, would first reduce the custom duties for imported industrial goods within twelve to twenty–two years gradually and finally reducing the duty to zero. It also has to adopt itself to the Common Customs Tariff of the Community in this way, while the Community would abolish all customs duties and charges having equivalent effect all at once. As a matter of fact, the Community fulfilled all its obligations two years before the enforcement of the Additional Protocol. Moreover, a new regime was developed that changed the structure of Turkish foreign trade. According to the principles of the new regime, Turkey would make deductions with respect to the years, as well as some implementations. Additionally, a Financial Protocol was arranged in order to help Turkey to fulfilll these obligations. According to the provisions of the Ankara Agreement, the "Final Stage," based on a customs union between Turkey and the EC, was to begin after the completion of the transition stage. The goal was to strengthen the economic policy cooperation during this stage, whose duration was not clarified and was left to the parties to decide.

Due to economic and political problems in the 1970s, Turkey could not fulfilll its obligations defined in the Additional Protocol, which outlines the modifications in the Ankara Agreement. On the other hand, Turkey encountered different problems after the accession of new countries to the Community. Although the coup d'état on March 12, 1971 did not result in frozen relations between Turkey and the EC, it increased negative discourse against Turkey among the public in many counties in Europe and in the European Parliament.[11] Nevertheless, Turkey has unilaterally frozen the fulfilllment of all obligations that arose from the Protocol of December 25, 1976.[12] The dates concerning tariff reductions designated in the Protocol changed. Great efforts were made to improve relations with the EC at the end of the 1970s. Yet another military takeover on September 12, 1980 suspended relations once again. The tension between Turkey and the EC resulted in Turkey's estrangement from the process of membership. The European public adopted a negative attitude towards Turkey immediately after the military takeover yet relations with EC were not broken after this coup d'état. Some EC members (France, Netherlands, and Denmark) assumed a negative attitude against Turkey, while others adopted the view that the army carried out a military takeover in order to stabilize democracy in Turkey. On the other hand, different views were defended in the European Parliament during the same period. Some of the members of Parliament criticized Turkey and demanded the suspension of relations with Turkey. Conservative and liberal deputies, on the contrary, opposed the views of the socialist and communist deputies.[13] The most important difference of this period from the 2000s is that some of the strong European countries showed a positive attitude in favor of Turkey.

However, some factors negatively affected the relations between Turkey and the EC in the last months of 1981. PASOK (The PanHellenic Socialist Movement) came to power in Greece, and Israel and the Jewish lobby did not support Turkey as a reaction to Turkey's developing warmer relations with the Arab countries. The activities of refugees that went to European countries from Turkey were highly negative towards Turkey. The Financial Protocol was suspended due to continued negative attitudes in the European Parliament and financial aid that was stipulated for Turkey was blocked. The relations between Turkey and the EC continued to be strained for a long time. Because, the civil government that took office following the military takeover pursued cooler policies towards the EC, not only did Greece increase its negative attitudes against Turkey (after it attained full membership to the EC), but Germany also did not want Turkey's membership due to worker movements. Consequently, the Association Council could not meet for a certain time, and the increasing economic problems in Turkey during the same period led to freezing of the relations between Turkey and the EC completely.[14] However, normalization began in the mid-1980s, and the EC-Turkey Association Council finally met in September 1986.

During the 1980s, the Community itself also experienced important developments. Portugal and Spain became members of the EC in 1986 after Greece became a full member in 1981. The new wave of globalization that began in the early 1980s also led to a review of the process of economic integration by the EC. This process underwent serious revision after the adoption of the Single European Act (SEA), which was the first major attempt made by member states to amend the arrangements made in the Treaty of Rome. Through the SEA, enforced in 1987, the EC aimed at a transition to a higher level of political and economic integration and preparations to establish a Single European Market began to accelerate.

Turkey applied for full EC membership on April 14, 1987, with the aim of reviving its relations under the influence of domestic developments and in foreign markets.[15] This application was of great importance in improving relations that deteriorated due to Turkey's failure to fulfilll its obligations. Financial aid stipulated to Turkey was not granted due to strained relations after the military takeover. Moreover, Greece, Spain, and Portugal were members of NATO, but not members of the EC, and these countries were economically less developed than the founding members of the Community. These factors resulted in a defensive feeling of insecurity and shortcoming. After these developments, Turkey decided to apply to the EC.

Most Turkish people received this application positively, while the UK and Belgium reacted to Turkey's application modestly. Yet many EC member countries, primarily Greece, regarded this application as an ill-timed initiative. The Council handed over the application to the European Commission, and the evaluation period of the European Commission was very long. The decision of the European Commission was announced on December 18, 1989.[16] The Commission accepted Turkey's competence in respect to its membership to the EC. Yet it stated that Turkey is inadequate in its economic, social, and political aspects. Moreover, it was stated that the EU was not in a position to accept new members due to efforts to deepen the integration, and it was proposed that Turkey should wait for the completion of the customs union process and the next enlargement. Specific concerns addressed by the commission were: "In the particular case of Turkey, these two aspects are all the more significant in that Turkey is a large country—it has a greater geographical area and will eventually have a bigger population than any Community Member State and its general level of development is substantially lower than the European average."[17] There were other factors that influenced the suspension of the application, in addition to the reasons explained above. First, an accelerated transformation began in the Central and Eastern European Countries (CEECs) in the late 1980s, and the Berlin Wall collapsed in 1989. The integration of the former "Eastern Block" countries to the West became one of the priorities of the EC under these conditions. Therefore, the accession of these countries to the Community would generate an additional financial burden on the Community's budget. Moreover integration in the Community and transition to liberal system were necessary for these countries that were governed under central planning for many decades. Significant and requisite financial support by the EC was necessary for systemic change in the CEECs. Since full membership of as great a country as Turkey would generate an additional financial burden, which would seriously affect the budget of the EC, and consequently, the European Commission postponed the full membership of Turkey.[18] The other reason was that Turkey's strategic importance against the expansion of communism during the Cold War disappeared. The Cold War was over, and the Soviet Union and CEECs were no longer threats for the West. Consequently, Turkey was no longer as strategically important against threats from these countries as it was during the Cold War years. Turkey's role has started to be defined as a "bridge" between Eastern and Western civilizations.[19]

FROM APPLICATION FOR FULL MEMBERSHIP TO THE CUSTOMS UNION (1987-1996)

During the 1990s, not only economic and monetary developments, but also some political developments occurred in the EU. In this period, relations between Turkey and the EU were influenced not only by the reasons mentioned above, but also by identity discussions all over Europe. This change was mostly experienced in Central and Eastern Europe at the beginning of the 1990s, and identity debates were intensified in many member countries. Some member countries of the Union claimed that Turkey was not a European country by stressing the importance of differences especially in religion. As a matter of fact, the EU started to include normative fields, such as human rights and minority problems more frequently[20] when an important step was taken about the new members, according to the provisions of the Treaty on the European Union (Maastricht Treaty).[21] The necessary conditions for accession to the EU were clarified in the 49th and 2nd Articles of the Treaty on the European Union (TEU)[22] and the conditions for full membership in the EU were stated at the Copenhagen Summit on June 21-22, 1993. Membership criteria mentioned in the related documents, such as the Copenhagen criteria, were critical and provided a clear framework, which the conditions for the candidate countries would be executed. The Copenhagen criteria consist of three groups, including political, economic, and acceptance of the Community acquis criteria, defined as:

- Political Criteria: stability of institutions guaranteeing democracy, a constitutional state, human rights, and respect for and protection of minorities;

- Economic Criteria: existence of a functioning market economy and the capacity to cope with competitive pressure and market forces within the Union;
- Acceptance of the Community acquis: ability to take on the obligations of membership, including adherence to the aims of political, economic, and monetary union.

Political criteria had special importance. If a candidate country did not fulfilll the political criteria, which were in fact a condition for initiating the accession negotiations on membership to the Union, it was impossible to become a full member.[23] The EU designates a detailed pre-accession strategy for countries to become a member and outlines that these countries are consequently required to fulfilll the Copenhagen criteria, and complete the Accession Partnership, National Program Progress Reports, and financial aid programs. Additionally, it provides for the continuation of the process towards full membership through accession negotiations. As a result, the dimension of relations between Turkey and the EU started to change in the 1990s.

On the other hand, the TEU included other changes that directly influenced relations between Turkey and the EU. For instance, the role of the European Parliament became more important as its legislative and supervisory powers increased with the introduction of the co-decision procedure and extension of the cooperation procedure. Considering the fact that Parliament had a negative position on many issues related to Turkey this meant the process would became more difficult. Furthermore, the Western European Union (WEU) was made a complementary part of common foreign affairs and of the security policy of the EU. Turkey was asked to become an associate member of the WEU, but would not have the right to speak on foreign policy and security fields in the EU decision-making mechanisms. This meant that Turkey, as a strong associate, would be excluded for a long time from defense and security policy areas.

All of these changes in the early 1990s also changed the membership conditions for Turkey to the EU. Moreover, after the 1989 Commission report, the EU decided to maintain its relations with Turkey on the customs union level, and doing so gave prominence to the customs union. Then, the Conclusion of the Presidency European Council in Copenhagen Summit stressed and demanded that relations with Turkey be maintained on the basis of a customs union. Also, it was emphasized, for the first time, that CEECs might become candidate countries. Thus, the EU proposed to maintain relations with Turkey on the customs union level, namely, on a lower level of integration rather than partnership aimed at full membership as stated in the 28th Article of the Ankara Agreement. The relations between Turkey and the EU were frozen after the Commission's report. The Association Council did not meet until 1992 in regard to the relations between Turkey and the EC.

On the other hand, negative attitudes against Turkey in the European Parliament began to harden after the conviction of the nine Democracy Party (DEP) deputies in 1994. The European Parliament approved a decision regarding the human rights and democracy violations in Turkey that were voiced, and recommended that the customs union be suspended, and decisions on the Parliament's approval process of the customs union were stipulated.[24] The tension between Turkey and Greece continued during these years, and clear messages began to be relayed that the Union would not accept new members in the short run.

Despite the negative developments, Turkey decided that it would continue its decisive attitude of reviving its relations with the Union and continue to work without deviating from the membership perspective. Meanwhile, the customs union became an important internal policy subject of Turkey because it was regarded as an important step for membership in the EU and would contribute to the economy of the country. Expectations grew for a more disciplined economy, for the promotion of the standards of Turkish goods, for facilitating the entrance to European markets, and for an increasing standard of living. This meant that Turkey would have a larger and stable foreign market, and thus the country would be stronger. As a result, Turkey increased its efforts to establish the customs union for both political and economic reasons. After serious deliberations in the European Parliament, the customs union between Turkey and the EU came into force on January 1, 1996 according to the Decision of the Association Council no. 1/95,[25] made at the Turkey-EU Association Council meeting on March 6, 1995. The customs union with the EU has also sparked a lively debate inside Turkey as nationalist sections of the society were adamantly against it, on the grounds that it would benefit the EU.

The customs union constitutes one of the most important phases of Turkey's integration to the EU.[26] The decision of the Turkey-EU Association Council received a positive response from the Turkish public, and even some circles stated that full membership had become guaranteed with the customs union. However, for the EU the customs union for industrial goods was only one part of the partnership relation and it was insufficient on its own for membership.

POST-CUSTOMS UNION PERIOD

After establishing the customs union, the European Parliament continued its negative attitude towards Turkey particularly regarding its human rights violations and problems in democratic practices. Additionally, while the EU accelerated its efforts on widening and deepening integration, it simultaneously enacted many regulations required by this process. This resulted in the

EU ignoring Turkey's membership application due to its concerns for deepening and enlargement. The most significant indication of this was the Agenda 2000 Report,[27] which was announced by the European Commission before the Luxembourg Summit on July 16, 1997 and included the EU's enlargement plans. The report clearly stated that Turkey had failed to fulfilll the criteria required for candidacy.

At the Luxembourg Summit, it was stressed that Turkey had the capacity for membership but failed to fulfilll the economic and political criterion. While the EU granted candidacy to the CEECs, Turkey was excluded from this process. The CEECs, which had been in the process of transition to a liberal system and were economically weaker, compared to Turkey, were included in the enlargement process, while Turkey, which had already gone through such a transition, was not included in this process. This fact was widely publicized in the national and international media. Unlike the EU's decision in 1989, the Turkish government perceived this second rejection as a clear case of discrimination.[28] Hence, the government of Turkey suspended political negotiations with the EU and stated that it would not participate in the European Conference that would be held the following year. In this way, relations accelerated until the 1997 Luxembourg Summit, were once again strained after the EU's disapproval of Turkey's status as a candidate. Despite the serious rupture in political relations, the customs union established between Turkey and the EU continued to operate. Furthermore, at the Cardiff Summit in 1998, a definition of Turkey's candidacy was created that had a positive slant, whereas at the Vienna Summit, negative expressions similar to those used at the Luxembourg Summit were restated. Then, the European Strategy for Turkey was published on March 4, 1998[29] and Turkey's eligibility for accession was once more stated. The strategy asserted that greater dialogue was needed in many fields such as industrial cooperation, participation of certain programmes and agencies, customs union, liberalization of capital movement, agriculture, and transport. This strategy paper was criticized because of its weakness that it was too one-dimensional as it focused on mostly the financial issues and customs union.[30]

In the post-customs union period while such developments occurred, important changes were also taking place in the EU. The Union continued to enlarge on one hand, and on the other, accelerated its efforts for deepening. The EU, considering the needs of both widening and deepening in the integration processes, made more amendments on the main treaties than previous periods. The Treaty of Amsterdam in 1997,[31] the Treaty of Nice in 2001,[32] and the Treaty of Lisbon (Reform Agreement)[33] in 2007 were signed. The Treaty of Lisbon entered into force on December 1, 2009,[34] after Netherlands and France resulted in a negative vote on European Constitution. The primary aims of the amendments made in the EU's basic agreements were: the EU's integration on a deeper level; rendering the mechanism of the EU more efficient and transparent; creating a more democratic structure; ensuring that the EU's structure is capable of protecting national interests; and creating a stronger voice for Europe in the international arena.

After establishing the customs union relations, a positive step for the membership of Turkey could be taken only in the final years of the 1990s. For the first time, EU member countries started to adopt a positive attitude towards Turkey's membership. This change in attitudes by the member countries primarily occurred because of external dynamics. The new government in Greece[35] initiated a more modest policy towards Turkey. Relations further developed after the devastating earthquake in Turkey in 1999 and lobbying activities influenced this policy change in Greece.[36] On the other hand, German foreign policy during Chancellor Schroeder was different from Chancellor Kohl. The new government in Germany was ideologically in favor of a more pluralistic structure and stressed that a country that was culturally different must not be excluded. After this political change, the German public adopted a more positive opinion towards Turkey. Nevertheless, Turkey's strategic position was the main factor in this change. Turkey's position in foreign policy became more important in this period, due to its veto power in NATO. Turkey was the second largest country in NATO and its geo-strategic location made Turkey an important player in terms of EU-NATO cooperation. Especially in view of the country's geographical proximity to existing and potential crisis areas, Turkey wielded its "veto power" in NATO to block the EU's access to NATO assets unless direct influence on all EU decision-making concerning matters affecting its security interests was guaranteed. Moreover, the USA's initiative and support for Turkey's membership increased.[37] Simultaneously, the importance of Turkey's geographical position came to light in regard to the Union's energy policies.[38] Positive developments in Turkey's economy and the capture of Abdullah Öcalan were regarded as important events by the EU.[39]

These positive developments were partially reflected in the Progress Reports[40] and included the statement that even though Turkey did not fulfilll all of the Copenhagen criteria, the country has a functioning market economy to a large extent.[41] The political atmosphere, generated in favor of Turkey, continued during the Helsinki Summit that was held on December 10-11, 1999, and a new period began in the relations between Turkey and the EU after Turkey assumed "candidate status." Thus, Turkey was in an equal position to the other candidate countries, would benefit from the pre-accession strategy, and participate in the EU programs and agencies.

Helsinki conclusions were highlighting the political matters that could make membership more complicated. Turkey was asked to solve the Cyprus problem and its outstanding border disputes with the help of the International Court of Justice.[42] Turkey did not accept any links between the efforts to find a solution to the Cyprus issue and its candidacy to the EU and stated that the

Cyprus issue was a problem between the Turkish Republic of Northern Cyprus and the Greek Cypriot Administration of Southern Cyprus on the island. Prime Minister Bülent Ecevit agreed to the Cyprus reference in the conclusions after the last-minute visit by Javier Solana, the EU's high representative for Common Foreign and Security Policy, and Verheugen, the EU commissioner responsible for enlargement on the night of December 9, 1999.[43] Yet the Aegean Sea and Cyprus conflicts continued to appear in the Conclusion of the Presidency of the European Council in Helsinki Summit. Moreover, in this report it was stressed that "critical subjects," such as minorities, freedom of expression, and human rights were included and that even after granting Turkey the status of candidacy, negotiations should begin only on the condition that the Copenhagen criteria are fulfilled.[44] On the other hand, according to the Conclusions of the Summit, the EU would prepare an Accession Partnership Document[45] for Turkey and Turkey would designate a National Program and explain in which form it would undertake the EU legislation.

Relations between Turkey and the EU entered in a new era after the Helsinki Summit. Turkey, a country with candidate status, was included formally in the pre-accession strategy of the Union. An Accession Partnership is based on the EU Acquis and the Copenhagen criteria and is prepared by the European Commission. The European Council approved the Accession Partnership in 2001 and a schedule for Turkey's candidacy process was created. However, the "Cyprus issue" was included under the political criteria in the Accession Partnership. An attempt to resolve the Cyprus problem was made through bringing the subject under the category "Priorities and Mid-term Targets" at the Council of Ministers meeting held in December 2000, following Turkey's statement of its discomfort on this subject.

The positive relations between Turkey and the EU, which continued and strengthened, had a positive impact on the domestic policy of Turkey, and the Turkish public's expectations regarding membership increased. Particularly some NGO's, such as Turkish Industry and Business Association (TÜSİAD), organized energetic activities for membership to the EU, hence they increased support for Turkey's membership both domestically and in European countries.[46] A National Program concerning Turkey's undertaking of EU Acquis was published for the first time on March 26, 2001.[47] Yet the crises in November 2000 and February 2001 severely affected the country's economy, and economic problems were added to the other political problems that were explained in the Progress Reports in detail. Nevertheless, comprehensive economic policies were put into practice after the 2001 crises and they were consistently pursued. Under the influence of the single party government—Justice and Development Party (AK Party) Government—that came into power with the 2002 elections, political stability was established and the Turkish economy began to improve. In this period, a sustainable high rate of growth, accompanied by macroeconomic stability, was mostly secured. Also, important steps were taken to fulfilll the Copenhagen economic criteria. Criticism of the Progress Reports on the Turkish economy gradually decreased due to the positive developments in the following years, particularly after 2005.[48] However, some criticism for failure to fulfilll the political criteria remained in the Progress Reports.

Reforms carried out since the Helsinki Summit secured the commencement of accession negotiations with Turkey on October 3, 2005 according to a decision made by the European Council on December 17, 2004 at the Brussels Summit. The controversial statement of the European Council was the reference to the open-ended character of the negotiations. It was stated, "These negotiations are an open-ended process, the outcome of which cannot be guaranteed beforehand. While taking account of all Copenhagen criteria, if the candidate state is not in a position to assume in full all the obligations of membership it must be ensured that the candidate state concerned is fully anchored in the European structures through the strongest possible bond."[49]

In addition to Turkey's political and economic stability, international developments, particularly in Central Asia and the Middle East (the invasion of Afghanistan and Iraq after September 11) increased the strategic importance of Turkey. Thus, with the adoption of the Negotiation Framework[50] by the European Council, accession negotiations were launched on October 3, 2005. This document stated that the common target of the negotiations, which would continue under 35 chapters, was accession to the EU, and that the negotiations were open-ended with no guaranteed end date.[51] The Commission's statement of open-ended process revealed the reluctance of the EU to consider Turkey as a full member and the negotiations would go on the basis of a differentiated procedure.[52] Turkey's Negotiations Framework also emphasized the EU's absorption capacity and the possibility of the permanent derogations in areas such as free movement of persons, agriculture, and structural funds.[53] But it is important to note that before the adoption of the Negotiation Framework, the European Commission addressed the potential impacts of Turkey on the Union and how Turkey's membership could be different from the other candidate states in its working paper in 2004. It was stated, "Turkey's accession would be different from previous enlargements because of the combined impact of Turkey's population, size, geographical location, economic, security and military potential, as well as cultural and religious characteristics."[54]

Hereafter, the Enlargement Strategy Paper prepared by the European Commission was published on November 9, 2005. In this paper the European Commission stated that Turkey: continued to fulfilll the Copenhagen criteria and made sufficient progress; realized important structural reforms in democracy and the rule of law; made some progress in human rights and minorities issues; and recently achieved success in the economy.[55] The 2005 Strategy

Paper includes positive evaluations concerning Turkey, and was the first and only Strategy Paper in which the Cyprus issue was not included.

Unfortunately, good relations that developed between Turkey and the EU did not last long. After 10 new candidate countries acceded into the EU[56] on May 1, 2004, Turkey signed the "Additional Protocol," which extended the Ankara Agreement to the new member states.[57] Nevertheless, on the same day, the phrase, "Republic of Cyprus" was used to describe the Greek Cypriots (Greek Cypriot Administration of Southern Cyprus) in the Introduction of the Protocol. Turkey, thereupon, released a declaration in which it announced that it did not recognize the Republic of Cyprus. The EU, in return, released a contra-declaration on September 21, 2005 indicating that Turkey's declaration was unilateral, did not form part of the Protocol and had no legal effect on Turkey's obligations under the Protocol.[58] Nevertheless, some countries, particularly France and Germany, clearly stressed that Turkey had to recognize Greek Cypriots as a condition for membership, and even proposed some solutions, including privileged partnership.[59]

Thus, the negotiation process, which started with the "Science and Research" chapter, reached a deadlock only a short time after it began. The documents prepared by the European Commission led to this result to a great extent. The Commission severely criticized Turkey in the Progress Report's section in which it was evaluated according to the Copenhagen political criteria and on November 29, 2006, reported that Turkey's performance concerning Cyprus was insufficient, and recommended partial suspension of membership negotiations.[60] As a matter of fact, according to the decision made at the EU's Summit on December 11, 2006, eight critical chapters out of 35 were suspended.[61] A majority of the chapters suspended would considerably affect the development of customs union relations. The Cyprus issue was an important problem in most of the documents of the EU. It can be said that the Cyprus issue has been Europeanized after that time. Also, the 2006 Enlargement Strategy Paper added two more conditions, which would have important influence on the membership of Turkey: European public support and the EU's absorption capacity.[62]

On the other hand, while the section on the evaluation of the economic criteria in the progress reports for Turkey narrowed, the sections about the political context gradually became more comprehensive. Considering that the Copenhagen political criteria are a precondition, in contrast to the other criteria, political developments are very important in regards to the realization of Turkey's course in the membership negotiation process. Although Turkey's deficiencies concerning legislative and economic criteria have been included in the Progress Reports in the following years, positive evaluations have also been part of the Progress Reports. Nevertheless, the political criteria that were submitted each year were the most problematic. The Progress Report in 2011 criticized the following: the Additional Protocol to Turkey's

Association Agreement was not approved by the Turkish Parliament yet; Turkey did not entirely fulfilll its obligations and without discrimination in spite of the calls of the Council and Commission; and limitations on direct transportation connections with Cyprus and obstacles to the free movement of goods continued to exist. Furthermore, the report criticized that Turkey did not make progress on the normalization of relations with the Greek Administration of Southern Cyprus, and Turkey did not remove its veto on the membership of the Greek Administration of Southern Cyprus to various international organizations.[63]

Today, one can easily see that there has been progress in the economic dimension of Turkey-EU relations. Also, having similar economic systems influenced positively the economic integration process between Turkey and the EU. In fact, the Turkish economy has been defined as a functioning market economy to a great extent since the first Progress Report.[64] Currently, economic integration between Turkey and the EU is being implemented by relying on Turkey's efforts to fulfilll membership conditions, primarily the Copenhagen criteria. This is necessary in order to make the customs union operate on the one hand, and on the other, to facilitate Turkey's transition to a higher phase of integration within the EU as a full member.

Also, Turkey has achieved a significant level of adjustment to the EU acquis communautaire in regard to its efforts in customs legislation. The European Commission notes this achievement in all the Reports since the first Progress Report prepared.[65] Turkey has removed all customs union taxes and taxes with equivalent effect, taxes on EU-origin industrial products, including industry shares taxed on processed agricultural products. It has begun to implement a Common Customs Tariff against third party countries, and put free trade agreements (FTAs) into practice, which it was required to do according to the 16th article of the Decision no. 1/95 of the Association Council. Turkey has signed these free trade agreements (FTAs) in spite of the fact that the EU has not supported it.[66]

One of the indicators of the level of economic integration with the EU is the trade volume between Turkey and member countries. The customs union established between Turkey and the EU contributed to the trade volume increase. Today, the EU is the most important trade partner of Turkey. Turkey's trade with the EU constitutes approximately half of its total trade.[67] Nevertheless, Turkey's share in the EU's total foreign trade is very low (4 percent as of 2010), and Turkey is ranked seventh in a list of EU trade partners.[68] While the share of the total exports to the EU was 46.2 percent at the end of 2010, the share of total imports from the EU was 41.7 percent in the same year. On the other hand, a great majority of foreign capital inflow to Turkey as foreign direct investments (FDI) is from the EU. 76 percent of FDI to Turkey in 2010 was of EU origin, although this capital in flow has decreased in recent years.[69] As can be seen, the economic dimension of the Turkey-EU relationship is far more important for Turkey than for the EU.

As mentioned before, all candidate countries must completely adopt the EU acquis and create the necessary institutional structure to implement the legislation. In fact, Turkey has taken critical steps to create the necessary institutional structure and to adapt its legislation to that of the EU. Turkey has made particular progress according to the provisions of the customs union that came into effect on January 1, 1996. This process further accelerated the initiation of negotiations. As of late 2012, Turkey has prepared nine harmonization packages.[70]

The first harmonization package entered into force on February 2, 2002 with regard to the criminal code, struggle against terror, and accusation procedures in state security courts. Later, new regulations were also accepted in a short time.[71] The ninth harmonization package generally covers regulations on civil-military relations and capital punishment. In addition to the harmonization packages, comprehensive legal reforms were made in many laws, including the Turkish Criminal Procedure Code and Turkish Criminal Code.[72] Thus, the positive developments that Turkey carried out regarding adaptation to EU acquis were given a place in the Progress Reports. Nevertheless, the EU criticized Turkey in certain aspects of the adaptation of these laws.

EU criticism during the negotiation process mainly focused on transparency, competition, state monopoly, privileges, and discrimination.[73] Although Turkey has generally reached a high level of adaptation to the EU legislation, it appeared considerably low in some fields such as the free movement of workers, free movement of services, agriculture-fishery, taxation, and regional policies. The lack of progress was mainly due to the chapters that were blocked. The political issues have been the most controversial part for Turkey in fulfillling the Copenhagen criteria. In the Progress Reports, the candidate country was evaluated in areas such as democracy, state of law, human rights, respect for minority rights and stability of institutions guaranteeing protection of minorities, assuming international obligations, regional cooperation, and relations with neighbors, enlargement countries, and member countries. All Progress Reports published to date included the expression "Turkey made certain progress in relation to political criteria" but again in all reports it was stated that existing shortcomings concerning human rights still existed. Nevertheless, the number of criticized fields increased from the middle of the first decade of 2000 in particular. For example, criticism of ongoing lawsuits began to find a place in the Progress Reports as new problem-laden fields (i.e., the method of dealing with the crime investigations regarding Ergenekon and similar lawsuits), implementation of criminal procedure methods that risk legal procedures, and the right to defense and the right to a fair trial.[74]

Table 1.1. Current Overview of Turkey's Accession Negotiations (As of the end of December 2011)

Closed Chapters (*)	Opened Chapters	Suspended Chapters
*Science and Research	*Enterprise and Industrial Policies (2007)	*Free Movements of Goods
	*Financial Controls (2007)	*Customs Union
	*Statistics (2007)	*Fisheries
	*Consumer and Health Protection (2007)	*Transport Policy
	*Companies Law (2008)	*External Relations
	*Intellectual Property Law (2008)	*Right of Establishment and Freedom to Provide Services
	*Free Movements of Capital (2008)	*Financial Services
	*Information Society and Media (2008)	*Free Movement of Workers
	*Culture (2009)	*Energy
	*Taxation (2009)	*Competition Policy
	*Environment (2009)	*Social Policy and Employment
	*Food Safety, Veterinary and Phytosanitary Policy (2010)	*Judiciary and Fundamental Rights
		*Justice, Freedom and Security
		*Public Procurement
		*Education and Culture
		*Agriculture and Rural Development (**)
		* Financial and Budgetary Provisions (**)
		*Institutions (**)
		*Regional Policy and Coordination of Structural Instruments (**)
		*Economic and Monetary Policy(**)

(*) Temporarily closed.
(**)Chapters blocked by France.
Source: http://www.senat.fr/rap/r10-677/r10-6771.pdf (10.09.2012).

Another key event in the course of Turkey-EU relations, in addition to the evaluations made in the Progress Reports, is the negotiation process that began on October 3, 2005. Although the negotiations have started in a very short span of time, they came to halt quite at the same pace. After the beginning of the negotiation process in 2005, it gradually slowed in the following year. The Council suspended eight negotiation chapters in 2006 declaring that Turkey was discriminatory in the implementation of the customs union with all the members of the EU. The Council charged that Turkey did not open its airports and harbors to Greek Cypriot vessels. In reaction to Turkey's policy of non-recognition and not allowing it to make use of Turkey harbors, Germany, France, Greece, and Cyprus decided to block some of the chapters. As of the end of 2011, on 19 of 35 acquis titles negotiations were blocked—more than half of the total number of the titles (Table 1.1). As a result, nearly seven years have passed since the beginning of the accession negotiation process and negotiations were started on only thirteen chapters.[75] The only chapter that is temporarily closed is the "Science and Research." Although Turkey and Croatia began accession negotiations on the same date, Croatia signed an Accession Agreement on December 9, 2011, after the completion of negotiations, and will become a full member on July 1, 2013.

Turkey has made clear progress in respect to economic integration and adaptation to EU legislation, considering current relations with the EU. This progress has been clearly stated in documents prepared by the EU institutions. Yet this lengthy negotiation process continues, and some of the EU member states have a negative influence on the Turkey-EU integration process. In fact, this situation influences the political criteria, which is the most trouble-ridden area between the EU and Turkey. Although all Progress Reports refers to the progress Turkey made in political criteria, the number of areas that are criticized has increased in recent years. Political criteria are sine qua non. They are a precondition for full membership, and failure to do so makes EU accession impossible, even if other criteria are fulfilled.

Although some assert that a strengthened political dialog continues between the two parties, this dialog is essentially unstable.[76] It has been affected by the international conjuncture, for sure, but mostly by the political approaches of the member states of the Union. Naturally, this instability in dialog influenced the negotiation process. However, the timing to adopt, enact, and implement the EU legislation is determined in the negotiation process. Actually, the only negotiated point is the schedule of implementation.[77] The negotiation process that began in 2005, including the amount of time Turkey needed to adopt and put into effect the EU legislation, is being determined. Thirty-five chapters would be discussed, yet continued on a different course from the negotiation process of other candidate countries.

After a period of stagnation in membership negotiations and political cooperation between Turkey and the EU, a New Positive Agenda that has been intended to bring fresh dynamics into the EU-Turkey relations was endorsed by the Council in December 2011, and launched in May 2012.[78] The objective of this process is to revive the stalled relationship between the EU and Turkey by rebuilding confidence and normalizing the process. The Positive Agenda could let the EU revisit its basic principles that have made recent enlargement rounds beneficial to stability in Eastern Europe. To that end it may consider proposing to Turkey a clear date for accession without which no initiative could be conclusive and sustainable. Within this framework, the Positive Agenda aims to contribute to Turkey's EU accession process especially by enhancing cooperation and by promoting reforms in Turkey in various areas such as fundamental rights, visa liberalization, mobility and migration, trade, energy, counter-terrorism, or dialogue on foreign policy. Within this framework, the European Union and Turkey have agreed to establish working groups with the aim to further support and accelerate the process of alignment of Turkey with EU policies and standards under eight chapters.[79] According to the latest Progress Report for Turkey published in the same year, six of the eight working groups, which have been established under the Positive Agenda, have already gathered for their first meeting.[80]

As it is seen, the relations between Turkey and the EU based on the Ankara Agreement seem to follow a fluctuating course due to the internal and external dynamics of the two parties. But, although these relations did not follow a stable course until today, Turkey-EU relations progressed,[81] and even accelerated, particularly after the customs union put into effect in 1996. At the same time, Turkey is one of the few countries that established a customs union with the EU before becoming a full member.[82] The relations particularly entered a different dimension by granting Turkey candidate country status in 1999. Thus, full membership to the EU for Turkey has become a strategic target after this date, and after receiving the candidate status, Turkey accelerated its attempts to modify its legal infrastructure and implement structural reforms to fulfilll the necessary conditions for full membership to the EU. However, the EU's treatment of handling of the negotiation process has by no means been fair when compared to the accession process of other candidates.

On the other hand, Turkey's approach to the membership has changed from government to government over time and the EU membership has turned into a daily topic of political debate. Nevertheless, Turkey's accession to the EU has become an even more ambiguous and controversial issue especially after 2006 as EU-Turkey relations have faced many difficult challenges. Because of the Cyprus dispute, and the suspension of eight chapters in the negotiation process, the AK Party government has showed reluctance in pushing the reform agenda forward. Hence, developments in the Middle

East have been carrying much greater urgency than Turkey's relations with the EU especially after 2010. The criticisms that the AK Party's axis has shifted from the West to the East also affect the relations between Turkey and the EU negatively.

Once again, the approaches of changing governments in some member countries in the EU, which affect the development of the EU integration, greatly influenced both the decisions of the EU institutions, and consequently, the course of the negotiation process. Consequently, it can be argued that the trend of the relations between Turkey and the EU has developed mostly as the reflection of the political approach of the governments. In the present state of affairs, the result of these developments has been that both sides have come to a point where Turkey-EU relations are being handled in a rather limited frame.

CONCLUSION

The relations between Turkey and the EU entered a different dimension after Turkey was granted candidate country status in 1999. After receiving the candidate status, Turkey accelerated its attempts to modify its legal infrastructure and implement structural reforms to fulfilll the necessary conditions for full membership to the EU. The EU decided to start accession negotiations in 2005 after the European Commission advised that Turkey sufficiently fulfilled the Copenhagen political criteria that were a prerequisite for these negotiations to be launched. Turkey, until the present phase, has made significant progress on the fulfilllment of the Copenhagen economic criteria and adaptation to the related legislation. This progress made in the economic field is stressed in the formal documents of the EU. However, the same successes in fulfillling the Copenhagen political criteria was not achieved, and the political criteria have remained the greatest criticism in the Progress Reports. Comparing the first Progress Report in 1998 with the 2012 Progress Report, it appears that criticism of Turkey has gradually increased over time. However, the Commission has never recommended that the negotiations be interrupted which it is required to do under the Negotiating Framework adopted at the time of the start of the negotiations, if it considers that Turkey no longer sufficiently fulfillls the Copenhagen political criteria.

. The negotiation process, during which thirty-five chapters would be discussed, began to follow a different course from the negotiation process conducted with other candidate countries. Nineteen chapters have been suspended until today. Due to the fact that Turkey did not extend the Additional Protocol to Greek Cypriots, some EU member countries that have a negative attitude towards Turkey's EU membership have politically blocked some chapters and the negotiations on these chapters were suspended, and the relations have come to the standstill.

The deadlock in Turkey-EU relations is not the first, when you look at the history of the relations and the relations between Turkey and the EU have not followed a stable course until today. Hence, after a period of stagnation in the relations, a New Positive Agenda intended to bring fresh dynamics into the EU-Turkey relations was launched in May 2012.

In fact, the highly erratic course of EU-Turkey relations can be interpreted as a reflection of the political decisions made by both sides. In the present state of affairs, both sides have come to a point where Turkey-EU relations are being handled in a rather limited frame. Both parties seem to be overlooking the multidimensional and dynamic nature of the relations; and while the Turkish front seems to have reduced the question to "should we become a member of the EU or not?" the EU appears to act in accordance with short term plans.

In effect, although the EU is an institution established on an economic basis to render peace and safety, it would not be an erroneous presumption to conclude that "the decisions that have been made in the course of enlargement have been based more on politics than economy." For example, doubts about Greece's level of economic development in its integration with the EU were expressed in the European Commission Report during the process of making the decision on its full membership in 1981. Furthermore, during the Central and Eastern European Countries' membership process like that of Romania and Bulgaria, political factors played an important role. In other words, the EU's decision on the membership of these latter countries was not based on the fulfilllment of all the Copenhagen criteria. Indeed, the decision made on the membership of the U.K. followed the same course. The decision for the full membership of the U.K., a country that is highly developed compared to Greece and the CEECs, was delayed due particularly to the objections from France, mainly on political grounds.

On the other hand, as it can also be seen clearly in the example of the Annan plan, although Turkey has made her best in the process, the EU, by way of Europeanizing the issue of Cyprus, has interestingly and consistently presented the issue to Turkey as a problem to be solved. In regards to this matter as well, the EU is acting in a way that is highly political rather than rational. However, if the EU had genuine intentions to solve this issue, they would not have set a date for the accession of the Greek Cypriot Administration of Southern Cyprus, right before the referendum regarding the Annan Plan. This conduct on the part of the EU, which is far from being rational, is contradictory to EU's objective of becoming an agent in the global arena.

Partly because of the inconsistent line adopted by EU institutions, enlargement is being blamed by the public in EU countries for all the economic problems faced by the Union at the moment. As a matter of fact, the results of public opinion polls conducted by the European Commission confirm this situation. In 2002 and 2003 while 75 percent and 80 percent of those who took the Eurobarometer survey respectively were leaning towards the enlargement of EU, by 2010, this percentage had dropped to 43 percent.[83] A similar case is also valid for the ratio of those who had an optimistic outlook on the future of the EU (while their number was 66 percent in 2009, in the spring of 2010 this had dropped to 57 percent).[84] Similarly, in Turkey, while the percentage of the people leaning towards becoming a member of the EU was 73 percent in 2004, it dropped radically to below 50 percent by 2011.[85]

Thus, it is seen that recent developments have caused despondency in both the European and Turkish public, resulting in negative attitudes toward membership from both parties. It is critical to recognize that a process devoid of a clear sense of direction would constitute an impediment for the completion of the integration process and would cause much more burden on the parties when the conditions change and become once again more favorable to enlargement.

NOTES

1. Senedi İttifak (Bill of Alliance-tr.) (1808), Tanzimat Fermanı (Edict of Improvement-tr.) (1839), Islahat Fermanı (Rescript of Reform-tr.) (1856)
2. Ziya Öniş, "Turkey's encounters with the new Europe: multiple transformations, inherent dilemmas and the challenges ahead," *Journal of Southern Europe & the Balkans,* 8 (2006), December 3: 279.
3. Later its name was changed to Organization for European Economic Co-operation and Development (OECD).
4. In this paper, it is used abbreviatedly as Ankara Agreement. It has consisted of a main document of 33 articles, an interim protocol in the appendix, a Financial Protocol and a Final Act, an Intention and Comment Notification, and a Letter.
5. The Agreement Creating an Association Between the Republic of Turkey and the European Economic Community (the "Ankara Agreement"), *Official Journal of the European Communities*, 16 (1973), No, 113, December 24, http://ec.europa.eu/enlargement/pdf/turkey/association_agreement_1964_en.pdf (22.10.2012).
6. Organization founded according to the provisions of Ankara Agreement was Council of Association.
7. Tuğrul Arat, "Avrupa Birliği ile Türkiye Arasındaki İlişkiler," *A.Ü. Hukuk Fakültesi Dergisi,* XLIV (1995): 588-592.
8. Ankara Agreement, art.2 (3).
9. Ankara Agreement, art.3.
10. Ankara Agreement, art.4.
11. Çağrı Erhan and Tuğrul Arat (a), "AET'yle İlişkiler," in Baskın Oran (ed.), *Türk Dış Politikası-Cilt 1*, İletişimYayınları, 2008:.847.
12. Turkey implemented the 60th article of the Additional Protocol.
13. Çağrı Erhan and Tuğrul Arat (b), "AT ile İlişkiler," in Baskın Oran (ed.), *Türk Dış Politikası-Cilt 2,* İletişimYayınları, İstanbul, 2008: 84.
14. Erhan and Arat (b), 2008: 87-88.
15. Application for full membership to the European Coal and Steel Community was made according to the 98th Article of the Paris Agreement, to the EEC according to 237th Article of the Treaty of Rome, and to the European Atomic Energy Community according to the 209th Article of the Euratom Treaty.

16. CEC, *Commission Opinion on Turkey's Request for Accession to the Community*, SEC (89) 2290 final/2, December 20, 1989.
17. CEC, 1989: 4.
18. Erhan and Arat (b), 2008: 96-101.
19. Didem Buhari, "Turkey-EU Relations: The Limitations of Europeanisation Studies," *The Turkish Yearbook of International Relations*, 40 (2009): 93-94; Metin Heper, "Turkey; between East and West," *Institute of European Studies Papers*, 2004, http://repositories.cdlib.org/ies/040516, (12. 08.2012).
20. Ian Manners, "Normative Power Europe: A Contradiction in Terms?," *Journal of Common Market Studies*, 40 (2002), 2:235-258.
21. According to the Maastricht Treaty which was signed on February 7, 1992 and entered into force on November 1, 1993, the Union is founded on the European Communities (first pillar), with two additional areas of cooperation (second and third pillars): the Common Foreign and Security Policy (CSFP) and Justice and Home Affairs (JHA). Also, the EEC became the European Community (EC). After the Maastricht Treaty, not only economic integration but also political integration was targeted and instead of the expression EC, the European Union (EU) started to be used. Consequently, in discussions on the relations between Turkey and the European Union, the phrase "European Union (EU)" was chosen.
22. The article numbers used are those changed by the Lisbon Treaty that made changes and annexes both in content and form on the main agreements (effective December 1, 2009) of the EU.
23. For full membership, not only the Copenhagen criteria, but also some other criteria, are necessary. New demands were developed through the Madrid (1995) and Luxemburg Summits (1997) in addition to the Copenhagen criteria. The Madrid Summit demanded harmonization of administrative structures in order to implement the Community policies of candidate countries (Absorption capacity criterion). At the Luxemburg Summit, the importance of both legislation harmonization and implementation of EU legislation were stressed. Thereby, some notions such as absorption capacity and permanent derogation were included in the formal documents of the EU after 1993.
24. Sanem Baykal and Tuğrul Arat, "AT'yle İlişkiler," in Baskın Oran (ed.), *Türk Dış Politikası-Cilt 2,* İletişimYayınları, İstanbul, 2008: 335-336.
25. The three basic subjects dealt with in this decision are: technical points concerning free movement of goods; enhancing cooperation not only in industrial products, but also in cultural, scientific, and environmental fields; and that financial aid that would be provided to Turkey.
26. For information about the effects of the customs union on Turkey see Ali Koçyiğit and Ali Şen, "The Extent of Intra-Industry Trade between Turkey and the European Union: The Impact of Customs Union, "*Journal of Economic & Social Research,* 9 (2007), 2: 61-84.
27. CEC, *Agenda 2000: For a stronger and wider Union*, http://europa.eu/legislation_summaries/enlargement/2004_and_2007_enlargement/l60001_en.htm (15.07.2007).
28. Narbone Luigi and Nathalie Tocci, "Running around in circles? The cyclical relationship between Turkey and the European Union, "*Journal of Southern Europe and the Balkans*, 9 (2007), December 3: 234.
29. CEC, *European Strategy for Turkey: The Commission's initial operational proposals,* COM (1998) 124 final, Brussels, 04.03.1998.
30. See Chris Rumford, "From Luxembourg to Helsinki: Turkey, the politics of EU enlargement and prospects for accession, " *Contemporary Politics,* 6 (2000), 4: 335.
31. Füsun Arsava, *Amsterdam Antlaşmasının Avrupa Birliği Hukukuna Katkıları,* A.Ü. Siyasal Bilgiler Fakültesi Yayınları, No: 589, Ankara, 2000:9-24. Gianni Bonvicini, "Making European Policy Work," in Martin Wetlake (ed.), *The European Union Beyond Amsterdam*, Routledge Press, 1998: 61-75.
32. A legal ground was established concerning the EU's enlargement according to the provisions of the Treaty of Nice, signed in 2001, and became a current issue shortly after the Amsterdam Agreement. With this agreement, the number of fields decided by a qualified majority increased, the voting strength of member countries changed, and the voting strength of the countries that became full members were determined. For more information on the Treaty

of Nice see. Füsun Arsava, "Nice Antlaşmasının Getirdikleri," *Ankara Avrupa Çalışmaları Dergisi,* 1 (2002), 2, Spring: 1-30.

33. The burden of administrative mechanisms increased gradually because the EU was enlarging and the rate of integration became higher. As a result some blockages occurred. Therefore the Union felt that it needed to reconsider its institutional structure, its authorities, and its targets, and as a solution accelerated discussions in relation to the designation of the Constitution. According to the decree made at the Laeken Summit in December 2001 the Union's structure must be more democratic, transparent, and efficient. Nevertheless, the view that the Constitution has to be re-analyzed in a different dimension came into question. Two factors influenced such a view: first, the referendums held in the Netherlands and France resulted in a negative vote on the European Constitution signed in Rome on October 29, 2004; and second, concerns that the referendums in other countries could possibly have the same results. See Sanem Baykal, "Reform Antlaşması ve Getirdikleri: Kurumsal Yapı Çerçevesinde Genel Bir Değerlendirme," *Ankara Avrupa Çalışmaları Dergisi*, 7 (2007), 1: 45-67.

34. The Lisbon Treaty provided important amendments and innovations in its basic agreements both in form and in content. The target was rendering the EU mechanism more efficient and transparent; creating a more democratic EU; generating a structure that allows the EU to protect national interests; and provide a stronger EU voice in the international arena. For more information see Belgin Akçay, "Ekonomik ve Parasal Birlik," in Belgin Akçay and Gülüm Bayraktaroğlu Özçelik (eds.), *Lizbon Antlaşması Sonrasında Avrupa Birliği: Serbest Dolaşım ve Politikalar*, second edition, Seçkin Publishing, Ankara, 2012:.327-383. Gülüm Bayraktaroğlu Özçelik, "Avrupa Birliğinin Kurumsal Yapısı ve Lizbon Antlaşması," in Belgin Akçay, Sevilay Kahraman and Sanem Baykal (eds.), *Avrupa Birliği'nin Güncel Sorunları*, SeçkinYayıncılık, Ankara, 2008: 204. Derya Büyüktanir, "Dış İlişkiler Kapsamında Avrupa Birliği'ninTüzel Kişiliği ve Lizbon Antlaşması," *Uluslararası İlişkiler,* 7 (2010), 27, Güz:102-106. Marchesi Daniele, 'The EU Common Foreign and Security Policy in the UN Security Council: Between Representation and Coordination,' paper presented at the 2008 International Studies Association (ISA) Convention, San Francisco, Mar 2008: 15.

35. Kostantinos Smitis Government (1996-2004).

36. Rumford, 2000: 340. For more information about the relations between Turkey and Greece after 1999 see Heinz-Jürgen Axt, "Relations with Turkey and Their Impact on the European Union," *Journal of Southeast European & Black Sea Studies,* 5(2005), September 3: 365-378.

37. Viktor Debnar and Alan Smith, "Why the US wants Turkey in the EU," *New Presence: The Prague Journal of Central European Affairs,* 7 (2006), 4, Winter: 20-21.

38. For the importance of Turkey for the EU in regard to energy security see Ali Tekin and Paul Williems, "EU-Russian Relations and Turkey's Role as an Energy Corridor," *Europe-Asia Studies*, 61(2009), March 2: 337-356. Ali Tekin and Paul Williems, "EU Energy Security: The Pipeline Connection," *East European Quarterly,* 42 (2008), 4, Winter: 419-434. Belgin Akçay, "Energy in the relations of Turkey with the EU: an Assessment in the context of Central Asia Region," *3. İzmir Economics Congress* organized by 9 Eylül University, February 29—March 2, 2012, İzmir, Turkey.

39. Baykal and Arat, 2008: 352-353.

40. Progress Reports, prepared annually by the European Commission, are reports that include: the evaluation of the Copenhagen criteria, namely: liberalization of political and economic order required for full membership of candidate countries to the EU, transposing the EU legislation into national legislation and effective implementation of the legislation through proper administrative and legal organizations. Progress Reports clarify the progress in regard to a large field of candidate countries. In Progress Reports, while evaluation concerning harmony with the Copenhagen criteria and political criterion include progress made in the candidate country after publication of the last Progress Report, the evaluation concerning economic criteria covers a longer period. Progress Reports for Turkey have been prepared since 1998. For more information see Belgin Akçay, The Economic Membership Criteria in Enlarged European Union: The Case of Turkey. *Juridicum,* 4 (2008), September: 196-203.

41. CEC, *Regular Report from the Commission on Turkey's Progress Towards Accession,* October 13, 1999: 46-47, http://ec.europa.eu/enlargement/archives/pdf/key_documents/1999/turkey_en.pdf (02.08.2012).
42. European Council, 1999, para. 4, 9a, 12.
43. Mustafa Türkeş and Göksu Gökgöz, " Reflections on the EU Strategy Paper 2003 – two approaches, moving conditions and a new juncture," 61-65, http://sam.gov.tr/wp-content/uploads/2012/02/5.-MustafaTurkesAndGoksuGokgoz.pdf (12.08.2012).
44. European Council, *Conclusions of the Helsinki European Council of December 10–11, 1999,* http://www.consilium.europa.eu/uedocs/cms_data/docs/pressdata/en/ec/ACFA4C.htm (02.09.2012).
45. The Accession Partnership Document is one of the important component parts of the enlarged accession strategy and it is based on the EU legislation and the Copenhagen criteria. The expectation from the candidate countries to act according to the values and aims clarified in the EU Treaty, which is a unilateral declaration of intention that binds the EU and negotiations, would not begin as long as political criteria are not fulfilled.
46. Öniş, 2006: 283.
47. National Programme has been revised in 2003 and 2008.
48. See Belgin Akçay, "Economy of Turkey in the Progress Reports," *Ankara Review of European Studies,* Fall issue. 7 (2007), 1: 19-44.
49. European Council, *Presidency Conclusions* – Brussels, December 16–17, 2004, 16238/1/04 REV 1:7, http://www.consilium.europa.eu/uedocs/cms_data/docs/pressdata/en/ec/83201.pdf (10.05.2012).
50. The Negotiating Framework Document of the EU defines the methods and principles of negotiations.
51. Ministry for EU Affairs, *Türkiye İçin Müzakere Çerçeve Belgesi ve İlgili Diğer Belgeler,* 2005, http://www.abgs.gov.tr/files/AB_Iliskileri/AdaylikSureci/MuzakereCercevesi/Muzakere_Cercevesi_2005.pdf. (12.08.2012).
52. Çiğdem Nas, "Changing Dynamics of Turkish Foreign Policy and the European Union," *Turkish Policy Quarterly,* 9 (2010), 4, Winter: 123. For more information about how the EU conditionality was used for Turkey and other counties see Kirsty Hughes, "Turkey and the European Union: Just another enlargement? (Exploring the implications of Turkish accession)" *Friends of Europe Working Paper,* June 2004. Frank Schimmelfennig and Ulrich Sedelmeier, "Governance by Conditionality: EU Rule Transfer to the Candidate Countries of Central and Eastern Europe," *Journal of European Public Policy,* 11 (2004), 4, 2004: 661-679. Frank Schimmelfennig et al., "Costs, Commitment and Compliance: The Impact of EU Democratic Conditionality on Latvia, Slovakia and Turkey," *Journal of Common Market Studies,* 41 (2003), 3: 495-518. Martin Brusis, "The Instrumental Use of European Union Conditionality: Regionalization in the Czech Republic and Slovakia," *East European Politics and Societies,* 19 (2005), 2: 291-316. Mustafa Aydın and Sinem A. Açıkmeşe, "Europeanization through EU Conditionality: Understanding the new era in Turkish foreign policy," *Journal of Southern Europe and the Balkans,* 9 (2007), December: 263-274. Viljar Veebe, "European Union's Positive Conditionality Model In Pre-Accession Process," *Journal of the Humanities & Social Sciences,* 13 (2009), 3: 207-231.
53. Luigi and Tocci, 2007: 236.
54. CEC, *Issues Arising From Turkey's Membership Perspective,* COM (2004) 656 final, Brussels: 4.
55. CEC, *2005 Enlargement Strategy Paper,* 9.11.2005, COM (561) Final: 28-33, http://eur-lex.europa.eu/LexUriServ/LexUriServ.do?uri=COM:2005:0561:FIN:EN:PDF (31.08.2012).
56. Czech Republic, Poland, Slovakia, Slovenia, Estonia, Latvia, Lithuania, Greek Administration of Southern Cyprus, Malta, and Hungary.
57. After European Enlargement, for Additional Protocol to the Agreement Creating Partnership Between Turkey and the European Economic Community see Ministery of Foreign Affairs, http://www.mfa.gov.tr/ek-protokol-ve-deklarasyon-metni.tr.mfa (10.08.2012).
58. European Council, *Enlargement: Turkey Declaration By The European Community and Its Member States,* Brussels, September 21, 2005, 2541/05 (Presse 243):1.

59. For Priviliged Partnership see Beril Dedeoğlu and Seyfettin Gürsel, "EU and Turkey: The Analysis of Privileged Partnership or Membership," http://betam.bahcesehir.edu.tr/en/wp-content/uploads/2010/05/EU-and-Turkey-The-Analysis-of-Privileged-Partnership-or-Membershipfinal.pdf (10.108.2012). Eurobserver, "Merkel says no to Turkey's EU bid," 04.12.2007, http://euobserver.com/tickers/106613 (12.09.2012). Erhan Içener, "Privileged partnership: An alternative final destination for Turkey's integration with the European Union?," *Perspectives on European Politics & Society*, 8 (2007), December 4: 415-438.

60. CEC, *Turkey 2006 Progress Report*, 2006, http://ec.europa.eu/enlargement/archives/pdf/key_documents/2006/package/sec_1426_final_progress_report_tr_en.pdf (15.08.2012).

61. Suspended titles are Free Movement of Goods, the Right to Business Establishment, Free Supply of Services, Financial Services, Agriculture, Rural Development, Fishery, Transportation Policy, Customs Union, and Foreign Relations.

62. CEC, *Enlargement Strategy and Main Challenges 2006 – 2007*, Including annexed special report on the EU's capacity to integrate new members, COM(2006) 649 final, Brussels, 8.11.2006: 8-17.

63. EC (a), *Turkey 2011 Progress Report*, SEC (2011) 1201 final 2011: 45, http://ec.europa.eu/enlargement/pdf/key_documents/2011/package/tr_rapport_2011_en.pdf (15.08.2012).

64. CEC, *1998 Regular Report from the Commission on Turkey*, 1998:4, http://ec.europa.eu/enlargement/archives/pdf/key_documents/1998/turkey_en.pdf (12.10.2012).

65. For economic integration of EU-Turkey see Belgin Akçay, "Economy of Turkey in the Progress Reports." *Ankara Review of European Studies*, Fall issue. 7 (2007), 1: 19-44. Belgin Akçay, "The Economic Membership Criteria in Enlarged European Union: The Case of Turkey," *Juridicum*, 4 (2008), September: 196-203.

66. See Mustafa Dönmez, "Türkiye-Avrupa Birliği İlişkilerinde Gümrük Birliği," in Belgin Akçay ve Gülüm Bayraktaroğlu Özçelik, *Lizbon Antlaşması Sonrası Avrupa Birliği; Serbest Dolaşım ve Politikalar*, Seçkin Yayınevi, Ankara, 2012: 501-523. Belgin Akçay, "Aday Ülke Statüsünün Kazanımı Sonrasında Türkiye'nin AB ile Ekonomik Entegrasyonu; Koşullar ve Kısıtlar," *Maliye Dergisi*, July-December, 40 (2011), 160:1-26.

67. EC(a), 2011:4.

68. EC(a), 2011: 4.

69. EC(a), 2011: 52.

70. The first Harmonization Package, draft law concerning "Harmonization Laws" was prepared according to the amendments in the Constitution of the Republic of Turkey on October 2001 and presented to the Speaker of Parliament by the Council of Ministers at the Turkish Grand National Assembly on January 15, 2002, and approved on February 6, 2002 by the Parliament after making some changes to it. For more information on Harmonization Packages see http://www.tbmm.gov.tr/develop/owa/haber_portal.aciklama?p1=14602 (10.08.2012).

71. Some of the laws made in relation to the prepared Harmonization Packages are: Law on Attaining Knowledge (October 9, 2003), Law on removing some articles of the Law on National Security Council and General Secretary of NSC (December 10, 2003), Law on Public Finance Administration and Control (December 10, 2003), Law on Banking (December 12, 2003), the Law on Establishing Children's Court and Its Functions and Accusatory Procedures (January 7, 2004). The eighth Harmonization Package that implements Constitutional Amendments was made on May 2004, Amendments on the Law on Public Officials' Trade Unions, Law on Social Security Institution (June 2004), Law on Association (July 2004), Public Administration Reform Package (July 2004), Law on Compensation of Detriments Generated from Terrorist Actions (July 2004), new Turkish Code of Criminal (September 2004) and the Law on Court of Appeal (September 2004).

72. For more information about the influence of the EU Harmonization Laws to the National Law and amendments made to the laws according to the EU adaptation see Ministry of Justice, *Avrupa Birliği'ne Aday Ülke Olarak Türkiye'de AB Uyum Yasalarının İç Hukuka Etki ve Katkısı*, Ankara, 2008.

73. The regulations made until today and those that shall be made in the future, according to the EU legislation predicted in the coverage of section titles, which were taken into account in the complementation of accession negotiations of Turkey, were given place in recently published "Turkey's Harmonization Program to EU Legislation (2007-2013)". For more informa-

tion see Ministry for EU Affairs, *Türkiye'nin AB Müktesebatına Uyum Programı (2007-2013)*, 2007, http://www.abgs.gov.tr/index.php?p=6&l=1 (11.08.2012).

74. CEC, *Turkey 2007 Progress Report*, 2007: 9, http://ec.europa.eu/enlargement/archives/pdf/key_documents/2005/package/sec_1426_final_progress_report_tr_en.pdf (02.08.10.2007); EC (a), 2011: 7.

75. See Ministry for EU Affairs's website, http//:www.ab.gov.tr (02.08.2012).

76. EC (a), 2011, p.4.

77. See European Council, *1995 Madrid Summit*, http://www.consilium.europa.eu/uedocs/cms_data/docs/pressdata/en/ec/00400-C.EN5.htm (15.08.2012).

78. EC (a), *Positive EU-Turkey Agenda*, MEMO/12/359, May 2012, http://europa.eu/rapid/press-release_MEMO-12-359_en.htm (12.10.2012).

79. These chapters are Judiciary and Fundamental Rights, Company Law, Financial Control, Statistics, Consumer and Health Protection, Information Society and Media, Justice, Freedom and Security, and Right of Establishment and Freedom to Provide Services.

80. EC (b), *2012 Progress Report*, COM(2012) 600 final, 2012: 4.

81. Mehmet Özcan et al., *Bundan Sonrası? Senaryo ve Analizleriyle Türkiye-AB ilişkileri*, USAK Yayınları, Ankara, 2009: 28-42. Ziya Öniş, "Turkey-EU Relations: Beyond the Current Stalemate," *Insight Turkey*, 10 (2008), 4: .35-50.

82. The countries that established a customs union with the EU before Turkey are Monaco (1958), Andorra (1991), and San Marino (1991), whose economies and territories are significantly smaller than Turkey's.

83. EOS Gallup Europe, *Flash Eurobarometer 140 Enlargement of the European Union*, 2003: 9. EC (b), *Eurobarometer 74 Autumn 2010 Public Opinion in the European Union*, Brussels, February, 2011: 62.

84. EC (b), 2011: 66.

85. The German Marshall Fund, *Transatlantic Trends*, 2011: 37-40. TAVAK, *Türk Halkının AB'ye Bakışı*, İstanbul, Ağustos, 2012: 2-3.

REFERENCES

Akçay, Belgin. "Ekonomik ve Parasal Birlik," in Belgin Akçay and Gülüm Bayraktaroğlu Özçelik (eds.), *Lizbon Antlaşması Sonrasında Avrupa Birliği: Serbest Dolaşım ve Politikalar*, second edition, Seçkin Publishing, Ankara, 2012: 327-383.

———. "Energy in the relations of Turkey with the EU: An Assessment in the context of Central Asia Region," 3. İzmir Economics Congress organized by 9 Eylül University, February 29—March 2, 2012, İzmir, Turkey.

———. "Aday Ülke Statüsünün Kazanımı Sonrasında Türkiye'nin AB ile Ekonomik Entegrasyonu; Koşullar ve Kısıtlar," *Maliye Dergisi*, July-December, 160, 2011: 1-26.

———. "Economy of Turkey in the Progress Reports," *Ankara Review of European Studies*, Fall issue. 7 (2007), 1: 19-44.

———. "The Economic Membership Criteria in Enlarged European Union: The Case of Turkey," *Juridicum*, September 4, (2008): 196-203.

Arat, Tuğrul. "Avrupa Birliği ile Türkiye Arasındaki İlişkiler," *AÜ Hukuk Fakültesi Dergisi*, XLIV (1995): 587-606.

Arsava, Füsun. *Amsterdam Antlaşmasının Avrupa Birliği Hukukuna Katkıları*. A.Ü. Siyasal Bilgiler Fakültesi Publishing, No. 589, Ankara, 2000.

———. "Nice Antlaşmasının Getirdikleri," *Ankara Avrupa Çalışmaları Dergisi*, 1 (2002), 2, Spring: 1-30.

Axt, Heinz-Jürgen. "Relations with Turkey and Their Impact on the European Union," *Journal of Southeast European & Black Sea Studies*, 5(2005), September 3: 365-378.

Aydın, Mustafa, and Açıkmeşe, Sinem A. "Europeanization through EU conditionality: Understanding the new era in Turkish foreign policy," *Journal of Southern Europe and the Balkans*, 9 (2007), December 3: 263-274;

Baykal, Sanem. "Reform Antlaşması ve Getirdikleri: Kurumsal Yapı Çerçevesinde Genel Bir Değerlendirme," *Ankara Avrupa Çalışmalan Dergisi*, 7 (2007), 1: 45-67.

Baykal, Sanem, and Arat, Tuğrul. "AT'yle İlişkiler, Türk Dış Politikası," in Baskın Oran (ed.), *Türk Dış Politikası-Cilt 2*. İletişim Publishing, İstanbul, 2008: 326-365.
Bonvicini, Gianni. "Making European Policy Work," in Martin Westlake (ed.), *The European Union Beyond Amsterdam*. Routledge Press, 1998, pp. 61-75.
Brusis, Martin. "The Instrumental Use of European Union Conditionality: Regionalization in the Czech Republic and Slovakia," *East European Politics and Societies,* 19 (2005), 2: 291-316;
Buhari, Didem. "Turkey-EU Relations : The Limitations of Europeanisation Studies," *The Turkish Yearbook of International Relations*, 40 (2009): 91-121.
Büyüktanır, Derya. "Dış İlişkiler Kapsamında Avrupa Birliği'nin Tüzel Kişiliği ve Lizbon Antlaşması," *Uluslararası İlişkiler*, 7 (2010), 27, Fall 2010: 87-110.
CEC. *Commission Opinion on Turkey's Request for Accession to the Community*, SEC (89) 2290 final/2, December 20, 1989.
CEC(a). *Progress Report 1998,* http://ec.europa.eu/enlargement/archives/pdf/key_documents/1998/turkey_en.pdf (17.08.2012).
CEC(b). *European Strategy for Turkey: The Commission's initial operational proposals,* COM (1998) 124 final, Brussels, 04.03.1998.
CEC. *1999 Regular Report from the Commission on Turkey's Progress Towards Accession,* October 13, 1999, http://ec.europa.eu/enlargement/archives/pdf/key_documents/1999/turkey_en.pdf (02.08.2012).
CEC. *Agenda 2000: For a stronger and wider Union* , 2000, http://europa.eu/legislation_summaries/enlargement/2004_and_2007_enlargement/l60001_en.htm (15.07.2007).
———. *Issues Arising from Turkey's Membership Perspective*, COM (2004), 656 final, Brussels.
———. *2005 Enlargement Strategy Paper,* COM (561) Final, 9.11.2005, http://eur-lex.europa.eu/LexUriServ/LexUriServ.do?uri=COM:2005:0561:FIN:EN:PDF (31.08.2012).
———. *Turkey 2006 Progress Report,* 2006, http://ec.europa.eu/enlargement/archives/pdf/key_documents/2006/package/sec_1426_final_progress_report_tr_en.pdf (15.08.2012).
———. *Enlargement Strategy and Main Challenges 2006 – 2007,* Including annexed special report on the EU's capacity to integrate new members, COM (2006) 649 final, Brussels, 8.11.2006.
———. *Turkey 2007 Progress Report,* 2007, http://ec.europa.eu/enlargement/pdf/key_documents/2007/nov/turkey_progress_reports_en.pdf (08.2012).
Daniele, Marchesi. 'The EU Common Foreign and Security Policy in the UN Security Council: Between Representation and Coordination,' paper presented at *the 2008 International Studies Association (ISA) Convention*, San Francisco, Mar 2008.
Debnar, Viktor, and Smith, Alan. "Why the US wants Turkey in the EU," *New Presence: The Prague Journal of Central European Affairs,* 7 (2006), 4, Winter: 20-21.
Dedeoğlu, Beril, and Gürsel, Seyfettin. "EU and Turkey: The Analysis of Privileged Partnership or Membership," http://betam.bahcesehir.edu.tr/en/wp-content/uploads/2010/05/EU-and-Turkey-The-Analysis-of-Privileged-Partnership-or-Membership_final.pdf (August 12, 2012).
Dönmez, Mustafa. "Türkiye-Avrupa Birliği İlişkilerinde Gümrük Birliği," in Belgin Akçay ve Gülüm Çelik Bayraktaroğlu, *Lizbon Antlaşması Sonrası Avrupa Birliği; Serbest Dolaşım ve Politikalar*. Seçkin Yayınevi, Ankara, 2012: 501-523.
EC (a). *Turkey 2011 Progress Report,* SEC (2011) 1201 final, 2011, http://ec.europa.eu/enlargement/pdf/key_documents/2011/package/tr_rapport_2011_en.pdf (15.08. 2012).
EC (b). *Eurobarometer 74 Autumn 2010 Public Opinion in the European Union*, Brussels, February, 2011.
EC (a). *Positive EU-Turkey Agenda,* May 2012, MEMO/12/359, http://europa.eu/rapid/press-release_MEMO-12-359_en.htm, (12.10.2012).
EC (b). *2012 Progress Report,* COM (2012) 600 final, http://ec.europa.eu/enlargement/pdf/key_documents/2012/package/tr_rapport_2012_en.pdf (20.10.2012).
EOS Gallup Europe. *Flash Eurobarometer 140 Enlargement of the European Union,* 2003.
Erhan, Çağrı and Arat, Tuğrul (a). "AET'yle İlişkiler," in Baskın Oran (ed.), *Türk Dış Politikası-Cilt 1*, İletişim Publishing, 2008: 808-853.

——— (b). "AT'yle İlişkiler," in Baskın Oran (ed.), *Türk Dış Politikası-Cilt 2*. İletişim Publishing, İstanbul, 2008: 83-101.

Eurobserver. "Merkel says no to Turkey's EU bid," 04.12.2007, http://euobserver.com/tickers/106613 (12.09.2012).

European Council. *Madrid Summit* 1995, http://www.consilium.europa.eu/uedocs/cms_data/docs/pressdata/en/ec/00400-C.EN5.htm (15.08.2012).

European Council. *Conclusions of the Helsinki European Council of December 10–11, 1999,* http://www.consilium.europa.eu/uedocs/cms_data/docs/pressdata/en/ec/ACFA4C.htm (02.09. 2012).

European Council. *Enlargement: Turkey Declaration By The European Community and Its Member States,* Brussels, September 21, 2005, 2541/05 (Presse 243).

European Council. *Presidency Conclusions* – Brussels, December 16–17, 2004, 16238/1/04 REV 1, http://www.consilium.europa.eu/uedocs/cms_data/docs/pressdata/en/ec/83201.pdf (10.2012).

Heper, Metin. "Turkey; between East and West," *Institute of European Studies Papers* , 2004, http://repositories.cdlib.org/ies/040516 (12.08. 2012).

Hughes, Kirsty. "Turkey and the European Union: Just another enlargement ? (Exploring the implications of Turkish accession)," *Friends of Europe Working Paper,* June 2004: 1-36.

Içener, Erhan. "Privileged partnership: An alternative final destination for Turkey's integration with the European Union?," *Perspectives on European Politics & Society* , 8 (2007), December 4: 415-438.

Koçyiğit, Ali, and Şen, Ali. "The Extent of Intra-Industry Trade between Turkey and the European Union: The Impact of Customs Union," *Journal of Economic & Social Research,* 9 (2007), 2: 61-84.

Luigi, Narbone, and Tocci, Nathalie. "Running around in circles? The cyclical relationship between Turkey and the European Union," *Journal of Southern Europe and the Balkans,* 9 (2007), December 3: 233-245.

Manners, Ian. "Normative Power Europe: A Contradiction in Terms?," *Journal of Common Market Studies*, 40 (2002), 2: 235-258.

Ministry for EU Affairs. *Türkiye'nin AB Müktesebatına Uyum Programı (2007-2013)*, 2007, http://www.abgs.gov.tr/index.php?p=6&l=1 (11.08.2012).

———. *Türkiye İçin Müzakere Çerçeve Belgesi ve İlgili Diğer Belgeler,* 2005, http://www.abgs.gov.tr/files/AB_Iliskileri/AdaylikSureci/MuzakereCercevesi/Muzakere_Cercevesi_2005.pdf (12.08.2012).

———. http//:www.ab.gov.tr (10.09.2012).

Ministry of Foreign Affairs. http://www.mfa.gov.tr/ek-protokol-ve-deklarasyon-metni.tr.mfa (10.08.2012).

Ministry of Justice. *Avrupa Birliği'ne Aday Ülke Olarak Türkiye'de AB Uyum Yasalarının İç Hukuka Etki ve Katkısı,* Ankara, 2008.

Nas, Çiğdem. "Changing Dynamics of Turkish Foreign Policy and the European Union," *Turkish Policy Quarterly,* 9 (2010), 4, Winter: 117-131.

Öniş, Ziya. "Turkey's encounters with the new Europe: multiple transformations, inherent dilemmas and the challenges ahead," *Journal of Southern Europe & the Balkans*, 8 (2006), December 3: 279-298.

———. "Turkey-EU Relations: Beyond the Current Stalemate," *Insight Turkey*, 10 (2008), 4: 35-50.

Özcan, Mehmet et al. *Bundan Sonrası? Senaryo ve Analizleriyle Türkiye-AB ilişkileri*. USAK Yayınları, Ankara, 2009.

Özçelik, Gülüm Bayraktaroğlu. "Avrupa Birliğinin Kurumsal Yapısı ve Lizbon Antlaşması," in Belgin Akçay, Sevilay Kahraman and Sanem Baykal (eds.), *Avrupa Birliği'nin Güncel Sorunları* , Seçkin Yayıncılık, Ankara, 2008: 203-234.

Rumford, Chris. "From Luxembourg to Helsinki: Turkey, the politics of EU enlargement and prospects for accession," *Contemporary Politics,* 6 (2000), 4: 331-344.

Schimmelfennig. Frank and Sedelmeier, Ulrich, "Governance by Conditionality: EU Rule Transfer to the Candidate Countries of Central and Eastern Europe," *Journal of European Public Policy,* 11 (2004), 4: 661-679.

Schimmelfennig, Frank et al. "Costs, Commitment and Compliance: The Impact of EU Democratic Conditionality on Latvia, Slovakia and Turkey," *Journal of Common Market Studies*, 41 (2003), 3: 495-518.

TAVAK. *Türk Halkının AB'ye Bakışı*. İstanbul, August, 2012.

Tekin, Ali, and Williems, Paul. "EU-Russian Relations and Turkey's Role as an Energy Corridor," *Europe-Asia Studies*, 61(2009), March 2: 337-356.

———. "EU Energy Security: The Pipeline Connection," *East European Quarterly*, 42 (2008), 4,Winter: 419-434.

The German Marshall Fund. *Transatlantic Trends*, 2011, USA.

Türkeş, Mustafa, and Gökgöz, Göksu. "Reflections on the EU Strategy Paper 2003 – two approaches, moving conditions and a new juncture": 61-82 http://sam.gov.tr/wp-content/uploads/2012/02/5.-MustafaTurkesAndGoksuGokgoz.pdf (30.06.2012).

Turkish Grand National Assembly.http://www.tbmm.gov.tr/develop/owa/haber_portal.aciklama?p1=14602 (10.08.2012).http://www.senat.fr/rap/r10-677/r10-6771.pdf (10.09.2012).

Veebe, Viljar. "European Union's Positive Conditionality Model In Pre-Accession Process," *Journal of the Humanities & Social Sciences*, 13 (2009), 3: 207-231.

Chapter Two

The Developments in Turkish Consumer Protection Law and the Effects of EU Law on These Developments

Şebnem Akipek

INTRODUCTION

When it comes to the concept of consumer protection, Turkey has an extensive history covering the notion, which actually dates back to the Ottoman Empire period. After the collapse of the Empire, consumer protection again played an important role in the young Turkish Republic. Though it has always been regarded as a very important idea, the first legislation directly enacted to regulate this concept only dates back to the year 1995. Until the enactment of this legislation, namely the Law on Consumer Protection, there was no direct provision to regulate matters about the consumers.

The notion and respective legislations regarding consumer protection have actually been developing in Turkey, parallel to the developments in the EU. During the preparation process of the Law on Consumer Protection, EU law has played the most important role. The primary aim in enacting this Law was to harmonize Turkish law with that of EU law on consumer affairs. In order to achieve this aim, before the codification of the Law on Consumer Protection, at the end of 1993 a commission was appointed by the State Planning Organization. This commission was named as the Commission for the Harmonization of EU law and Turkish law in the Field of Consumer Protection, and it was composed of academics, bureaucrats, persons from public and private sectors, and NGO representatives. The common tie between these people was their interest and previous work on consumer issues and also EU law. The writer of this article also acted as a member of this commission and acted in the capacity of the reporter of the commission. Following an intense study that lasted nearly two years, a report was prepared by this commission that covered all the history and development of EU law on consumer protection and the respective proposals for the intended legislation to be enacted in Turkey. In addition to the above mentioned studies, all the directives and the regulations of the EU were analyzed and examined to be adopted in Turkish legislation. Following the submission of this report, the existing draft Law on Consumer Protection was amended to include the views given by this report and then the Law was enacted.

Therefore, it could easily be stated that all the directives and regulations, as well as the main principles of EU law related to consumer protection, affected the development of consumer law in Turkey and were all reflected in the Law on Consumer Protection.

Following the enactment of the Law on Consumer Protection in 1995, there have been extensive developments in the field of consumer protection both in the world and in the EU. Turkey followed the same pattern and in order to satisfy the need of revision in the existing Law, commenced studies that resulted, in 2003, with a major amendment in the Law on Consumer Protection, which also bore the urge to provide the continuation of the harmonization with the EU law. From the year 2003 again there have been very important developments in the area of consumer protection both in the EU and in the world. Again there is an ongoing process in Turkey for the amendment of the existing Law on Consumer Protection. A draft has already been prepared, but it is still under examination. It could very easily be mentioned that EU law has affected the preparations of the draft and has been highly taken into consideration.

Considering all these explanations it could be stated that the effects of EU law on the Turkish consumer protection law is huge. The Turkish law is in line with the EU law and the application of the law is also in line. In particular, the dispute solving mechanisms are functioning perfectly and as a candidate member, Turkey is well prepared in the issues regarding consumers.

This article will attempt to analyze both the developments in Turkish and EU law in the field of consumer protection and will brief on historical and current developments, followed by an explanation of the effects of EU law on the Turkish system including comparisons. Finally, some suggestions for the future regarding the concept will be provided.

DEVELOPMENTS IN THE TURKISH LEGAL SYSTEM VIS A VIS CONSUMER PROTECTION LAW

Developments before the Foundation of the Turkish Republic

As is well known, the roots of the Turkish Republic go back to the Ottoman Empire. When we go back to the Ottoman Empire period, especially by way of "professionals' organizations" there were many efforts to protect consumers. The professionals working in various fields, such as tailors, shoe makers, barbers, butchers, etc., were gathering together and forming some chambers that resemble the commercial chambers of today.[1] These chambers were given a special name, i.e. "Ahi[2] Birlikleri."[3] Though they were the "professionals' organizations" and mainly aimed to protect the rights of the people in that working field, the rules set by these organizations were indirectly protecting the consumers as well. In order to promote the job of their members and the production and the sales of goods and services, these organizations tried to build a strong tie between their members and the consumers.[4] They also formed the roots of another organization that was very effective in the Ottoman Empire and that developed mainly during the fifteenth century, namely "Lonca Örgütü."[5]

Starting with the fifteenth century, the same professionals working in the same field of production and sales started to come together, and under the name of their profession, started to open their shops in the same market place close to each other. This was named a "lonca" and with the help of this organization the first roots of competition took hold. In that way, the consumers had a wide range of choices and they got the chance to compare the goods and/or products by their value and quality. Again, it should be mentioned that this was not a direct protection, but since it promoted competition, the consumers were indirectly protected.

At the end of the fifteenth century, a law on regulation of the Municipality of Bursa was published and this law was the first piece of legislation that brought the concept of "standards" to the Ottoman Empire. Most of the standards brought by this law were related to the health and safety protection of the consumers, whereas some also covered the economic rights of the consumers as well.

With the dawn of the seventeenth century, the state introduced new measures to protect the consumers by instituting certain limits for the sales prices of certain goods. The state declared a maximum price on the respective goods and it was forbidden to sell these goods over the stated price, which aimed for the stabilization of market prices.

This initial system vis a vis consumer protection, actually worked perfectly until the nineteenth century. However, with the beginning of the collapse of the Ottoman Empire, firstly "lonca" were affected, and then, in 1839, they were abolished. Following this, the maximum price was lifted and all the state control over the sellers and the producers ceased. Together with all these developments a well functioning system came to an end and as a result the consumers were left without any protection.[6]

Developments after the Foundation of the Turkish Republic

The last years of the Ottoman Empire were full of wars and there was huge instability all over the country. Following the years of struggle, the Turkish Republic was founded in 1923, but the economic situation was too bad and the consumers were having great difficulty. Most of the people in the country were undereducated and they no longer had any wish to protect their rights. Though there was a need of urgent protection it was not one of the primary concerns of the government to deal with the consumers, since they were trying to overcome the effects of the war.[7]

One of the most important developments in the first years of the Turkish Republic was actually the adoption, in 1926, of two very important codes from Switzerland, namely the Civil Code and the Code of Obligations. The Code of Obligations was especially essential for the protection of consumers and it brought many provisions that also provided cover vis a vis the consumers. However, during those years as consumers and consumer protection were not regarded as a specific subject, the need of providing specific provisions to protect consumers was not deemed necessary. Not only in Turkey, but also in the world, there were not many direct codes or laws to protect consumers. For that reason the Code of Obligations was not targeting specifically the consumer, but all persons—both real and legal, entering into legal transactions and building obligations.[8]

Following all these developments, with the beginning of the 1930s, some new legislation was enacted that provided not a direct but an indirect protection for consumers.[9] The common feature of all of this legislation was actually to provide state control over the economy, together with the aim of achieving an advanced control to protect the public order, only indirectly aiming at the protection of the consumer.

In the 1950s, the consumption habits of the consumers started to change and the economic situation of the country gradually improved. Industry grew rapidly and parallel to that private consumption expenses started to increase. In light of all these developments, the notion of consumer protection once again started to gain importance.[10]

During the following twenty years, the government tried to bring certain regulations regarding consumers, but these were all weak efforts and did not have any successful results. In the modern sense, the concept of consumer protection was considered for the first time by a draft law regarding the consumers in 1971.[11] However, the Grand National Assembly did not even discuss it, so it was not possible to enact.

When constitutional rules are considered vis a vis the consumers, it should first be mentioned that after the founding of the Turkish Republic, three different Constitutions were enacted. The first one was enacted in 1924, the second one in 1961, and the last one in 1982. In the first two Constitutions, there were no direct rules regulating consumers or consumer protection. In this sense, the 1982 Constitution is very important, since it is the first Constitution that brings a direct provision regarding consumers. Therefore, it is considered to be a milestone in the protection of consumers and a very important development. With regard to the aforementioned, the Turkish Constitution Article 172 guarantees the protection and counselling of the consumer by the State and encourages the consumer to take the initiative in protecting themselves. Together with this provision in the Constitution, the protection efforts of the consumers gained speed and as a result, some NGO's were founded.

Subsequent to the 1982 Constitution, Turkey narrowed the gap with the EU again. When the historical development of the relations between the EU and Turkey are considered, it could easily be stated that they began with the enactment of the Ankara Treaty in 1963. Though it has a long history, the relations between the two nearly came to a stop between the beginning of the 1970s until the mid-1980s. Together with the Customs Union in 1995, relations improved again and as a result Turkey became a candidate country trying to harmonize its legislation to that of the EU. Many areas of law have been affected with these harmonization efforts, but one of the first to be affected is actually in the area of consumer protection. It could, without any hesitation, be stated that the Law on Consumer Protection is a result of these harmonization efforts, and is in line with the EU law on consumers. Actually the enactment of this law is the most important development in the protection of consumers.

THE LAW ON CONSUMER PROTECTION

The Enactment and the Purpose of the Law on Consumer Protection

Together with the establishment of the Customs Union between Turkey and the EU in 1995, the first direct law in the field of consumer protection was enacted by the Turkish Grand National Assembly. This Law was enacted on February 23, 1995, and published in the Official Gazette on March 8, 1995. The Law on Consumer Protection, which entered into force on September 8, 1995, aimed specifically at the harmonization with the EU legislation, as the Customs Union necessitated harmonization especially in the areas of consumer protection, competition, and intellectual and industrial property law.[12]

Actually in the explanatory memorandum of the Law, it was clearly stated that the first and second consumer programs of the EU were taken into account together with the Council Resolution of June 23, 1986, concerning the future orientation of the policy of the EU for the protection and promotion of consumer interests.

The purpose of the Consumer Protection Law is stated under Article 1 that reads *"to take measures aimed at protecting the health, safety and economic interests of consumers in line with the public good, building consumer awareness, indemnifying losses incurred by consumers and protecting them against environmental hazards; to promote consumer initiatives aimed at protecting consumer interests and to encourage volunteer organizations aimed at devising consumer-related policies."* This purpose clearly reflects itself in the five main consumer rights program accepted by the EU.[13] All of these rights are regulated and protected by the Law, but the chief aim of the law is to bring better and quicker ways of redressing consumer disputes and to protect the economic interests of consumers. The Law consists of 34 articles and some of these provisions also have an aim to protect the public welfare together with consumer interests.

The Context of the Law on Consumer Protection

Article 2 of the Law on Consumer Protection provides that the law covers all the subjects specified in Article 1, as well as all consumer-related transactions in the goods and services to which a consumer is one of the parties. Therefore, consumers are the core persons in this Law. Whenever a consumer is a party to a transaction then principally the provisions of this Law should be the primary ones to be applied, and only in the absence of a provision in this Law, the general codes like the Code of Obligations and the Commercial Code should be applied.

As far as the term "consumer" is concerned, pursuant to the definition given under Article 3, the consumer can either be a real person or a legal person being a party in purchasing, using, or benefiting from a good or service without having any profession-oriented or commercial purpose. The definition of the "consumer" covers both the real and the legal persons and this aspect of the Turkish law could be regarded as one of the most important aspects that differ from the EU Law. Nearly in all of the directives and other pieces of legislation related to consumers in the EU, a consumer is mostly taken as a real person.[14]

Though the definition of consumer covers both real and legal persons, it should also be evaluated according to Turkish law as to whether all legal persons may be considered as consumers.

Accordingly, the wording of this Article may be interpreted so as to mean that even a corporation or a limited liability company can be entitled to benefit from the rights granted to the consumer. However, considering the related provisions of the Turkish Commercial Code, which stipulates that all obligations of a merchant are commercial and further, the exception to this general rule is only for real person merchants, a corporation, a limited liability company, a limited partnership or any other commercial entity, are not entitled, regardless of their nature, to enter into agreements having consumer-based character. In this regard, the Turkish Court of Appeals has generally ruled that trading companies, whether corporations or limited liability companies or ones similar in nature, can in no way be considered within the frame of the respective scope of the Law on Consumer Protection and, therefore, are not able to benefit from the rights granted to the consumers by such law.[15] Consequently, "legal persons," which are referred to in Article 3 of the Law on Consumer Protection, are deemed to be foundations and societies that are not entitled to conduct any commercial activities. As a result, it could be stated that, for example, a society buying furniture for the general assembly meetings should be regarded as a consumer.

Although a broad meaning is given to the consumer, a relatively narrow meaning is given to the term "good." Until the amendments made in the Law in 2003, a good was defined as a movable property that may be subject to trade, so none of the immovable property was included in this concept.

Another important characteristic of the Law is that consumers are not only protected in legal transactions concerning the sale of goods, but they are also protected in legal transactions concerning the supply of services. The other party of these transactions can be a seller, a provider, a producer, or any other real or legal person who supplies a service, such as a bank giving consumer credit. When the other party is a legal person, it can be either a private law or a public law legal person, such as the state itself or a municipality supplying for example water utilities or providing transportation.

The provisions of the Law are arranged in two different groups, one set of provisions aim to prevent any damage on behalf of the consumers, i.e., the protective provisions, and the other aim to compensate the damages suffered by the consumers as a result of a transaction between the consumer and the seller. Therefore, the second section of the Law on Consumer Protection incorporates the first set of provisions, which outlines protecting and informing the consumer, lays down the legal status as well as rights and obligations of both parties with respect to defective goods; instalment sales; campaign sales; door-to-door sales (doorstep sales); consumer credits; periodicals; subscription agreements; warranty certificates; user guides; after sales services; commercial advertisements; and hazardous and dangerous goods and services. The other sections of the Law include the second set of provisions. In these sections there are provisions governing consumer organizations; legal proceedings-penalties; and miscellaneous provisions.

A further importance is given by the Law, to compensating the damages of the consumers. In order to comply with this aim the Law introduces a new dispute resolution method in Turkey, to be used only in the field of consumer protection. This is an extra-judicial method which leads to the formation of Arbitration Committees. The aim is to form these Committees in every province in Turkey and to solve the consumer disputes with a relative ease leading to the acceleration of proceedings. The Committees, which are composed of five members, mitigate the problem solving of the consumers in case of a dispute.[16] Also filing to these Committees is free of charge.

The Law also introduces specific consumer courts[17] to the judicial system and when a consumer or a consumer union applies to these courts the application is exempt from all duties and charges.

The Amendments on the Law on Consumer Protection

Due to the European Council's granting Turkey official status as an accession state in 1999, Turkey started to bear the burden of giving more effort to harmonization in the legal sense, including the application of the existing laws. Also, in the passing years some failures of the Law on Consumer Protection were felt and a need to add certain provisions to the Law emerged. The harmonization need also worked as an igniting factor.

Therefore, following the enactment of the Law on Consumer Protection in 1995, major amendments were passed in 2003 in order to ensure a higher level of protection for consumers and to harmonize Turkish consumer protection legislation with that of the EU.

With these recent amendments made to the Consumer Protection Law in 2003, defective services are with a separate provision incorporated into the scope of the Law alongside the defective goods. A defective service is defined as *"a service containing material, legal or economic deficiencies that influence the quality or the quantity that affects the quality specified in the advertisements or announcements made by the supplier, or established in the standards or technical regulations, or decrease or eliminate its value or the benefits expected from such service by the consumer."*

Another important amendment is in the definition of both consumer and good terms. Both of them gained a wider concept with the amendment.[18] The immovable properties in particular were included, not in every sense, but when they were subject to transaction for using them as a domicile or for holiday purposes. For example, if a consumer takes credit to buy a house, this transaction will fall into the content of the Law. The intangible assets designed for use in an electronic environment are also included in the Law. By that way online transactions are covered by the Law.

Distance selling was also not regulated by the Law and with these amendments a specific provision regulating distance selling was added. This provision is directly taken from the Distance Selling Directive of the EU. The distance selling contract is defined as a contract concerning the delivery of goods or performance of services concluded in a written, audiovisual, telephonic and electronic environment or by using other means of communication without physically meeting the consumer. In these contracts, consumers should be provided with certain information specified in the Law itself. This provision is exactly the same as that of the provision of the EU Directive.

A further development is the inclusion of credit cards to the Law. Disputes between banks and consumers regarding credit cards are regulated by the Law with a specific provision.

By these amendments, a great loophole in the Turkish legal system is filled with a provision about the unfair provisions of a contract, again directly affected by the EU system. According to this article, any provision in a contract inserted by one party without negotiating with the consumer and that distort the balance against the latter, and that violate the principle of good faith are considered unfair. Therefore, these provisions are not binding for consumers.

Two more inclusions to the Law are time-share vacations and package tours. These are two of the most problematic and frequently used concepts for the consumers. If a consumer is faced with a problem or a dispute is created during a holiday and because of a package tour, this should be solved quickly and in the best interest of the consumer. Also it is common for many people to obtain an immovable for time-share vacations. Two articles are added to the Law to regulate these two notions.

With regard to product liability, the liability for defective goods and services is widened, even though this part may still be regarded as one of the weakest points of the Law, since a distinction could still not be clearly made among tortuous liability and strict liability.

Though in its first enactment the Law included the Arbitration Committees, their decisions were not directly enforceable. This created a difficulty for the consumers, and having seen this need the lawmaker corrected the mistake by bringing a couple of very important amendments. First of all, up to a certain amount it is mandatory to file a dispute to the Arbitration Committees, and this amount is increased and published every year according to the inflation. Again up to this amount the decisions of the Committees are directly enforceable, they are binding decisions and if one of the parties wants to appeal against these decisions the appellate court is directly the consumer court being the last instance.

The disputes above the stated amount could directly be sued at the consumer court as first instance court or they could also be taken to the Arbitration Committee and in that case the decision of the Committee will be regarded as a strong proof by the judge if the parties still take the dispute to a consumer court.

THE NEW CODE OF OBLIGATIONS

One of the latest developments in the Turkish legal system is the enactment of the new Code of Obligations.[19] The new Turkish Code of Obligations had been enacted in January 2011 and it entered into force on July 1, 2012. It may also be regarded as very important for the protection of the consumers.

The Code of Obligations is taken from Switzerland by way of reception in 1926 as stated above. However, it had only minor amendments in the passing years and it became out of date. The harmonization efforts with the EU urged the law-maker to undertake major changes in the Code itself. A draft had been prepared, but waited long years to be enacted. In January 2011 the Turkish Grand National Assembly achieved a huge progress by enacting it. This change in the eighty-five-year-old Code of Obligations is one of the most sought after changes in Turkish legislation. The new Code of Obligations is also parallel to the Swiss Code of Obligations. The new Code consists of 649 articles and 22 chapters.

The new Code of Obligations is also a general code and not only treats consumers, but in comparison with the previous code, it includes some provisions that both directly and indirectly protect them. It is in that sense harmonized with the EU law and tries to satisfy the increasing need of consumer protection in Turkey.

Regarding the standard contracts, that is to say the contracts pre-drafted by one party of the legal transaction and that are not negotiable, the weaker party is protected more by the Code against the party that pre-prepared the contract, such as a bank, insurance company, car rental company, etc.

Another important aspect of the new Code is that, for the first time in Turkish law, the "general conditions of the transactions" are specifically regulated. These general conditions are the conditions drafted by one of the parties of the transaction and are not negotiated.

The dominant party of a legal transaction should not act against the interests of the other party and must obtain the consent of the other party. At least this provision will help to protect the interests of the consumers more. If the dominant party of a legal transaction violates this provision, the transaction shall be partially or wholly null and void. In addition, any ambiguous wording shall be interpreted in favor of the signing but not the drafting party.

The above mentioned provisions are only some examples from the new Code. However, besides this progress, there are also some failures of the new Code. One of the most notable ones in the field of consumer protection is the Code's not building a completely parallel line together with the Law on Consumer Protection. It was a hope for all the academics studying consumer protection that the Code and the Law would have common features, but still there are certain collisions and contradictions between the provisions of the two.

COMPARISON BETWEEN THE EU AND TURKISH LEGISLATION ON CONSUMER PROTECTION

The Acquis on Consumer Protection

In the EU, the acquis in this area of consumer protection actually covers protection of the economic interests of consumers (including misleading and comparative advertising, price indications, consumer credit, unfair contract terms, distance and doorstep selling, package travel, time-share, injunctions for the protection of consumers' interests, certain aspects of the sale of consumer goods and associated guarantees), as well as general product safety (liability for defective products, dangerous imitations, and general safety of goods) and distance marketing of consumer financial services.[20] Together with these the *acquis* in the area of consumer protection cover easy access to justice.

The Member States of the European Union (EU) must effectively enforce the acquis through appropriate judicial and out-of-court dispute resolution mechanisms as well as administrative systems, including market surveillance and an active role for consumer organizations.[21]

Member States need to transpose the *acquis* into their national legislations. The implementation and enforcement of consumer and health protection policies require adequate administrative capacities and infrastructure at national, regional, and local levels. With regard to consumer protection, this refers to effective market surveillance and appropriate independent judicial and out-of-court (extra-judicial) dispute resolution mechanisms. It is also necessary to raise public awareness, consult with the public, and involve consumers and consumer organizations actively in effective policy implementation, thus informing and educating the consumer and ensuring a role for consumer organizations.

Turkish Legislation and Position on Consumer Protection with regard to the Acquis

During the harmonization process, Turkey acknowledged that regarding the consumer protection she could easily accept the *acquis*, since the legislation is almost in line with the *acquis* of the EU. Actually no difficulty is expected in implementing the measures of consumer protection by accession.[22]

As stated above, first of all the Turkish Constitution (Article 172) guarantees the protection and information of consumer by the State and also encourages consumers to take initiatives for protecting themselves. In line with the EU approach and policy on consumer protection, a first law on consumer protection was adopted by Turkey in 1995. The amendment to the Law in 2003 aimed at further harmonization with the *acquis*. The enactment of the new Code of Obligations may also be considered as a last step in the harmonization efforts. Together with Code's coming into force, the protection level for the consumers is hoped to be increased further.

For every five year period, a development plan is prepared by the Turkish State Planning organization, and the Turkish strategy on consumer protection for the period 2007–2013 is included in general terms in the ninth Development Plan officially published on July 1, 2006.

Turkey gives a report to the European Commission regularly about the achievement realized in the field of consumer protection and according to the latest report submitted in 2012,[23] through the EU accession process Turkey expects to reach all consumer rights as regulated by the EU legislation and to strengthen the health system of consumers, to develop a social dialogue also focussing on support of consumer NGOs and their local networks, and to establish more consumer courts. As stated above, the Law on Consumer Protection established a consumer court in every province, but still the State could not yet achieve to establish a court in every province.

Concerning the institutional framework, till 2011 the main actor was the General Directorate for Protection of Consumers and Competition of the Ministry of Industry and Trade established in 1993. In 2011 there was a change[24] due to structural aspects and the organization of the government following the elections, and the Ministry of Industry and Trade was divided into two by forming two ministries. The General Directorate dealing with the consumers is now organized under the Ministry of Customs and Trade with a new name, Directorate General of Consumer Protection and Market Surveillance. Its task is to ensure the compatibility of the Turkish legislation with the *acquis* regarding especially the promotion of the economic interests of the consumer.[25] In this context, it also has direct enforcement functions, i.e., supervising and monitoring the whole Turkish market, undertaken by its own inspectors based in Ankara. There are also decentralised units of the Ministry for the Protection of the Consumers' Economic Interests at the Provincial Directorates in 81 provinces which act as an enforcement body. Besides this institutional framework, the municipalities are empowered to check price labelling.

With regard to the safety of products, the Ministry of Customs and Trade is in charge of market surveillance for a broad range of products including energy labelling, textiles and footwear, but excluding detergents, cosmetics, toys, medical devices, and medicinal products which the Ministry of Health is responsible for and food, feeding stuffs, fertilisers and veterinary medicinal products that fall under the competence of the Ministry of Agriculture and Rural Affairs. There are also other institutions that perform market surveillance such as the Telecommunication Authority (radio and telecommunication equipment), the Tobacco, Tobacco Products and Alcoholic Beverages Market Regulatory Authority (tobacco and tobacco products, alcoholic beverages, ethyl alcohol) and the Ministry of Labor and Social Security (personal protective equipment).

There is a Market Surveillance and Product Safety Assessment Board under the Ministry of Economy that is responsible for the coordination between the different authorities. The Board also monitors the preparation and implementation of technical legislation and takes advisory decisions relating to market surveillance.[26]

In 1995, together with the enactment of the Law on Consumer Protection, a Consumer Council is established and this Council acts as an advisory body to the Ministry of Customs and Trade. In this Council there are representatives from public institutions, universities, professional chambers, and consumer organizations.[27] Another institutional body again introduced with the Law on Consumer Protection is the Board of Advertisement.[28] This Board composed of representatives from public organizations and NGOs, sets up principles for commercial advertisement/notices and monitors/examines this area of advertising.

The Law on Consumer Protection urges consumers to come together and form organizations, being aware that by that way the consumers are better represented and have a possibility to be heard better, which leads to a higher degree of protection. Consumers have achieved this ideal quite well and today in Turkey there are around fifty Consumer NGO's and six of the bigger ones already came together and established a national federation.[29]

As far as the EU *Directive on Injunctions* is concerned, Turkey reached minimum legal alignment together with the amendments in 2003. As for the consumers' access to justice, Turkey has a dual structure. Firstly, there are the Arbitration Committees. These semi-judicial and semi-administrative provincial committees deal with consumer complaints, as part of the extra-juridical and out of-court settlement for consumer disputes. According to the data regarding 2010, there are 974 committees which are located in 81 provinces and 893 districts of Turkey.[30] The number of consumer complaints reaches up to around 50,000 per year.[31] Secondly, twenty-four consumer courts in nine provinces as first instance single judge civil courts deal with consumer cases. In the other provinces, First Instance Civil Commercial Courts are provisionally authorized to act until the establishment of specialised consumer courts. Legal actions brought before the courts by consumers, their organizations, or the Ministry are exempt from any duties or charges. This is a very important development in the Turkish judicial system that the consumer organizations are entitled to file lawsuits, also for precautionary injunctions to terminate violation in the collective interest of consumers.

Together with the Law on Consumer Protection, the Law on the Preparation and Implementation of Technical Legislation on Products enacted in 2001 constitutes a regulatory framework in the area of product safety. It could be stated that these two Laws are to a large extent in line with the EU

Directive on General Product Safety of 1992 and of 2001. They lay down the rules and procedures for the placing on the market of products, conformity assessments, and market surveillance. They fix the obligations of the producers and distributors as well as the rights of the enforcement bodies and their instruments.

Concerning the liability for defective products and dangerous imitations, the amendments adopted in 2003 filled the gap, and the Turkish legislation came closer to the *acquis*.

Regarding the unfair terms in consumer contracts, there were no direct provisions in this field, until the amendments made in 2003. Together with the amendments, a provision had been added to the Law on Consumer Protection and following this, a by-law was issued. With that means, the Turkish legislation came in line with the EU Directive, concerning Unfair Terms in Consumer Contracts. The courts started also to render decisions in favor of the consumers to eliminate unfair terms in contracts.

With respect to the EU Directive on Indication of Prices, in Turkey the indication of the prices of services and alignment goes far beyond the EC law, as it also requires the labelling of the prices of services. In addition, in Turkey there are no exceptions for small companies, craftsmen, and individual traders on stating the unit price for the product's unit of measure.

Both of the EU Directives about doorstep sales and distance sales[32] were implemented into the Turkish legal system with the Law on Consumer Protection. In 1995, the doorstep sales were regulated with this Law, however, the amendments developed the idea and the provisions regarding the distance sales were also incorporated into the Law in 2003.

With regard to consumer credit, the 10th article of the Law on Consumer Protection is totally in line with the EU Directive on Consumer Credits. Even in Turkish law there is a broader range of protection, since the credit taken for the immovable property to be used for settlement purposes is also included in the concept. Besides, there is a specific provision brought in 2003 about credit cards.

The EU Directives on Time-share and on Package Travel are also implemented by the Law on Consumer Protection together with two separate bylaws.

Assessment of the Degree of Alignment with the Acquis

Considering the above explained development of the Turkish consumer protection law, it could easily be noticed that the whole system has developed according to EU law, taking into consideration all the strategies and values of the EU. First of all, the enactment of the Law on Consumer Protection has led to major improvements in the field of legislative harmonization.

Therefore, Turkey has reached a satisfactory level of alignment with the *acquis*. The EU views are also in line with this evaluation, despite the fact that there are still certain problems in the application and implementation of the legal provisions. Therefore, the administrative capacity of enforcement and application should be strengthened and consumer movement and organization should be urged. In particular, the cooperation and partnership among the existing consumer NGO's should be achieved. It is a necessity to take certain measures to improve the cooperation and partnership. Another important problem is that many NGO's are financially weak. Support should be given to these NGO's. The ties between these NGO's and the state bodies need also be improved. The consumer organizations must be supported in taking part in the formation of consumer policies. The consumers taking part in the consumer organizations should be promoted.[33]

While strengthening the administrative and also the judicial capacity, the number of legally qualified experts in the aforementioned fields should be increased. The Law on Consumer Protection started to be a compulsory subject taught in some of the Law Faculties. At least in many law faculties it is given as an optional subject. Law students must be urged to study consumer protection. By way of education, the number of experts will be increased. When the arbitration committees are considered, it could easily be noticed that they lack experts and experienced personnel. Additional legal training should be given to the existing personnel and the committees should be better equipped and supported by the state.

In the field of consumer protection, the education of consumers should be taken seriously. An informed consumer will find it easier and natural to protect his/her rights. This education should also start at the primary school level. Receiving information is important for the consumers as well. They should be better informed by the companies, merchants, and public institutions about the unsafe or dangerous products in the market.

Implementation of the decisions of the Consumer Council is also important. This needs to be improved by the relevant organizations. Market surveillance should be considered more, and the products that are considered unsafe should be withdrawn from the market as soon as possible.

In the specific fields regarding the consumer protection such as doorstep sales, product safety, consumer credit, distance sales, etc., I believe, Turkey has reached a degree of harmonization. Of course there are still some loopholes or missing parts compared to the related Directives in the field. However, the reason for this is more or less because of regulating a whole field of consumer protection with one huge law. The EU has separate directives on every related issue. Therefore, it is possible to bring detailed provisions by that way. On the other hand, the Turkish legislator preferred to regulate every related field with one or two provisions in the general law. For that reason these provisions are not detailed like the directives. This gap is being filled by the by-laws issued by the Ministry of Industry and Trade.

In its evaluation reports, the European Commission also reported progress in the legal field, but still mentioned the need to transpose and apply the existing rules. According to 2012 report, the biggest failure is in the field of market surveillance, since the activities remain inadequate. The report mentions that The National Market Surveillance Strategy Document was revised for the years 2012-2014 and adopted by the Market Surveillance and Product Safety Assessment Board, consisting of Ministers and heads of market surveillance authorities, which held its first meeting in July 2012. But still according to the Report no progress is achieved on the revision of general product safety legislation.[34]

The Commission also points out the fact that regarding the economic interests of consumers, the level of alignment with European legislation is high. Turkey has shown a very important development in the judicial system as well about the consumer cases. However, the Commission notes that the legislation should be interpreted more consistently. Especially the capacity of consumer courts and arbitration committees needs to be further strengthened.[35]

CONCLUSION

Though Turkey has a long process in the development of the consumer protection, the position reached is quite satisfactory on a legal basis. It is one of the unique fields of law that directly followed the pattern of the EU counterparts. With the increasing relations after the 1990s between Turkey and the EU, the gap of not having a direct legislation regulating consumer protection has been filled with a Law, the Law on Consumer Protection, that reflects the values and the rules of the EU. All the provisions of the mentioned law are affected by a related EU directive or regulation.

The need for consumer protection and the increasing importance given to this field influenced the new Code of Obligations, and the Code provided many provisions in favor of consumers or at least indirectly protecting them.

A commission consisting of academics and civil servants has been established to continue work on drafts of consumer protection legislation in line with EU requirements. As a result a draft has been prepared, but it is still under discussion. The new Law on Consumer Protection has not yet been adopted. When it is adopted it will further strengthen the position of consumers. But the law-maker should be careful in keeping this new legislation in line with the other existing legislation.

As to a comparison between the *acquis* and the Turkish law on the notion of consumer protection, it could easily be stated that Turkey has reached a rather satisfactory level. The problem does not arise from the existing legislation, but sometimes in its application and enforcement.

To solve the stated problem, education of both consumers and the people, especially the lawyers who will be in a position to enforce the application, should be taken more seriously.

A final remark should be made on the importance given to the development of the judicial system. The more learned and experienced the judges become, the better the existing legislation will be interpreted and applied.

NOTES

1. TUSİAD, *AT'de Tüketiciyi Koruma Politikaları ve Türkiye'de Durum*, İstanbul 1990: 112.
2. The word "ahi" is actually from Arabic and it means brotherhood.
3. Şebnem Akipek, *Türk Hukuku ve Mukayeseli Hukuk Açısından Tüketici Kredisi*, Ankara 1999:108.
4. Ali Ceylan, *Tüketicinin Korunması*, Bursa, 1988: 27-28.
5. Ceylan, 1988: 28.
6. Ceylan 1988: 32.
7. Akipek, 1999: 110.
8. As mentioned above the Code of Obligations is adapted from the Swiss law together with the Civil Code. But unfortunately the Turkish legislator was a bit late to follow the amendments made by the Swiss legislator and both codes became at least partially out of date with the passing years. Especially after the 1980s some drafts were prepared for both codes, but until 2001 none of them had the chance to be enacted. In December 2001, the Civil Code had altogether been changed and a new code was enacted and become effective on the first day of 2002. Until very recently the draft Code of Obligations waited to be enacted by the Turkish Grand National Assembly. As will be explained below it was enacted in January 2011, but still has not become effective. The specific characteristic of the new Code of Obligations is the extensive importance given to the consumer, which also directly protects them.
9. The first one of this legislation dates back to 1928 and it was about medical services and the production of medicine. This law was followed by two other laws in 1930, namely the Public Health Law and Law on Municipalities. Several other laws were also enacted in 1933, 1936, and 1938 following the mentioned ones.
10. TUSİAD, 1990: 113.
11. Haluk Tandoğan, "İç ve Dış Ticaretin Düzenlenmesine İlişkin Kanun Tasarısı ile Ticarette Dürüstlüğün Korunması Hakkında Kanun Tasarısının Tüketicinin Korunması Açısından İncelenmesi", *BATIDER* 10(1980), 4: 10.
12. Yesim Atamer and Hans Micklitz, "Implementation of the EU Consumer Directives in Turkey," 27 *Penn State Int. Review*, 2008-2009:551.
13. At this point the development of the Community Consumer Policy should also be evaluated. The founding Treaty of the Community did not have any direct provision regarding consumer protection, as it was not among the purposes of the newly formed economic community. At a very early stage this gap was noticed and the EC Commission proposed the establishment of a Consumers' Consultative Committee. The absence of any specific reference to consumer protection in the Treaty of Rome also created the absence of continuous policy in the field of consumer protection for quite a long period of time. As a result, the provision of the new article 100A of the EC Treaty started a high priority on the issue of consumer protection for the purpose of establishing an internal market. With the creation of the EU consumer protection program, the concept gained further importance. Even before all these developments some programs had been prepared for the protection of the consumers and the main rights of consumers were stated in the first community consumer protection program. According to this,

the five main rights of the consumers are consumer health and safety, the protection of the economic interests of consumers, consumer information and education, consumer representation and the right to be heard, and lastly consumer redress. For more information on the subject see: David Oughton and John Lowry, *Textbook on Consumer Law*, second edition, Oxford University Press, Norfolk 2000: 62-72, P. S. R. F. Mathijsen, *A Guide to European Union Law*, ninth edition, Sweet and Maxwell, London 2007: 433-437.

14. In most of its decisions especially the European Court of Justice points out the fact that the concept of consumer should be taken narrowly and only real persons should be considered as a consumer: http://www.laweuropa.com/133-Avrupa-Birliginde-Tuketicinin-Tanimi (12.12.2012).

15. Court of Appeals, 19th Law Chamber, file no. 1999/3932, decision no. 1999/4621, date 6.7.1999.

16. S. Murat Çelikten, "Consumer Protection in Turkey," *Liability for Products in Global Economy*, Center for International Legal Studies, Kluwer Law International, Netherlands 2005: 35-59.

17. But unfortunately it should be mentioned that in most of its decisions the Court of Appeals in a way narrows down the jurisdiction of the consumer courts. For example, the definition of consumer under Article 3 refers to the "purchasing," "using," or "benefiting from" by the consumer of a good or service. Though this definition actually includes all types of services, in one of its established precedents, the Turkish Court of Appeals rules out any claim by the consumers based on "freelance contracts" (general service contracts such as a construction contact) saying that the services provided within the framework of a freelance contract are not to be considered as a "consumer transaction" to which the relevant provisions of the Law on Consumer Protection can apply. For instance, a claim arising from a repair work provided by a service station to a vehicle is not subject to consumer protection legislation and, thus, such a lawsuit should be heard before the general first instance courts and not consumer courts. In the last few years the Court of Appeals wrote wider decisions which may be regarded as a hope for the future.

18. Hasan Seçkin Ozanoğlu, "4822 sayılı Kanunla 4077 sayılı Tüketicinin Korunması Hakkında Kanunun Uygulama Alanında Getirilen Değişiklikler Üzerine," http://www.e-akademi.org/makaleler/hsozanoglu-1.htm (18.10.2010).

19. The Code of Obligations (no. 6098) was enacted by the Turkish Grand National Assembly on January 11, 2011 and after promulgated by the President of the Republic, it was published in the Official Journal on February 4, 2011 (OJ no. 27836). It entered into force approximately after one and a half years after its enactment on July 1, 2012.

20. http://europa.eu/pol/cons/index_en.htm (02.12.2012).

21. http://europa.eu/legislation_summaries/enlargement/ongoing_enlargement/community_acquis_turkey/e16113_en.htm (15.12.2012).

22. http://www.turkishweekly.net/news/34612/detailed-screening-on-consumer-protection-starts.html (10.01.2011).

23. http://ec.europa.eu/enlargement/pdf/key_documents/2012/package/tr_rapport_2012_en.pdf (05.11.2012).

24. This change is realized by the Statutory Decree on the Organization and Duties of the Ministry of Custom and Trade published in the Official Journal on June 8, 2011, http://www.gumrukticaret.gov.tr/altsayfa/mevzuat/94/kanun-khk.html (05.12.2012).

25. http://www.gumrukticaret.gov.tr/icerik/263/28/tuketicinin-korunmasi-ve-piyasa-gozetimi-genel-mudurlugu.html (09.12.2012).

26. http://www.ekonomi.gov.tr/index.cfm?sayfa=0E66979A-D8D3-8566-4520C0246A7D5A3C (05.11.2012).

27. Up to now this Council held 16 meetings and the last one of these meetings was held in May 2012. For more information see: http://www.gumrukticaret.gov.tr/altsayfa/icerik/309/1629/16-tuketici-konseyi.html (17.12.2012).

28. http://www.gumrukticaret.gov.tr/altsayfa/kategori/133/reklam-kurulu.html (10.11.2012).

29. http://www.tudef.org.tr/ (13.12.2012).

30. http://www.sanayi.gov.tr/Pages.aspx?pageID=518&lng=en (19.09.2012).

31. http://ec.europa.eu/enlargement/pdf/turkey/screening_reports/screening_report_28_tr_internet_en.pdf (05.11.2012). This was the situation when this screening report was submitted, for the year 2012 in November this number is more than 120,000.
32. Namely the EU Directive on Contracts Negotiated away from the Business Pemises and the EU Directive on Distance Sales.
33. http://ec.europa.eu/enlargement/pdf/key_documents/2012/package/tr_rapport_2012_en.pdf (05.11.2012).
34. http://ec.europa.eu/enlargement/pdf/key_documents/2012/package/tr_rapport_2012_en.pdf (05.11.2012).
35. http://ec.europa.eu/enlargement/pdf/key_documents/2012/package/tr_rapport_2012_en.pdf (05.11.2012).

REFERENCES

Akipek, Şebnem. *Türk Hukuku ve Mukayeseli Hukuk Açısından Tüketici Kredisi*. Ankara. 1999.

Atamer, Yesim, and Micklitz, Hans. "Implementation of the EU Consumer Directives in Turkey." *27 Penn State Int. Review*, 2008-2009, 551 ff.

Ceylan, Ali. *Tüketicinin Korunması*. Bursa, 1988.

Çelikten, S. Murat. "Consumer Protection in Turkey," *Liability for Products in Global Economy*, Center for International Legal Studies, Kluwer Law International, Netherlands, 2005, 35-59.

Mathijsen, P. S. R. F. *A Guide to European Union Law*. Ninth edition. Sweet and Maxwell, London, 2007.

Oughton, David, and Lowry, John. *Textbook on Consumer Law*. Second edition. Oxford Univesity Press, Norfolk, 2000.

Ozanoğlu, Hasan Seçkin. "4822 sayılı Kanunla 4077 sayılı Tüketicinin Korunması Hakkında Kanunun Uygulama Alanında Getirilen Değişiklikler Üzerine," 2003, http://www.e-akademi.org/makaleler/hsozanoglu-1.htm (18.10.2012).

Tandoğan, Haluk. "İç ve Dış Ticaretin Düzenlenmesine İlişkin Kanun Tasarısı ile Ticarette Dürüstlüğün Korunması Hakkında Kanun Tasarısının Tüketicinin Korunması Açısından İncelenmesi." *BATIDER*, 10 (1980), 4:10 ff.

TUSİAD (Türk Sanayici ve İş Adamları Derneği). *AT'de Tüketiciyi Koruma Politikaları ve Türkiye'de Durum*. İstanbul, 1990.

http://www.laweuropa.com/133-Avrupa-Birliginde-Tuketicinin-Tanımı (12.12.2012).

http://europa.eu/pol/cons/index_en.htm (02.12.2012)

http://europa.eu/legislation_summaries/enlargement/ongoing_enlargement/community_acquis_turkey/e16113_en.htm (15.11.2012).

http://www.turkishweekly.net/news/34612/detailed-screening-on-consumer-protection-starts.html (10.01.2011).

http://ec.europa.eu/enlargement/pdf/key_documents/2012/package/tr_rapport_2012_en.pdf (05.11.2012).

http://www.gumrukticaret.gov.tr/altsayfa/mevzuat/94/kanun-khk.html (05.12.2012).

http://www.gumrukticaret.gov.tr/icerik/263/28/tuketicinin-korunmasi-ve-piyasa-gozetimi-genel-mudurlugu.html (09.12.2012).

http://www.ekonomi.gov.tr/index.cfm?sayfa=0E66979A-D8D3-8566-4520C0246A7D5A3C (05.11.2012).

http://www.gumrukticaret.gov.tr/altsayfa/icerik/309/1629/16-tuketici-konseyi.html (17.12.2012).

http://www.gumrukticaret.gov.tr/altsayfa/kategori/133/reklam-kurulu.html (10.11.2012).

http://www.tudef.org.tr/ (13.12.2012).

http://www.sanayi.gov.tr/Pages.aspx?pageID=518&lng=en (19.09.2012).

http://ec.europa.eu/enlargement/pdf/turkey/screening_reports/screening_report_28_tr_internet_en.pdf (05.11.2012).

Chapter Three

Competition Law in Turkey From Association to Accession

Turning into a teenager with the same role model "Nineteen year old Turkish Competition Law following EU Competition Law"

Gamze Öz

INTRODUCTION

This article aims to set forth the developments in Turkish Competition Law ("TCL") in its nineteenth year, in the light of Turkey-EU relations and the candidacy process of Turkey. It concentrates on the sources and basic principles of TCL and provides how EU Competition Law (the "ECL") has influenced the emerging and development of TCL. In that respect, in this article the author compares TCL to a teenager ("Teen") who has been following the ECL since its very early days like the role model of a teen to grow into.

The growth of competition law in recent years has been enormous in Turkey. With the impact of privatisation and liberalisation attempts in the last two decades, in the Turkish economy competition law has turned out to be a major concept for state owned enterprises as well as private ones. The influence of ECL on this development has been not only in the enactment stages of Law No. 4054 on the Protection of Competition (hereinafter "Competition Law" or the "Law") but also in the process of application of the Law. The Turkish Competition Authority ("TCA"), the institution authorized to enforce the Law, follows the developments in ECL and also refers to the EU case law as a complementary source in its decisions. Thus it has been significant to understand the impact of ECL on TCL not only for the TCA, judiciary, and the business cycles but also for the state departments and lawyers through the candidacy process.

Competition Law has been important for Turkey not only as a developing economy but has been one of the key issues in the Progress Reports of the Commission[1] concerning Turkey. Since 1996 the Commission has been observing Turkey's progress in competition law and it has set forth serious critism as well as appraisal regarding the Turkish authorities on the enforcement of TCL. The criticism has been mostly related to the failure in certain regulations such as the surveillance of state aids which has been an important component of the EU Competition Policy and has been requested to comply with from the associate and candidate countries.

In the first part below, the sources of TCL will be described in order to introduce the main rules and regulations which form TCL, and in the second part, the features of TCL will be evaluated.

SOURCES OF TURKISH COMPETITION LAW

Primary Sources: Constitional Background and Legislative Acts

Political Background

As far as the economic reasons behind TCL are concerned, parallel to the EU Competition Law, the free market economy as the economic regime applied after the 1980s would itself be sufficient as the economic model, to explain the need for legislation on the regulation of the markets for goods and services. Thus, the main economic reasoning for the Law is the economic system which is in effect in Turkey today. Obviously, within this economic reasoning, the new approach of the EU concerning the social market economy phenomenon, regardless of the ambiguities it bears in its nature, had not been considered at all in the drafting process of the TCL. Nevertheless if the social market economy phenomenon plays a role in the interpretation of the EU Law, one wonders whether that may have an impact on the interpretation of the TCL.

In addition to the economic grounds, the role that international agreements played in the enactment of the Turkish competition legislation should not be underestimated. Obviously Turkey-EU relations towards the customs union had accelerated the effectiveness of the TCL.

Despite this explicit impact, comparing the two systems, one may see that it is not only the economic grounds and level of development which differs from that of the EU but unlike the EU system, there is not an ultimate purpose of integration in Turkey. Thus to start with the analysis, one should first set forth the major difference between the two systems that makes the settings considerably different. The integration goal of the EU which is a unique goal compared to the unitary states' competition laws has played a significant role in the interpretation and enforcement of the ECL. Furthermore the level of economic development in both jurisdictions and the supremacy of EU Law which has shaped the application of unified rules throughout the EU jurisdiction, make the two systems considerably different from each other. These differences may have an impact both at the policy making level and the interpretation of the rules.

Just two decades ago, Turkey did not have a Competition Law. Despite a few drafting attempts in the 1970s and 80s, none of those drafts had passed in the Parliament. Ultimately the draft of the Law was prepared by a team of law professors in 1992, who were all experts of competition law and economics, and further studied by the directorates of the Ministry of Trade and Industry[2] before it was presented to the Parliament. As a country in the process of Association, the team had modelled TCL on the ECL. Nonetheless it has been the Customs Union Decision No. 1/95[3] ("Decision No. 1/95") which had a significant impact on the enactment of the Law[4] in the Parliament in December 1994. Turkey's competition law and policy is mainly governed by the Law. TCL authorizes the establishment of an autonomous institution, namely the "TCA" which includes the Competition Board, "TCB" to enforce the law and issue communiqués for the implementation of the Law.[5]

Constitutional Basis

Article 167/2 of Turkish Constitution 1982 on the economic duties of the State sets forth the constitutional basis of the Law as:

> *. . . The State should take all necessary measures to provide and improve the sound and orderly functioning of the markets for goods, services, capital, credits and money and to that end, should avoid actual or contractual cartel agreements and monopolies in the markets . . .*

From the reading of Article 167, the provision sets forth three duties for the State authorities. First is to provide the necessary conditions so that private enterprises will have the possibility to improve themselves within a competitive environment. Secondly, to avoid statutory or actual monopolies. Thirdly, to avoid cartels. Surprisingly, despite this wording of the reasoning of Article 167, the Law neither refers to cartels nor to monopolies. The term used in Article 6 is "abuse of dominant position" as parallel to ECL, and Article 4 prohibits restrictive agreements, decisions, and concerted practices. A "cartel" is not referred to in the Law but it is defined in the by-laws issued by the TCB.[6]

International Agreements: Treaties Building Turkey-EU Relations

Although it has entered in the agenda of the State prior to the explicit requirement in the Decision No. 1/95 that the enactment of legislation on the protection of competition in Turkey should be in compliance with the EU competition rules,[7] earlier than the Decision No. 1/95, the Association Agreement which initially sets forth the frame for the association relation of Turkey with the European Economic Community (EEC)[8] requires that the Contracting Parties maintain the applicability of the provisions of the Rome Treaty on the harmonisation of competition, tax, and the laws.

Moreover, the Additional Protocol between Turkey and the EEC[9] requires that for the purposes of approximation of the economic policies of the Parties, the Association Council, within six years following the effectiveness of the Additional Protocol, should take the necessary measures for the implementation of the relevant articles of the Rome Treaty on competition matters[10]—namely, Articles 81 and 82 (now Articles 101 and 102) on the prohibition of agreements, decisions, and concerted practices and the abuse of dominant position which distorts competition and Articles 86-88 (now Articles 106 and 108) which refer to state aids.[11]

Article 32 and 33 of the Decision No. 1/95 sets forth that restrictive trade practices and abuse of dominant position that may affect customs union between Turkey and the EU is prohibited. Article 34 in particular regulates state aids and lists compatible and incompatible state aids and requires Turkey to align its state aid policy with the EU.

Legislative Acts

Law No. 4054 on the Protection of Competition

In terms of its scope, TCL is applicable to all restrictive agreements, decisions, behavior of all undertakings, and of association of undertakings ,and there are no exceptions in the Law for certain sectors or areas of the economy.[12] Broadly speaking, in terms of the sectors that it applies to, TCL covers all sectors and areas of the economy, including state undertakings.

In the days since TCL has been enacted, Turkey has been and it still is going through extensive privatisation policies. The density of the public enterprises in the economic system in the 1990s had led to the question of whether or not TCL would apply to such public enterprises. There is not an explicit provision in the Law on the exclusion of state undertakings from inclusion within the Law. Furthermore both the reasoning of the Constitutional basis of the Law and Turkey's commitments[13] under the Decision No. 1/95[14] require that the TCL should also apply to state undertakings. In accordance with these requirements, the TCB interpreted the Law in such a way that, despite the lack of explicit provisions on that matter, public undertakings[15] and the undertakings to which certain privileges or exclusive rights[16] are provided by the State are also covered by the Law. Although in its first couple of years, the TCB has been reluctant to initiate investigations against or impose fines on the public undertakings,[17] in the following years, the TCB has rendered several decisions[18] that the public undertakings are within the scope of the Law and even fined public undertakings for several infringements.[19]

STATE AIDS RULES IN TURKEY : A NEWLY BORN SISTER TO THE COMPETITION LAW

Law No. 6015 on the Monitoring and Supervision of State Aids

As stated both in the Ankara Agreement and in the Additional Protocol, the adoption of legislation compatible with the acquis communitaire in EU competition law including EU state aids law has been one of the commitments of Turkey. Further, in the Decision No. 1/95 Turkey has undertaken to align all aids with the principles set forth in Articles 107 and 108 of the TFEU.[20]

Despite the existence of a specific provision in the Decision No. 1/95, monitoring state aids was neither regulated in the Law nor in a separate specific law until 2010. Monitoring of state aids has been regulated under a Competition Chapter in the TFEU ("Treaty on the Functioning of the European Union") and under the Approximation of Legislation Chapter in the agreements regulating Turkey-EU relations.

Lack of a system of supervision and surveillance of state aids in Turkey has long been criticised by the European Commission. Having observed the lack of an enactment, not only in the consecutive Progress Reports but also in the Accession Partnership Documents dated 2001, 2003, 2006, 2008, and 2009 Turkey has been critised for her failure in this area.

In accordance with the EU requirements, legislation on the monitoring and supervision of state aids had been expected to be the twin sister of the Competition Law. Nevertheless despite a rapid growth in the area of competition law, the law on monitoring state aids had not been on the agenda of the governments for more than a decade. Finally the Parliament enacted a law on the surveillance of state aids. Law No. 6015 On the Monitoring and Supervision of Subsidies ("Law No. 6015)[21] enacted in October 2010, sets forth the principles and procedure to regulate the state aids in accordance with the agreements between Turkey and the EU and to make the notifications to the relevant authorities where necessary. The principles and procedure of monitoring and supervision have been modelled upon the Commission's duties concerning state aids.

State aids are defined to be any aid, provided directly by the state or through state sources to certain enterprises or to the production of certain products by way of creating discrimination which distorts or may distort competition which may affect trade between Turkey and the EU.

Thus from the wording of the Law No. 6015, it is clear that there are two exceptions within the scope of Law No. 6015. The first exception relates to sectors; the agriculture and fisheries sectors are not within the scope of the Law No. 6015. The second exception arises from the scope of the Law No. 6015, as Law No. 6015 has been enacted to regulate state aids which may affect trade between Turkey and the EU. Thus those aids which do not have any impact on trade between Turkey and the EU do not fall within the scope of this Law.

Law No. 6015 sets forth the establishment of a Board for the Monitoring and Supervision of State Aids, composed of members appointed from the Ministry of Finance, Ministry of Trade and Industry, Undersecreteriat of State Planning Organization, Undersecreteriat of Treasury, Undersecreteriat of Foreign Trade, and the Competition Authority and the General Director of State Aids.

One of the reasons for the delayed enactment of this Law is said to be the status and structure of the Board authorized to monitor the state aids and its impartiality. Thus the enforcement will prove or disprove the earlier hesitations on its impartiality. Compared to the TCA, whose jurisdiction covers the activities of public undertakings as well as private undertakings, the area of jurisdiction of this Board is mostly related to the State's decisions on subsidies. Thus its impartiality and independence will be as important as that of the TCB, and probably more difficult as the structure of the Board so whispers. Furthermore in the EU, both state aids and antitrust are governed by the same organ of the EU, the Commission. Whereas under the Turkish regime, at least theoretically at this stage, there may be discrepancies in the interpretations of the two institutions of the competition related concepts.

In the light of the above, state aid rules can be said to be part of the competition policy in the EU whereas in Turkey it is not clear from the wording of Law No. 6015 whether this would have an aligned application with the Competition Law. Thus the enforcement will show how much compliance there will be in the enforcement of the two enactments. Furthermore, Law No. 6015 specifically refers to the Turkey-EU Customs Union process, therefore Law No. 6015 has a limited scope as the impact of the relevant state aid to the customs union will affect the applicability of the Law.

OTHER LEGISLATIVE ACTS

TCL is the main law which governs competition law and policy. Nevertheless there are also other legislative acts enacted earlier or later than the Law No. 4054. For example regarding the energy markets, the Energy Market

Regulatory Board is authorized to impose preventive measures to protect fair competition amongst market players. Specific measures for such purpose is ensured in the relevant energy market legislation, such as the Electricity Market Law No. 4628,[22] Natural Gas Market Law No. 4646,[23] and Petroleum Market Law No. 5015[24] which are all enforced by the Energy Market Regulatory Board. Other examples for such specific sector related competition rules are also found in the Telecommunications Law No. 4673, Privatisation Law No. 4046, and Banking Law No. 5411. Although it is not explicitly stated in any of the relevant legislation nor in the TCL, in all of these examples, to coordinate the monitoring of anticompetitive behavior, full cooperation among these agencies must be achieved.[25]

One of the questions which has not yet created significant problems in practice, but still stands unresolved, is the allocation of jurisdiction between TCA and sectoral regulators, and more generally the relations between all related institutions with the TCA.

The second question recalls the term "competition advocacy" which deserves a separate section. Competition Advocacy seems to have gained priority in the practice of the TCA in the last couple of years which is expected to have a positive impact in the cooperation between the TCA and the regulators. There is only one statutory provision concerning a specific situation where cooperation and coordination is a statutory requirement. Under the privatization process, taking the opinion of the TCA before the tender process is a formal requirement the failure of which may be considered as a failure in the formal requirements thus may cause the cancellation of the relevant administrative decision on privatization.[26]

ADMINISTRATIVE ACTS

In addition to the relevant statutory provisions, since the TCB is authorized to set forth the implementing rules, it issues communiqués and by-laws[27] in order to show the enforcement rules of the Law and take decisions in accordance with the Law. Both the investigative powers and its procedural rules are modelled upon the rules that govern the European Commission's enforcement procedures. As the TCB has followed the Commission's enforcement model in issuing the secondary legislation, the experts regularly follow the developments in the EU as well as the case law. The TCB has issued several communiqués some of which have a general nature, some of which are more specific.[28]

In addition to the TCB communiqués, it has been a recent practice of the TCA to issue explanatory guidelines[29] in order to facilitate compliance to the law. This practice of the TCA is also modelled on the EU Commission's practice of issuing quidelines for guiding the enterprises.

In 2009 the TCB enacted two by-laws[30] both of which had been modelled on counterparts in the EU. One of these is the Leniency By-laws where it regulates the principles, procedure, and the consequences of leniency in case of anticompetitive practices, and the other one is on the principles of calculation of fines. However despite the enactment and enforcement of both, within the last two years, there have been serious discussions on the lawfulness of both of these by-laws even among the TCB members as there have been dissenting votes in the decisions where these by-laws have been applied. The firms that have been fined based on these by-laws have challenged the legality of these rules before the Council of State and those cases are still pending.

BASIC FEATURES OF TURKISH COMPETITION LAW

Prohibition on restrictive agreements, concerted practices, and decisions of association of undertakings (Article 4 of TCL)

In addition to its regulatory acts, the TCB, as the decision making organ of the TCA, takes decisions on violations together with sanctions; approval of mergers and acquisitions; renders negative clearance and exemption decisions.

The prohibition in Article 4[31] is modelled upon Article 101 of TFEU. As in the EU, the Law makes no distinction between horizontal or vertical agreements as both may fall within the scope of the Law. Thus the Law follows the general principles that apply in Article 101 ECL but differs in the enforcement of violations as there exists a presumption for concerted practices.

The Law sets forth the major examples of violations as in Article 101 of TFEU and does not provide a definition for hard core cartels. Nevertheless the TCB had made this distinction in the relevant by-laws issued in 2009 and in its several decisions. Despite the lack of an explicit reference to the term "cartel" in the Law, the TCB had defined cartels in the two by-laws enacted in 2009.

There are no specific rules or exceptions governing cartel behavior in the respective sectors, nor are there any *de minimis* rules. Although *de minimis* has been argued for in theory, as to the debates due to the lack of a statutory ground in the Law it has never been applied. However the TCB considers introducing the legal basis for *de minimis* with the amendment of the Law.

Not only contracts and other looser forms of agreements, such as oral agreements or gentlemen's agreements but also concerted practices of the undertakings are covered by the Law. Article 4 (last two paragraphs) together with Article 59 introduce a "presumption of concerted practice." According to this presumption, where there is a lack of sufficient proof for the existence of an agreement and a similarity regarding the price changes or the balance of supply and demand or other activities of the undertakings between the markets concerned and the markets where competition is prevented or distorted or limited, the undertakings concerned shall be deemed to have performed a concerted practice. TCB had applied the presumption in its several decisions.

Despite the fact that TCL is to a considerable extent based on EU competition law, this presumption of concerted practice creates a fundamental difference in terms of the burden of proof[32] and it is widely criticized in academia.

As a result of this presumption, the burden of proof is shifted from the TCB to the undertakings which are accused to have engaged in such a parallel action. In other words, if it is not possible to prove the existence of an agreement which distorts competition, but where there is still an indication, explicit or disguised, of an anti-competitive activity in the markets, the TCB will be able to take an action against the undertakings that are deemed to have been involved in such activities. In such cases, it is the undertakings that will have to rebut the presumption of concerted practice and will have to prove either that they have not engaged in such a parallel conduct or if they did, that they had justified their conduct on economic reasons. There are several decisions of the TCB where undertakings were alleged and have been found to have conducted a concerted practice.[33]

The Board has claimed in several cases that the relevant undertakings have been engaged in concerted practices. In some relevant decisions, the TCB had investigated yeast manufacturers for the uniform prices they have applied,[34] had investigated collusive action between newspaper publishers and based on documentary evidence stated explicitly in its decision that oligopolistic interdependence alone is not sufficient to trigger the concerted practice presumption.[35] In other decisions involving the cement and ready-mix concrete markets, the Board cited circumstantial evidence and employed economic analysis to support its determinations of collusion. The TCB, upon lack of an agreement to that effect, has fined three major cement producers[36] operating in the Aegean cement market and two enterprises operating in the cement market in the Mediterranean Region for refusing to deal (provide clinker) in the relevant geographic market to a smaller player through a concerted practice.[37]

Despite a considerable number of decisions, there is still serious academic debate on the constitutionality of the presumption and its compliance with EU Law.

As well as horizontal agreements, vertical agreements are also subject to and covered by Article 4 of the Law.[38] The TCB explicitly makes a distinction between the effect of vertical and horizontal agreements in the market and thus between the respective fines for each category of agreements. The Board has investigated several vertical agreements and charged fines in some of those investigations where the agreement, although vertical, was not within the scope of one of the exemption regulations and either not applied for an individual exemption or even if applied, did not qualify for it. Compared to its earlier decisions regarding vertical agreements, where the TCB had rendered more *per se* decisions, within the last couple of years it has moved towards an effect-based analysis for the vertical agreements. Although this can still be regarded as not a sufficient improvement, compared to its earlier years, at least the attempts should count.

Article 5 of the Competition Law provides exemptions to the Article 4 prohibitions. As this provision is parallel to Article 101/3 of the TFEU it can be either an individual exemption provided by a decision of the TCB or a group (block) exemption provided by a Communiqué of the TCB.

As it was the case in ECL, in its earlier years the TCB had regulated the vertical agreements with different regulations such as regulations for exclusive purchasing and sales agreements separately, all of which have been rendered ineffective upon the enactment of the general Communiqué for vertical agreements.[39]

PROHIBITION OF ABUSE OF DOMINANT POSITION (ARTICLE 6 OF TCL)

Article 6 prohibits abuse of a dominant position, whether perpetrated by a single firm or by several firms acting jointly. Benefiting from the definitions of the EU jurisprudence "dominance" is defined as the power to act independently of competitors and customers in determining parameters such as price, output, and amounts distributed.[40] The non-exclusive list of abusive practices in Article 6 is also modelled on the EU Article 102. Nevertheless there are differences in the wording and contents of the examples. The Law does not define a particular market share test for presuming or identifying dominance.

There are a considerable number of cases where statutory monopolies or dominant firms have been found to have abused their dominance. In its landmark cases, TCB had ruled against a company that had concessionary rights;[41] in another decision it concluded that two firms exercised joint dominance over the "essential facility" infrastructure necessary to provide national roaming capability for GSM mobile telephone services;[42] and in another Article 6 decision it fined Turkish Telekom, once the state-owned monopoly provider of land line telephone infrastructure for excluding competition in the dial-up internet services provider ("ISP") market.

TCB also fined the statutory monopoly BELKO authorized as the sole coal provider in and around Ankara city for excessive pricing. This is one of the early decisions of the TCB where it challenged the costs and the pricing policy of a company of the local authority and it is the only decision of the

TCB where excessive pricing of a dominant firm has been considered to be an abuse. Although the decision has been criticised from several aspects, it seems to have cured the excessive prices created as a result of a failure of price regulation in the relevant market where a monopoly has been created by an administrative decision of the municipal authority.

CONTROL OF MERGERS AND ACQUISITIONS (ARTICLE 7 TCL)

Concentrations which may restrict competition are regulated in Article 7 of TCL. As to Article 7 TCB is authorized to issue communiques to announce which concentrations are subject to review and therefore should be notified to the TCA. To that end, the new Communiqué on the Control of Mergers and Acquisitions No. 2010/4[43] entered into force on January 1, 2011. Communiqué No. 2010/4 repealed the previous Communiqué No. 1997/1 which had been in force since 1997.

There has already been a need for a change of the earlier Communiqué as it had been applied since 1997. It is not only the thresholds which needed an adjustment but there was a need for the clarification of certain concepts as well. With the new Communiqué, Turkish merger control rules got closer to the relevant EU legislation. Nevertheless, it is expected that there will be areas or questions which will need the Board's further explanation either on case-by-case analysis or by issuing guidelines or both.

In the earlier version of the Communiqué, there was an alternative criteria for notification based on turnover or market share. Communiqué No. 2010/4 adopted only "a turnover-based system" and also updated the previous figures in the Communiqué by setting forth national and worldwide figures. Adoption of turnover criteria provides further legal certainty as most companies mostly relied on the turnover criteria in their assessment.

Pursuant to Article 7 of the Communiqué No. 2010/4, a merger or acquisition shall be notified to the Competition Board (the "Board") to get approval either if:

1. the total turnover of both parties in Turkey exceeds TL 100,000,000 and the individual turnovers of at least two parties separately exceed TL 30,000,000, or
2. the global turnover of one party exceeds TL 500,000,000 and individual turnover of at least one other party in Turkey exceeds TL 30,000,000.

The affected market test, although tried in the earlier version of the Communiqué, has been amended with the Communiqué 2012/3 and it is no longer an explicit criterion for notification of mergers and acquisitions.

Procedure for controlling mergers and acquisitions

Legal base: Law No. 4054 Article 7 and TCB Communiqué No. 2010/4
Notification

- Mandatory for all concentrations that meet the turnover criteria set forth in Article 7 of Communiqué 2010/4.
- Such concentrations shall not be implemented either before its notification or until it has been declared compatible with the Law pursuant to the decision of the TCB.
- Those mergers and acquisitions which do not cause change of control need not be notified.

Upon Notification

- The TCB can approve the concentration if it deems that it does not cause any threat to competition in the market.
- In the course of its assessment, where the TCB finds out that the concentration may create anticompetitive effects, it may request that the firms comply with some undertakings to avoid/cure the possible anticompetitive impact (conditional approval).
- The TCB where it deems necessary may request information from all related third parties and carry out on the spot investigation.
- The TCB is to render its decision within 30 days after receipt of the complete notification.

The decisions of the TCB concerning mergers and acquisitions are, as are all other TCB decisions, subject to the judicial review of the administrative courts.

Privatization and Competition Law

In the late 1990s and early 2000s the Turkish Parliament launched a number of privatisation, deregulation, and market reforms with a significant impact on a number of sectors such as energy and telecommunications sectors.[44]

The privatisation process in Turkey is subject to the involvement of the TCA both as rendering an opinion at pre-tender stage and approving the transfer of assets/shares from public to private, based on Privatisation Law No. 4046, Competition Law and Communiqué No. 1998/4 regulating privatisations. TCB, before the tender process, opines on the privatisations and after the privatisation process TCB reviews the transaction as a concentration.

The opinion of the TCA delivered under the privatisation process is not binding. Thus, the opinion delivered by the TCA during the privatisation process becomes binding only when it is reflected in the tender documents or in the final decision of the TCB while approving the acquisition of the state owned property.[45]

ENFORCEMENT OF COMPETITION LAW

The Teen has changed its structural form several times: Turkish Competition Authority and the decision making body Turkish Competition Board

Following the Brussels school of competition law, TCL sets forth the enforcement of the Law by a central administrative authority, TCA. Despite the enactment of competition law in 1994, the actual enforcement started only after 1997.

The TCA, which existed since 1997, is an independent authority which is statutorily granted financial and administrative autonomy. The TCB is the decision making organ of the Authority.[46] The structure of the TCB and the authorities that nominate candidates for Board membership have changed a few times since its establishment.

Today the TCB is composed of seven members, The members of the TCB are appointed by the Council of Ministers among the candidates nominated by the Ministry of Customs and Trade, the Ministry of Development, the Court of Appeals, the Council of State, and by the Turkish Union of Chambers and Exchanges.[47]

The Teen is Proactive and Dynamic: Powers of the TCB

The TCB is empowered to interfere with any infringement of the Law, either upon a notification or a complaint or the request of the Ministry of Customs and Trade, and can also act upon its own initiative.[48] The general functions of the TCA are set out in Article 27 of TCL. The primary role of the TCA is in the sphere of detection of anticompetitive behavior. However the TCA with a gradually increasing effort, shows great interest in competition advocacy in the last years.

Not only for the Turkish Competition Policy but also from the viewpoint of administrative law, the procedural rules in the Law play a very important role as the Law has been the first set of rules codified under one statutory document which regulates administrative procedural rules. The Council of State in reviewing the acts of the TCA has ruled that these provisions are mandatory and that the TCA should comply with these rules in the process of its decision making, the failure of which may cause the cancellation of the relevant decision by the Court.

The TCB where it deems necessary starts a preliminary investigation which should be concluded within a thirty days period. Upon the completion of the preliminary investigation report by the committee of competition experts authorized by the TCB, the TCB announces whether or not it will start an investigation. The investigation should be completed within six months that can be extended for another six months, which is usually the case in the investigations. During the process of an investigation, the accused parties are given the rights to submit three written defense petitions and also following the completion of the written phase, the right to appear in the oral hearing before the TCB.

To perform its tasks and duties, the TCB has been given very extensive examination and investigative powers. To that end, it can authorize the experts to conduct dawn raids and to examine books and other records, take copies, ask for written and oral explanations and carry out on the spot investigations regarding the undertakings subject to investigation.[49] In case an on-the-spot inspection is hindered or likely to be hindered, the on-the-spot inspection is performed with the decision of a magistrate.

During the course of an investigation, the TCB has the authority to request any information from all public institutions and private companies and association of undertakings and those companies and public undertakings, should provide the information requested within the given time period.[50] The refusal to cooperate with the investigating experts or rejection of investigation on the premises may cause a fine.

The Teen May Hurt Sometimes: Sanctions and Penalties

The sanctions of Competition Law violations are limited to administrative monetary fines only and competition law violations do not constitute crimes. Thus, there are no criminal law sanctions under Competition Law, unless the claimed action also constitutes a crime under criminal laws. On the basis of the fact that competition law violations are not considered as crimes, there are no surveillance operations. Nevertheless, there are decisions of the TCB where the telephone tapping records of the relevant criminal authorities obtained in criminal investigations have also been referred to in the investigation carried out by the TCB.[51]

The TCB is empowered to impose fines and periodic penalty payments on the undertakings for the violation of the Law.[52] Since lack of consistency and transparency in the enforcement of administrative fines have been criticised[53] for a long time, the TCB had issued a Communiqué to set forth the fining principles for anticompetitive practices.

If the fines that the TCB may impose for the violation of the Law can be classified under two headings, these would be the periodic penalty payments and one-off penalties. One-off penalties can further be classified as those fines which can be charged for procedural violations such as failure to notify, providing misleading information, etc., and those which can be charged for the violations of the substantive provisions of the Law, including the cartel arrangements.

The periodic penalty payment amounts up to five per ten-thousandth of the annual gross revenue of the undertakings concerned, and of associations of undertakings and/or the members of such associations, which is generated by the end of the preceding financial year and where it is not possible to calculate such revenue, of the revenue which is generated by the end of the closest financial year and which shall be determined by the Board.

Where undertakings or associations of undertakings are assessed administrative fines, executives or employees of the undertaking or association of undertakings which is detected to have had a determining impact on the violation are assessed administrative fines up to five percent of the fine imposed on the undertaking or association of undertakings.

In deciding an administrative fine, the Board takes account of factors such as the repetition and duration of the violation, the market power of the undertakings or associations of undertakings, their determining impact on the occurrence of the violation, whether they conform to the commitments made, whether they assist with the inspection, the gravity of the damage which has occurred or is likely to occur. Further the TCB had issued by-laws in 2009 on the calculation principles for cartel cases.

On the grounds of the Leniency by-laws issued in 2009, undertakings or associations of undertakings or their executives and employees which actively cooperate with the Authority for uncovering the violation of the Law may be held immune from the fines or be granted reductions on the fines to be levied pursuant to the relevant paragraphs, taking into account the nature, effectiveness, and timing of the cooperation and with the reasoning thereof clearly presented.

Since the Leniency Communiqué has recently been issued and it is a new practice for firms, there are very few decisions of the TCA in which the leniency program has been applied. The most notable decision of the TCA involving leniency has been in the industrial and medical gases sectors.

The recent amendment of the Law has substantially changed the fining policy of the Law as the previous version of the Law had fixed amounts of fines for procedural violations whereas now these violations will be fined on the grounds of the gross revenue of the undertaking concerned.

Further the Law also sets forth fines for those managers and employees who has disclosed a decisive influence on the conduct of the infringement. These changes aim at providing efficient compliance. In these amendments the TCB had again followed the EU approach in order to have a discouraging mechanism and by this way have firms refrain from violating the Law.

The fines set forth in the Law are all administrative fines. In addition to the administrative fines explained above, unlike some other jurisdictions there are no other (criminal or civil law) sanctions such as disqualification of managers or imprisonment.

The Actions of the Teen are Subject to Review: Appeal/Judicial Review of TCB Decisions

With an amendment in the Council of Law,[54] a specific chamber (13th Chamber) had been established and it took office by the beginning of 2005 in order to review the decisions of most of the regulatory authorities including the TCA. The Council of State 13th Chamber is not at all a specialised court authorized to deal exclusively with competition law disputes, as it acts more like a court reviewing the decisions of all the regulatory institutions in the Turkish legal system. The decisions of the TCB on interim measures, fines and periodic penalty payments, and all its final decisions had been challenged before the Turkish Council of State (the highest administrative court in the Turkish legal system) until the recent amendment regarding a judicial reform.

Nevertheless a recent amendment in the judicial system has changed the judicial review model explained above and made Council of State the appeal court to review the decisions of the relevant administrative court that will have jurisdiction to review the decisions of the TCB.

The statutory time period for taking a legal action against the decision is 60 days commencing from the date when the reasoned decision is served to the parties. An appeal application does not stop the enforcement unless an injunction decision is given by the Court.

The administrative court can either cancel the decision of the TCB or reject the request of the parties. Thus, if the administrative court cancels the decision on any ground, the decision including the fine shall be considered non-existent. Unlike the authority of the European Courts, the court cannot reduce the fines by its decision. Even if the fine has been found disproportionate or unlawful, this would lead to the cancellation of the whole decision.

CONCLUSION

There has been significant development not only in TCL but also in ECL in the last decade. In EU Law it is not only the procedural rules and the shared competence of the Commission with the national member states which have changed since the beginning of 2000 but also the emphasis made to the competition rules with the amendment of the founding treaties. With the effectiveness of the TFEU the old Article 3(g) of the Rome Treaty has been amended and the new Article 3(1)(b) of the TFEU states that as well as other areas stated in Article 3, the Union shall have exclusive competence in establishing the competition rules necessary for the functioning of the internal market.

Article 3 of the new TFEU states that the EU shall work for the sustainable development of Europe based on, among other things, a highly competitive social market economy. This is considered to be a new approach which is different than the characteristic enforcement policy in the early years of the EU, focusing on preventing barriers between national markets emerging and protecting competitors from dominant companies.[55]

It is a well established fact that the EU Competition Policy has a significant impact on other economic policies of the EU. A relatively recent example on that can be seen in the Commission's Europe 2020 Paper setting forth the economic priorities of the EU for 2020. According to the Europe 2020 Paper, efficient use of sources such as energy; development of certain standards encouraging the improvement of technology and innovation in the area of intellectual property rights; the need to coordinate the financial policies especially during the times of crisis and the use of state aids policy at such times are all closely related with the competition policy.

All these developments may gradually have an influence on the application of competition rules not only in the early EU member states but also in the newcomers and also in Turkey as an association country negotiating for accession. Nevertheless the implementation of the substantial rules which have been in effect for more than fifty years by now in a developed, multilayered legal system has been the role model for Turkish Competition Law as well as many other jurisdictions.

Time has shown that the Teen who was born nineteen years ago, had her first baby steps forward. Today, it seems it is time to sit back and review what has been done. Setting up priorities, adjustment of its institutional design to the set priorities, and aiming at more efficient work with strengthening its capacity for sound economic analysis are the areas that should be taken into account regarding a teenager towards the end of its second decade.

NOTES

1. 1 EC, *Turkey2009 ProgressReport*, 14.10.2009, http://ec.europa.eu/enlargement/pdf/key_documents/2009/tr_rapport_2009_en.pdf (20.01.2010).
2. As of this date, that Ministry is called the Ministry of Customs and Trade.
3. Decision No. 1/95 Article 16.
4. Published in the Official Gazette No. 22140 dated December 13, 1994.
5. Article 27 of Law No. 4054 authorizes the TCB to issue Communiques to show the application of the Law.
6. Article 3 of the By Laws defines "Cartel" as "competition-restrictive agreements and/or concerted practices between competitors for fixing prices; allocation of customers, providers territories or trade channels; restricting the amount of supply or imposing quotas, and bid rigging."

7. Nurkut İnan and Gamze Öz, "Turkish Competition Law and the Impact of the Customs Union Decision" in Subidey Togan and V.N. Balasubramanyam (eds.), *Turkey and Central and Eastern European Countries in Transition Towards the Membership of the EU*, Palgrave, 2001: 259-267.

8. Association Agreement between Turkey and the EEC, September 12, 1963 OJ 217, 29.12.1964.

9. Additional Protocol dated November 23, 1970 published in the Official Gazette dated 31.12.1977 OJ EC L361/1.

10. These Articles should be read as Article 101 and 102 with the effectiveness of TFEU.

11. Additional Protocol, Article 43.

12. Gamze Öz and Zeynep Cakmak, "Turkey" in Mater Dabbah (ed.), *Cartels Project*, Sweet and Maxwell Publishers, London, 2010: 102. Gamze Öz; "Legal and Institutional Aspects of Competition Policy in Turkey and Its Impact on Investment" in Shyam Khemani (ed.), *Competitiveness and Regulation in Turkey*, TEPAV (2005): 61-67, http://www.tepav.org.tr. Gamze Öz, *AB ve Türk Hukukunda Hakim Durumun Kötüye Kullanılması*, Rekabet Kurumu Yayını, 2000.

13. For further analysis of the competition rules of the Customs Union : İnan and Öz, 2001, p. 262.

14. Decision No. 1/95 Article 39.

15. For e.g. Competition Board Decision No. 02-60/755-305 dated October 2, 2002 (TTnet Decision), published in the Official Gazette No. 25431 dated April 12, 2004.

16. For e.g. Competition Board Decision No. 03-72/874-373 dated November 10, 2003 (ÇEAŞ Decision).

17. Gamze Öz, "Hakim Durumun Kötüye Kullanılması" *Rekabet Forumu*, www.rekabetdernegi.org.tr.

18. Decisions No. 06-02/47-8 dated 5.1.2006 and No. 60/755-305 dated 2.10.2002 Türk Telekom kararları.

19. Decision No. 01-17/150-39 dated 06.04.2001 regarding BELKO where TCB had fined BELKO (a monopoly concession to import and sell coal for heating purposes in and around Ankara region) for excessive pricing.

20. Melike Demirkaya Özmen, *State Aids Policy in the EU : With Specific Reference to the Banking Sector in the Post 2008 Crisis*, Unpublished Masters Thesis submitted to the Graduate School of Social Sciences of Middle East Technical University, 2010.

21. Devlet Desteklerinin İzlenmesi ve Denetlenmesi Hakkında Kanun No. 6015 (Law No. 6015 on the Surveillance and Supervision of State Aids' enacted on 13.10.2010 published in the Official Gazette No. dated 23.10.2010.

22. Published in the Official Gazette No. 24335 dated March 3, 2001.

23. Published in the Official Gazette No. 24390 dated 2 May 2001.

24. Published in the Official Gazette No. 25322 dated December 20, 2003.

25. Restructuring, Competition and Regulation in the Turkish Electricity Industry, part of the Project on Competitiveness and Regulation in Turkey, TEPAV/EPRI publication (2006): 147.

26. For further details see Gamze Öz; "Regional experiences and lessons learnt in fastening competition in regulated sectors, focusing on the link between competition agencies and regulated bodies," Seminar Paper presented in Sao Paolo, Brazil, in the Seminar on Competition Law and Policy in Latin America: addressing development priorities UNCTAD/IDRC/Getulio Vargas Foundation Law School November 30–December 1, (2006).

27. A list of the Communiqués issued by the Competition Authority can be found in the website of the Competition Authority: www.rekabet.gov.tr.

28. Can be reached from the web-site of the TCA www.rekabet.gov.tr The following are the TCB Communiqués which are of general nature:

- Communiqué on the Mergers and Acquisitions No: 1997/1 (Amended by the TCB Communiqués No. 1998/2, 1998/6 and 2000/2, 2010/4)
- Communiqué on the Completion of the organization of the Competition Authority No. 1997/5

- Communiqué on the Procedures and Principles to be Pursued in Pre-Notifications and Authorisation Applications to be Filed with the Competition Authority in order for Acquisitions via Privatisation to Become Legally Valid (Amended by the Competition Board Communiqué No. 1998/5) No: 1998/4
- Block Exemption Communiqué on Vertical Agreements (Amended by the Competition Board Communiqué No. 2003/3) No: 2002/2

The following TCB Communiqués are relatively more specific:

- Block Exemption Communiqué No: 2003/2 on Research and Development Agreements
- Block Exemption Communiqué No. 2005/4 on Vertical Agreements and Concerted Practices in the Motor Vehicle Sector
- Block Exemption Communiqué No. 2008/2 on Technology Transfer Agreements
- Block Exemption Communiqué No. 2008/3 in relation to the Insurance Sector.

29. Guidelines on the Explanation of the Block Exemption Communiqué on Vertical Agreements No. 2002/2
Guidelines on Certain Subcontracting Agreements between Non-competitors
Guidelines on the Definition of Relevant Market
Guidelines on Optional Notification of Agreement, Concerted Action and Enterprise Union Decisions
Guidelines on the Explanation of Block Exemption Communiqué on Vertical Agreements and Concerted Practices in the Motor Vehicle Sector No. 2005/4.

30. By-Laws on Leniency and By-laws on the Calculation of Fines, both published in the Official Gazette No. 27142 dated February 15, 2009.

31. "Article 4—Agreements and concerted practices between undertakings, and decisions and practices of associations of undertakings which have as their object or effect or likely effect the prevention, distortion or restriction of competition directly or indirectly in a particular market for goods or services are illegal and prohibited. Such practices are especially as follows:

a. Fixing the purchase or sale price of goods or services, elements such as cost and profit which form the price, and any terms of purchase or sale,
b. Partitioning markets for goods or services, and sharing or controlling all kinds of market resources or elements,
c. Controlling the amount of supply or demand in relation to goods or services, or determining them outside the market,
d. Complicating and restricting the activities of competing undertakings, or excluding firms operating in the market by boycotts or other behaviour, or preventing potential new entrants to the market,
e. Except exclusive dealing, applying different terms to persons with equal status for equal rights, obligations and acts,
f. Contrary to the nature of the agreement or commercial usages, obliging to purchase other goods or services together with a good or service, or tying a good or service demanded by purchasers acting as intermediary undertakings to the condition of displaying another good or service by the purchaser, or putting forward terms as to the resupply of a good or service supplied.

In cases where the existence of an agreement cannot be proved, that the price changes in the market, or the balance of demand and supply, or the operational areas of undertakings are similar to those markets where competition is prevented, distorted or restricted, constitutes a presumption that the undertakings are engaged in concerted practice.
Each of the parties may relieve itself of the responsibility by proving not to engage in concerted practice, provided that it is based on economic and rational facts."

32. İzak Atiyas and Gönenç Gürkaynak, "Presumption of Concerted Practice": *A Legal and Economic Analysis*, 2006, http://myweb.sabanciuniv.edu/izak/files/2008/10/atiyas-gurkaynak-

concerted-practice-may-2006.pdf (24.01.2011), also in IVth Annual Symposium on Recent Developments in Competition Law, Erciyes University and the Competition Authority (2006). Gönenç Gürkaynak, "Shifting the Burden of Proof in Turkish Competition Law, Feature Turkey," www.global-competition.com (12.03.2003).

33. Competition Board Goltas and Denizli Cimento Decisions No. 07-76/908-346 dated September 29, 2007.

34. Competition Board Maya Decision No. 00-24/255-138 dated June 27, 2000.

35. Competition Board Decision No.00-26/291-161 dated July 17, 2000.

36. Competition Board Cement II Decision of the TCB No.02-06/51-24 dated January 2, 2002

37. Competition Board Decision No.05-05/42-17 dated January 13, 2005 regarding Denizli Çimento and Goltas announced on date 25.01.2005 (reasoned decision not yet published).

38. Sanem Şimşek and Tarkan Erdoğan, "An Effects-Based Approach to Exclusivity Agreements: The Case of Coca-Cola Turkey," *European Competition Law Review*, 29 (2008), 10, p. 570.

39. Block Exemption Communiqué No. 2002/2 on Vertical Agreements issued on July 14, 2002 and published in the Official Gazette No. 24815.

40. See Article 3 of the Law.

41. OECD, *Peer Review Report on Turkey's Competition Law and Policy*, Global Forum on Competition, DAF/COMP/GF(2005)4, dated January 27, 2005.

42. OECD, 2005, p.44.

43. Published in the Official Gazette No. 27722 dated October 7, 2010.

44. Öz; "Regional experiences and lessons learnt in fastening competition in regulated sectors, 2006).

45. Gamze Öz, "The impact of Competition Law in the Privatizations Process in Turkey," Conference Paper presented in a Conference on Competition Law and Privatization in Cairo, Egypt, January 28, 2008.

46. Law No. 5388 amending Article 22 of Law No. 4054 published in the Official Gazette No. 25874, dated July 13, 2005.

47. Article 22 of the Law.

48. Article 40 of the Law.

49. Articles 14 and 15 of the Law.

50. Article 14 of the Law.

51. No. 07-24/236-76 dated March 16, 2007.

52. Articles 16-19 of the Law.

53. OECD, 2005, p.24.

54. Law No. 5183 dated June 2, 2004.

55. http://competitionlawblog.blogspot.com/2010_01_01_archive.html (24.01.2010).

REFERENCES

Atiyas, İzak, and Gürkaynak, Gönenç. "Presumption of Concerted Practice": A Legal and Economic Analysis; May 17, 2006, http://myweb.sabanciuniv.edu/izak/files/2008/10/atiyas-gurkaynak-concerted-practice-may-2006.pdf) (24.01.2012), also in IVth Annual Symposium on Recent Developments in Competition Law organized by Erciyes University and the Competition Authority, Ankara, 2006.

Competition Authority. *Report on Implementation of Competition Policy in Turkey 1997-2003*. Ankara 2004, www.rekabet.gov.tr (15.01. 2010).

EC. *Turkey 2009 Progress Report*, 14.10.2009, http://ec.europa.eu/enlargement/pdf/key_documents/2009/tr_rapport_2009_en.pdf (20.01.2010).

Gellhorn, Ernest, and Kovacic, William E. *Antitrust Law and Economics in a Nutshell*, Fourth Edition. West Pub. Co., St. Paul, 1994.

Güney, Esat Serhat. *Restructuring, Competition and Regulation in the Turkish Electricity Industry* part of the Project on Competitiveness and Regulation in Turkey, TEPAV/EPRI publication, Ankara.

Gürkaynak, Gönenç. *Shifting the Burden of Proof in Turkish Competition Law*, Feature Turkey in www.global-competition.com (12.01. 2003).

İnan, Nurkut, and Öz, Gamze. "Turkish Competition Law and the Impact of the Customs Union Decision" in Subidey Togan and V.N. Balasubramanyam (ed.), *Turkey and Central and Eastern European Countries in Transition Towards the Membership of the EU*. Palgrave, 2001: 259-267.

Khemani, Shyam R. *Overview and Recommendations, Competitiveness and Regulation in Turkey*. TEPAV, Ankara, 2005.

OECD. *Turkey Peer Review of Competition Law and Policy*, 2005, http://www.oecd.org/dataoecd/26/7/34645128.pdf (20.01.2010).

Öz, Gamze. "Legal and Institutional Aspects of Competition Policy in Turkey and Its Impact on Investment" in Khemani, Shyam (ed.) *Competitiveness and Regulation in Turkey*. TEPAV, Ankara, 2005:61-67, www.tepav.org.tr (10.03.2008).

———. *AB ve Türk Hukukunda Hakim Durumun Kötüye Kullanılması*. Rekabet Kurumu Yayını, Ankara, 2000.

———. "Hakim Durumun Kötüye Kullanılması" *Rekabet Forumu*, www.rekabetdernegi.org.tr (01.01. 2007).

———. "Regional experiences and lessons learnt in fastening competition in regulated sectors, focusing on the link between competition agencies and regulated bodies." Seminar Paper presented in Sao Paolo, Brazil, in the Seminar on Competition Law and Policy in Latin America: addressing development priorities organized by UNCTAD/IDRC/Getulio Vargas Foundation Law School, Sao Paolo, November 30–December 1, 2006.

———. "The Impact of Competition Law in the Privatizations Process in Turkey." Conference Paper presented in a Conference on Competition Law and Privatization in Cairo, Egypt on January 28, 2008.

Öz, Gamze, and Cakmak, Zeynep. "Turkey" in Mater Dabbah (ed.), *Cartels Project*. Sweet and Maxwell Publihers, London, 2010.

Özmen Demirkaya, Melike. *State Aids Policy in the EU : With Specific Reference to the Banking Sector in the Post 2008 Crisis*. Unpublished Masters Thesis submitted to the Graduate School of Social Sciences of Middle East Technical University, Ankara, 2010.

Şimşek, Sanem, and Erdoğan, Tarkan. "An Effects-Based Approach to Exclusivity Agreements: The Case of Coca-Cola Turkey." European Competition Law Review, 29 (2008), 10.

Yenisey, K.D. "Prohibitions of Cartels in Turkey." European Competition Law Review, 2002: 26-34.

http://competitionlawblog.blogspot.com/2010_01_01_archive.html

http://ec.europa.eu/enlargement/pdf/key_documents/2009/tr_rapport_2009_en.pdf

www.rekabet.gov.tr

www.rekabetdernegi.org

Chapter Four

The Dispute Settlement Procedures in the Ankara Agreement

Decision No. 1/95 and the Jurisdiction of the European Court of Justice

A. Aslı Bilgin

INTRODUCTION

Turkey made its first application to join the European Economic Community (EEC), known as the European Union (EU) now, in 1959. This application resulted in the signature of the Ankara Agreement[1] (Agreement Creating an Association Between the Republic of Turkey and the European Economic Community), which was composed of three titles and thirty-three articles, including main institutions of this Association in 1963, instead of an accession treaty. The Ankara Agreement is being accepted as a framework agreement on the way to the full membership. Article 28 of the Ankara Agreement also confirms that the ultimate aim of the parties is Turkey's full membership to the Union.[2] In order to prepare Turkey for membership, the Ankara Agreement envisaged the establishment of a Customs Union in three phases (preparatory phase, transition phase, and completion phase) which would also pave the way to a closer relationship between Turkey and the EU.[3] The preparatory phase lasted from 1964 to 1973. At the end of this phase an Additional Protocol[4] which aimed to remove customs duties between both parties was adopted. The transitional period began in 1973 and ended with the adoption of Decision No. 1/95 of the EC–Turkey Association Council on implementing the final phase of the Customs Union.[5] No sooner had the Customs Union decision entered into force in 1996 than the final phase was initiated and is still going on. Despite Turkey's application for full membership in 1987, Turkey was finally declared as a candidate country in 1999 at the Helsinki Summit and is still waiting at the EU's entrance gate.

In accordance with Article 6 of the Ankara Agreement, the establishment of the Association Council which ensures the implementation and the progressive development of the Association is envisaged. It should be noted that the only institutional body with legislative features described in the Agreement is the Association Council.[6] On the other hand the Council of Association is also entitled to set up committees to assist its tasks and to ensure the proper functioning of the Association under Article 24 of the Ankara Agreement.[7] As a result of this provision, the Association Committee has been established to prepare the agenda of the Association Council and make analysis regarding technical issues that the Association Council needs. Furthermore, the Turkey-EU Joint Parliamentary Commission has been entitled to examine the annual activity reports prepared by the Association Council and to exchange views on the issues regarding association relations and to make recommendations to the Association Council. Finally, the Customs Cooperation Committee has been formed to monitor the implementation of the provisions related to Customs Union of the Ankara Agreement.[8] In addition to these committees, the Association Council also established a Customs Union Joint Committee under Articles 50-51 of Decision No. 1/95, "to carry out exchange of views and information, to formulate recommendations to the Association Council and to deliver opinions with a view to ensure the proper functioning of the Customs Union." Even though the Association Council and the other committees aim at securing proper functioning of the Association between Turkey and the European Union, a dispute settlement procedure is not discussed in detail under the Ankara Agreement. The only provision envisaged for dispute settlement is Article 25 under the Ankara Agreement. Pursuant to this Article, the Association Council has been authorized for dispute settlement in two ways. It can resolve a problem either by giving a decision itself or submitting the dispute to the European Court of Justice (ECJ) or to any other existing court or tribunal. Besides the Ankara Agreement, Decision No. 1/95 also foresees a procedure for dispute settlement under Articles 61-62. The main difference between the Articles related to dispute settlement is their scope of application. While Article 25 under Ankara Agreement is a general provision that can also be applied for the disputes arising from decisions of the Association Council unless specified otherwise, Articles 61 and 62 are provided for special situations stated in the provisions. Article 25/2 of the Ankara Agreement must be interpreted in conjunction with Article 6 as meaning that the words "application and interpretation of the Agreement" covers the application and the interpretation of the decisions of the Council of Association. Moreover, the initiation of the procedures also differ from each other due to the authorized institution to apply and the applicant.

Along with these procedures, the European Court of Justice has a discrete status which will be examined under two headings. Even if it is hard to submit the dispute to the European Court of Justice through the dispute settlement procedures provided in the Ankara Agreement and Decision No. 1/95 of the Association Council, the European Court of Justice has the right to interpret the two documents by the preliminary ruling procedure.

This paper analyzes the dispute settlement procedure stipulated in the Ankara Agreement and Decision No. 1/95 in general. In this respect, in the first part of the paper the procedure and the institutions figured under the terms of the Ankara Agreement for dispute settlement are examined while the second part is devoted to the dispute settlement procedure in Decision No. 1/95. The positive and negative features of both procedures will also be considered. In the last part of the paper, first, the position of the European Court of Justice in the dispute settlement procedure envisaged in the Ankara Agreement and Decision No. 1/95 is discussed. Secondly, the jurisdiction of the European Court of Justice on the EC-Turkey Association Agreement and Decisions of the Council of Association is argued.

DISPUTE SETTLEMENT PROCEDURE IN THE ANKARA AGREEMENT

The dispute settlement procedure has been established under Article 25 in the Ankara Agreement.

Article 25 of the Ankara Agreement reads as follows:[9]

> *1. The Contracting Parties may submit to the Council of Association any dispute relating to the application or interpretation of this Agreement which concerns the Community, a Member State of the Community, or Turkey.*
>
> *2. The Council of Association may settle the dispute by decision; it may also decide to submit the dispute to the Court of Justice of the European Communities or to any other existing court or tribunal.*
>
> *3. Each Party shall be required to take the measures necessary to comply with such decisions.*
>
> *4. Where the dispute cannot be settled in accordance with paragraph 2 of this Article, the Council of Association shall determine, in accordance with Article 8 of this Agreement, the detailed rules for arbitration or for any other judicial procedure to which the Contracting Parties may resort during the transitional and final stages of this Agreement.*

The Article reflects some crucial limitations in order to submit any dispute to the Council of Association in two issues. First of all, the dispute should be about the application or interpretation of the Ankara Agreement and it should concern the Union, a member state of the Union, or Turkey. Secondly, contracting parties who are the Union, a member state of the Union, or Turkey, are the only applicants entitled to apply to the Council of Association for a dispute settlement.[10]

As it is also defined in the Article, the competent authority to determine the way to settle the dispute is the Association Council. Pursuant to Article 25, it has two options. Besides settling the dispute by its own decision, the Association Council can also convey the dispute to the Court of Justice of the European Union or to any other existing court or tribunal. Due to the interpretation of the Article 25/2, if the Council of Association prefers to submit the dispute to any judicial authority rather than resolving it by giving a decision itself, it can easily be said that in addition to the European Court of Justice, the Association Council is free to submit the dispute to whatever existing judicial institution it would prefer.

According to some authors, the former is called political and the latter is called judicial procedures.[11] Even though this entitlement can be acceptable, it should be kept in mind that the selection of the procedure belongs to the decision of the Council of Association which has a binary role as a decision maker and an arbitrator of the conflicts.[12] At first, the appointment of the Council of Association as the dispute settlement authority can be seen as appropriate, but the decision making process in the Council of Association indicates the opposite. Article 23 of the Ankara Agreement regulates the composition and the decision making process of the Association Council. In accordance with this Article, the Association Council consists of members of the Turkish Government on the one hand and the members of the Governments of the Member States and members of the Council and of the Commission of the Community on the other hand. Unanimity is required for all decisions. In terms of provision, it is clear that there are two parties and each party has one vote. Even though there are only two parties, each party consists of more than one member and this composition makes it hard to determine the way the parties vote because first of all, each party has to decide how to vote with its members. In other words, they need to get their members' consent before declaring their votes. To sum up, the Council of Association, in order to settle a dispute envisaged under article 25 either by giving its own decision or by assigning it to any other judicial authority, should act unanimously either way.

Apart from this, Article 25 regulates another remedy to settle a dispute in its last paragraph which can be resorted to after exhausting the procedures envisaged under Article 25/2 during the transitional and final stages of the Ankara Agreement. The relevant article's last paragraph gives the Council of Association the right to determine the rules for arbitration or any other judicial procedure to which the Contracting Parties may resort. Thus, the Association Council regulates the rules to submit the dispute to an arbitration board with the Decision No. 1/95. With reference to Article 25/4, arbitration or any other judicial procedure has become a dispute settlement procedure just for transitional and final stages of the Ankara Agreement only if the dispute cannot be settled by political or judicial procedure under Article 25/2.

The dispute settlement procedures regulated in the Ankara Agreement are inadequate and ineffective because of the entitlement of the Council of Association as the decision making authority. In other words, the veto option given to the each Party can cause the dispute to get stuck in a deadlock where unanimity is required. In addition to this, envisaging a judicial procedure by entitling a political institution to decide whether to appeal makes the procedure political rather than legal.

DISPUTE SETTLEMENT PROCEDURE IN DECISION NO. 1/95

The Council of Association has adopted an arbitration procedure under Article 61 of Decision No. 1/95 due to the right given to it by Article 25/4 of the Ankara Agreement. It sets forth the conditions under which the arbitration procedure may be applied. Besides Article 61, the establishment and the functioning of the arbitration board was enacted under Article 62. Along with Article 61, there is also another situation registered under Article 39/4 that contracting parties have a right to appeal arbitration.

The Competence of the Arbitration Board

Article 61 of Decision No. 1/95 mentions the competences of the Arbitration Board in detail which provides that:

> *Without prejudice to paragraphs 1 to 3 of Article 25 of the Ankara Agreement, if the Association Council fails to settle a dispute relating to the scope or duration of protection measures taken in accordance with Article 58 (2), safeguard measures taken in accordance with Article 63 or rebalancing measures taken in accordance with Article 64, within six months of the date on which this procedure was initiated, either Party may refer the dispute to arbitration under the procedures laid down in Article 62. The arbitration award shall be binding on the Parties to the dispute.*

Pursuant to Article 61, the contracting parties have a right to appeal arbitration where a dispute arising from the scope or duration of a protection, safeguard, or rebalancing measure which was taken under Article 58/2, 63 or 64 unless the dispute can be settled by the Council of Association within six months from the date of initiation of the proceedings.

The Customs Union is a kind of trade agreement to remove trade barriers, and reduce or eliminate customs duty on mutual trade and to levy common external tariffs on trade with non-members.[13] The proper functioning of the Customs Union requires not only the harmonization of member states' legislations but also the same implementation of them in the areas of direct relevance to the functioning of the Customs Union. Otherwise, the discrepancies between member states' legislations or differences in their implementation may engender the disablement of free movement of goods, trade deflections, or economic problems. Thus, Article 58/2 is envisaged in order to explain the rights Contracting Parties have when one of these situations emerges or when a possibility of any of these situations occurs between Turkey and the Community. Contracting Parties can take protection measures by informing the Customs Union Joint Committee which has the right to change or remove the measures taken. In this situation, when a dispute arises between contracting parties based on this Article first, they have to submit the problem to the Council of Association. If the dispute cannot be settled during the aforementioned duration, each party has the right to appeal to the arbitration board.

Article 63 refers to the safeguard measures taken under Article 60 of the Additional Protocol. Article 60 of the Additional Protocol gives contracting parties the right to take protection measures:

- if serious disturbances occur in a sector of the economy of the Community or of one of more Member States or the Turkish economy or prejudice one of their external financial stability or,
- if difficulties arise which adversely affect the economic situation in a region of Turkey or the Community.

Even though each party has the right to decide whether to take protection measures or not, each of them shall notify the Council of Association immediately of those measures and of the rules for their application. While Article 63 reaffirms that the mechanism and modalities of safeguard measures set forth in Article 60 of the Additional Protocol remain valid, Article 61 enables the Parties to appeal to the arbitration board if a dispute related to safeguard measures emerges.

Furthermore, apart from safeguard and protection measures, Article 64 defines rebalancing measures that can be adopted by one of the contracting parties if an imbalance occurs between the rights and obligations of the Parties originated from Decision No. 1/95 because of a safeguard or protection measure taken by one side. The procedure for taking rebalancing measures envisaged in Article 64/2 by referring Article 60 of Additional Protocol which means that the only condition is to notify the Council of Association immediately of rebalancing measures and of the rules for their application. The Contracting Parties can submit a dispute arising from rebalancing measures to the arbitration board under the conditions set forth in Article 61.

In addition to Article 61, another way to appeal to arbitration is regulated under Article 39/4. This article is related to the aids granted by Turkey. The Community has the right to object against the aids granted by Turkey if they are considered as a breach of EU law when they had been granted by a member state. In this situation, the Parties can resort to the arbitration, if Turkey does not agree with the Community's opinion and the dispute cannot be solved within thirty days.

The Establishment of the Arbitration Board

While Article 61 determines the situations where the contracting parties can resort to arbitration, the composition of the arbitration board is established in Article 62. The arbitration board consists of three arbiters. Each contracting party shall appoint one arbitrator within thirty days. The arbitrators so appointed, shall appoint a third umpire whose nationality is different from the contracting parties.

The relevant Article also describes the procedure that will be applied if the two arbitrators cannot agree upon the third one in two months time starting from their appointment. In this case, the two arbitrators choose the umpire from a list of seven people prepared by the Council of Association. Notwithstanding the list, if the two arbitrators cannot determine the third one even from the list, the Decision No. 1/95 does not include any provision for the fulfilllment of the appointment. According to some authors,[14] this absence should be construed that two arbitrators have to agree upon a name from the list.

The functioning of the arbitration board is also described in the Article. The Arbitration Board adopts its rules of procedure unless prescribed otherwise by a decision of the Contracting Parties. The meetings of the Board are held in Brussels and decisions are taken by a simple majority, which means having at least 2 votes of 3 members.

Both the required majority and the composition of the Board ensures the settlement of the dispute under Article 61 and Article 39/4 contrary to Article 25 of the Ankara Agreement. As it is discussed above, under Article 25, the empowered authority for dispute settlement is the Council of Association and the required majority to act is unanimity which is difficult to ensure. Therefore, the procedure set forth under Articles 61 and 39/4 in the Additional Protocol is convenient to settle the dispute whereas it is difficult to say the same thing for the procedure set forth under the Ankara Agreement.

THE JURISDICTION OF THE COURT OF JUSTICE OF THE EUROPEAN UNION

The European Court of Justice has been one of the most efficient institutions of the European Union since the beginning of the integration. Its tasks are described under Article 19/3 the Treaty on European Union[15] (consolidated text) as follows:

> *3. The Court of Justice of the European Union shall, in accordance with the Treaties:*
>
> *a) rule on actions brought by a Member State, an institution or a natural or legal person;*
>
> *(b) give preliminary rulings, at the request of courts or tribunals of the Member States, on the interpretation of Union law or the validity of acts adopted by the institutions;*
>
> *(c) rule in other cases provided for in the Treaties.*

With respect to Article 19, it can clearly be understood that only the ECJ has the competence to interpret the Treaties and the secondary legislation of the European Union. In addition to the tasks assigned to the European Court of Justice under the Treaties, the Court as the driving force behind the integration process also shapes the direction of the integration by its decisions. As it is well known, two indispensable doctrines, called supremacy[16] and direct effect,[17] were created through a decision of the Court even there is no such right entrusted to the Court in the Treaties.[18] Therefore, the Court of Justice is also being accused of extending its competences beyond the competences given to it in the treaties and acting like a judicial activist.[19]

The European Court of Justice has been entrusted in the dispute settlement procedure provided for in Article 25 of the Ankara Agreement and Article 39 of Decision No. 1/95 of the Association Council. However, it is really troublesome to bring a dispute before the European Court of Justice because of the application procedure which requires a unanimous decision of the Association Council. Thus, the competence of the Court is considered ineffective in this procedure. Nevertheless, only the Contracting Parties who are Turkey on one side, the Member States and the Union on the other, can initiate this procedure because of the essence of the dispute provided in the Articles. In other words, the dispute settlement procedure under Article 25 only contains the disputes arising from the application and the interpretation of the Ankara Agreement while Article 39/5 of Decision No. 1/95 of the Association Council includes the disputes concerning illegal aids granted by one of the member states of the Community. Even if an individual is affected by a dispute provided in the Articles above, he/she has no right to initiate the procedures because dispute settlement procedures do not involve any provision for individuals.

On the other hand, although there is no provision about preliminary ruling in the Ankara Agreement and decisions of the Association Council, the European Court of Justice has a right to interpret the Ankara Agreement and the decisions of the Association Council under Article 267 of the Treaty on Functioning of the European Union (TFEU).[20] However, this competence is totally different from the dispute settlement procedures envisaged in the Ankara Agreement and Decision No. 1/95 of the Association Council in some aspects. Under Article 267 TFEU, the ECJ has the opportunity to interpret the Association Agreement and the decisions of the Association Council through the preliminary ruling procedure in which the national courts from all the EU Member States can refer a question on interpretation of the Treaties and secondary legislation to the ECJ.[21] Not only the nationals of the member states, but also the third country nationals are eligible to initiate this procedure. It should be noted that by the preliminary ruling procedure, the European Court of Justice has given a great number of decisions regarding the Association Agreement and Decision No. 1/95 of the Association Council.

As a Dispute Settlement Institution in Accordance with the Provisions under the Ankara Agreement and Decision No. 1/95

Similar to Article 39/4, Article 39/5 of Decision No. 1/95 mentions disputes emerging from the aid granted by one of the member states of the Community which it deems to be unlawful under EC law. Even though the subjects of the Articles are the same, the procedures set forth in the Article are different. This time only Turkey is entitled to initiate the procedure by raising an objection and convoking the Association Council. Unless the problem can be solved within three months by the Council of Association, it can determine unanimously to refer the case to the European Court of Justice.

As it can be understood from the Article 39/5, there are some differences between Article 39/5 and Article 39/4.[22] Firstly, in Article 39/4 the only dispute settlement institution is the arbitration board, whereas in Article 39/5 the European Court of Justice is entitled as the ultimate dispute settlement institution after the Association Council. Secondly, the parties can refer the case to the arbitration board directly, without needing a decision taken by any institutions, whereas in Article 39/5 Turkey needs to bring the case before the Association Council and in order to appeal to the European Court of Justice Turkey needs an Association Council decision. Thirdly, the duration envisaged for the parties to submit the dispute to the arbitration board is thirty days which begins with the initiation of the procedure under Article 39/4, while the period set under Article 39/5 is determined three months from the application to the Association Council.

These remarkable differences between two Articles indicate an imbalance and inequality between Parties and can also be criticized for making the procedure ineffective and redundant for Turkey. While the Community can easily bring the dispute before the arbitration board in accordance with Article 39/4, Turkey is deprived of the opportunity to bring the dispute before the dispute settlement authority by its own decision. A general competence is given to the Association Council to decide whether to refer the dispute to the European Court of Justice or not. For sure, as it is discussed above, the quorum required for taking decisions in the Association Council is unanimity which means that it is apparent that the Community has the chance to block the process.

Hence, the requirement for a decision of the Council of Association makes Article 39/5 of Decision No. 1/95 inessential. In a nutshell, Article 39/5 does not only mention anything new but it is also nothing more than a duplication of Article 25/2 of the Ankara Agreement.[23]

The Jurisdiction of the European Court of Justice under Article 267 of the Treaty on Functioning of the European Union

Under the Ankara Agreement and Decision No. 1/95 it is really hard to bring any dispute within the framework drawn by the Articles before the European Court of Justice without a decision taken in the Association Council by unanimity. As a conclusion of the Articles relating dispute settlement under the Ankara Agreement and Decision No. 1/95, it seems that unless the Parties would prefer to bring the dispute before the European Court of Justice, the European Court of Justice does not have jurisdiction on the interpretation of the Association Agreements. Either Party has the right to veto and can easily cause a deadlock.

However in the context of the European Union law, the preliminary ruling procedure[24] is established under Article 267 of the Treaty on Functioning of the European Union (TFEU) (ex Article 234 Treaty establishing the European Community (TEC)), to ensure the uniformity in the interpretation of Community law.[25] The preliminary ruling procedure is based on the cooperation between the Court and national courts.[26] It is up to the national courts whether to submit the questions to the European Court of Justice for a preliminary ruling[27] except in cases where there is not any court or tribunal to appeal against the national court's decision. Thus, the cooperation between two courts is vital to the success of this procedure. Article 267 TFEU provides:

The Court of Justice of the European Union shall have jurisdiction to give preliminary rulings concerning:
a) the interpretation of the treaties
b) the validity and interpretation of acts of the institutions, bodies, offices or agencies of the Union.
Where such a question is raised before any court or tribunal of a Member State, that court or tribunal may, if it considers that a decision on the question is necessary to enable it to give judgment, request the Court to give a ruling thereon.
Where any such question is raised in a case pending before a court or tribunal of a Member State against whose decisions there is no judicial remedy under national law, that court or tribunal shall bring the matter before the Court.
If such a question is raised in a case pending before a court or tribunal of a Member State with regard to a person in custody, the Court of Justice of the European Union shall act with the minimum of delay.

As indicated in the Article, while the references for interpretation may be made with regard to treaties and Union acts, the references for validity do not include the Treaties.[28] On the other hand, in accordance with the Article it is not clear whether the ruling of the Association Agreements may be referred to the European Court of Justice through preliminary ruling procedure or not. The European Court of Justice held whether it has a jurisdiction over the interpretation of the Association Agreements or not in the *Haegeman*[29] case. The Court was asked to interpret certain provisions of the Association Agreement between the European Economic Community and Greece signed in Athens on July 9, 1961. First, the Court determined whether its jurisdiction includes Association Agreements. The ECJ stated as follows:[30]

2. Under the first paragraph of article 177 of the EEC Treaty[31] *the Court of Justice shall have jurisdiction to give preliminary rulings concerning the interpretation of acts of the institutions of the Community*
3. The Athens Agreement was concluded by the Council under articles 228[32] *and 238*[33] *of the treaty as appears from the terms of the decision dated September 25, 1961.*
4. This Agreement is therefore, in so far as concerns the community an act of one of the institutions of the Community within the meaning of subparagraph (b) of the first paragraph of article 177.
5. The provisions of the agreement, from the coming into force thereof, form an integral part of community law.
6. Within the framework of this law, the court accordingly has jurisdiction to give preliminary rulings concerning the interpretation of this agreement.

It is obvious that the ECJ based its decision on Article 267/2 of TFEU. In reference to this Article, the ECJ accepted the Association Agreement as an act of institution as it was concluded by the Council.[34] Reading Article 218 (ex Article 300) with Article 217 of TFEU (ex Article 310), the competence to conclude agreements between the Union and third countries or international organizations is given to the Council which is also to form the basis of the Court decision.

According to Hartley,[35] in the *Haegeman* case, the Court interpreted the Agreement itself not the Council decision. As indicated above, the contracting parties to the Association Agreements are the European Union and its member states on one side, the third country or an international organization on the other. However the European Court of Justice considered the Council as if it is the contracting party and accepted the Association Agreement as an act of the institutions of the Community.

After the *Haegeman* case, the Court gave a similar decision with a small difference in the *Demirel* case.[36] The *Haegeman* case is known as the Court's first ruling on the interpretation of international agreements whereas the *Haegeman* case concerned a mixed agreement[37] like the *Demirel* case, where the term 'mixed agreement' was used to describe the Association Agreement for the first time.[38]

Two questions concerning the interpretation of Articles 7 and 12 of the Agreement establishing an Association between the European Economic Community and Turkey were referred to the European Court of Justice. The Court first considered its jurisdiction before ruling on the questions by referring to the *Haegeman* case as follows:[39]

> *It should be first pointed out that, as the court held in its judgment of April 30, 1974 in case 181/73 Haegeman v. Belgium (1974) ECR 449, an agreement concluded by the Council under articles 228 and 238 of the treaty is, as far as the Community is concerned, an act of one of the institutions of the Community within the meaning of article 177 (1) (B), and, as from its entry into force, the provisions of such an agreement form an integral part of the Community legal system; within the framework of that system the Court has jurisdiction to give preliminary rulings concerning the interpretation of such an agreement.*

On the other hand the German Government and the United Kingdom alleged that even if it is accepted that the ECJ has jurisdiction over provisions of a 'mixed' agreement, it does not include the provisions whereby member states have entered into commitments in the exercise of their own powers.[40] The Court rejected the claim, ruling that,[41]

> *In that connection it is sufficient to state that that is precisely not the case in this instance. Since the agreement in question is an association agreement creating special, privileged links with a non-member country which must, at least to a certain extent, take part in the community system, article 238 must necessarily empower the community to guarantee commitments towards non-member countries in all the fields covered by the treaty. Since freedom of movement for workers is, by virtue of article 48 et seq of the EEC treaty, one of the fields covered by that treaty, it follows that commitments regarding free-*

dom of movement fall within the powers conferred on the community by article 238. Thus the question whether the court has jurisdiction to rule on the interpretation of a provision in a mixed agreement containing a commitment which only the member states could enter into in the sphere of their own powers does not arise.

It should be stated that as a result of this decision, it seems that the European Court of Justice has declared that the Association Agreements are mixed agreements and it has jurisdiction over all provisions of mixed agreements without considering whether the decisive provisions fall in the exclusive competence of the Member States or not.[42] But later cases[43] show that even though the ECJ has broadened the scope of its jurisdictional power over mixed agreements, it is not allowed to interpret a provision if it falls within the exclusive competence of the Member States.[44] After considering itself competent to interpret all provisions of a mixed agreement as long as the provision falls in the exclusive competence of the Union,[45] another question was asked to the European Court of Justice through preliminary ruling procedure in the *Sevince*[46] case. The question is whether the court has jurisdiction to interpret the Decisions taken by the Association Council which is the institution of the Association between Turkey and the European Community. The court explained its views as follows:[47]

8. By way of a preliminary observation, it should be borne in mind that, as the Court has consistently held, the provisions of an agreement concluded by the Council under Articles 228 and 238 of the EEC Treaty form an integral part of the Community legal system as from the entry into force of that agreement (see judgments in Case 12/86 Demirel [1987] ECR 3719, paragraph 7 and in Case 30/88 Greece v Commission [1989] ECR 3711, paragraph 12)

9. The Court has also held that, since they are directly connected with the Agreement to which they give effect, the decisions of the Council of Association, in the same way as the Agreement itself, form an integral part, as from their entry into force, of the Community legal system (see judgment in Case 30/88 Greece v Commission, supra, paragraph 13).

10. Since the Court has jurisdiction to give preliminary rulings on the Agreement, in so far as it is an act adopted by one of the institutions of the Community (see judgment in Case 181/73 Haegeman [1974] ECR 449), it also has jurisdiction to give rulings on the interpretation of the decisions adopted by the authority established by the Agreement and entrusted with responsibility for its implementation.

11. That finding is reinforced by the fact that the function of Article 177 of the EEC Treaty is to ensure the uniform application throughout the Community of all provisions forming part of the Community legal system and to ensure that the interpretation thereof does not vary according to the interpretation accorded to them by the various Member States (see judgments in Case 104/81 Kupferberg [1982] ECR 3641 and in Joined Cases 267 to 269/81 SPI and SAMI [1983] ECR 801).

As it is indicated in the decision, the Court of Justice has declared that it has jurisdiction to interpret not only the provisions of Association Agreements (the Ankara Agreement), Additional Protocol to the Ankara Agreement, but also the provisions of Association Council decisions.[48] The justification for the ruling was based on the direct connection between the Agreement and the decisions of the Council of Association. According to the Court, the Agreement and the decisions adopted by the institution established by the Agreement could not be subject to different rules. Therefore, the judgment establishes that the decisions of the Council of Association also form an integral part of EU law, like the Ankara Agreement, and the European Court of Justice has jurisdiction on them.

After the *Demirel* and *Sevince* cases, the national courts have referred to the ECJ a series of questions relating to the Ankara Agreement and the decisions of the Association Council.[49] In this way, the European Court of Justice has also the chance to interpret the Ankara Agreement and the decisions of the Council of Association in all aspects. In recent years, many preliminary rulings related to ongoing problems between Turkey and the EU such as visas and resident permits have been brought before the European Court of Justice by individuals instead of brought before the Council of Association by Turkey as envisaged under dispute settlement procedure in the Ankara Agreement. It is due to the fact that Turkey knows the inefficiency of the procedure because the member states still do not accept the meaning of the "standstill clause." It would be awkward to discuss the dispute in the Association Council hoping the member states would agree to settle or refer the dispute to the Court or any other tribunal.

In the *Sosyal and Savatli* case,[50] two Turkish lorry drivers, working in a Turkish company engaged in the international transport of goods, were refused the visa they needed to gain access to Germany with their vehicles.[51] Both of them alleged that the refusal is contrary to the Article 41/1 of the Additional Protocol to the Ankara Agreement with Turkey which prevents Contracting Parties from imposing more restrictions on free movement of services and the right of establishment than those which applied at the time when the Additional Protocol entered into force. The Court has held that Turkish nationals had the right to enter Germany without a visa for the purposes of free movement of services and the right of establishment until 1980. The legislation accepted in 1980 has been replaced with the legislation on aliens as of January 1, 2005 in order to implement an act of secondary Community legislation, Regulation No 539/2001.[52] In this respect, the Court concluded that even if it is adopted to implement Community legislation, it worsens the situation of Turkish nationals at the time when the Additional Protocol entered into force within the meaning of infringement of Article 41, called the standstill clause.

In 2010 the Court concluded a dispute related to Article 13 of Decision 1/80 which prohibits the introduction of any new measures which would make Turkish nationals' and their families' residence conditions stricter than those which applied at the time when Decision 1/80 entered into force in relation to the Member State concerned. This provision also contains a standstill clause similar to Article 41/1 of the Additional Protocol to the Ankara Agreement. In the *Toprak* and *Oguz* cases,[53] the Netherlands amended its Law on foreign nationals which regulates the admission and residence of foreign nationals in the Netherlands in 1982 and 2000 after the entry into force of Decision 1/80. While the amendments brought with the circular in 1982 improved the residence conditions of Turkish nationals, the one adopted in 2000 worsens the conditions applied at the time when Decision 1/80 entered into force. The court declared that a standstill clause prohibits the adoption of new measures only if they worsen the situation at the time when the relevant rule entered into force which means that the measures that improve the conditions are always welcomed and must be applied.

Consequently, references for a preliminary ruling procedure also serve to enable Turkish nationals to bring disputes in accordance with the direct effect principle before the Court of Justice of the European Union arising from the Ankara Agreement, the Additional Protocol, and the Decisions of the Association Council. However, it is not a convenient way for all disputes related to the relationship between Turkey and the EU.

CONCLUSION

The dispute settlement rules and procedures have a significant role in every agreement, treaty, or decision. The significance of this role is derived from the need to protect the rights envisaged in agreements, treaties, or decisions. This reason is also valid in the relation between Turkey and the EU. The Contracting Parties signed an Association Agreement, the ultimate aim of which is full membership of Turkey in the EU, and also determined the steps that should be taken in order to achieve this goal. Until the goal is attained, some disputes can arise on the application or on the interpretation of the steps taken. In order not to impede the aim provided in the agreement, effective remedies and enforcement become essential elements in a dispute settlement procedure.

As it is indicated above, the dispute settlement procedure stipulated in the Ankara Agreement and Decision No. 1/95 of the Council of Association is neither effective nor applicable for implementation. The requirement of unanimous Association Council decision for settling a dispute is cumbersome *per se*. If one of the Parties wants to prevent the process, there is nothing for the other Party to do. This negative feature emanates from the political aspect of the process that entitles both Parties to act in accordance with their own will. In other words, neither Party may compel the other to settle a dispute by force. Besides this negativity, the private applicants are not entitled to submit any dispute concerning the interpretation or application of the Ankara Agreement and decisions of the Association Council even if it affects their rights through the dispute settlement procedures. Therefore, it should be noted that in no way are the private applicants accepted as a part of the dispute settlement procedures.

These ineffective processes are also preventing the disputes being brought before the European Court of Justice. Hence, it would not be wrong to say that the European Court of Justice is a secondary institution for the dispute settlement procedure provided in the Ankara Agreement and Decision No. 1/95. Despite its secondary position in dispute settlement procedures, the European Court of Justice declared that it has jurisdiction on the Ankara Agreement and the decisions of the Association Council through preliminary ruling procedure provided in the Treaty on Functioning of the European Union. After this declaration, the Court of Justice has ruled on many disputes concerning the provisions of the Ankara Agreement and the Decisions of the Association Council.

In conclusion, the entitlement of the Association Council as the main authority for dispute settlement indicates that the preferred procedures are political rather than legal. In this respect in order to settle a dispute through these procedures both parties' interests should be in the same direction, because there is no compulsive provision to effectively enforce the procedures. In spite of the fact that the European Court of Justice has declared that it has jurisdiction on the Ankara Agreement, the Additional Protocol, and the Decisions of the Association Council through preliminary ruling, it is inadequate when the appealing conditions and the entitled applicants are considered. Lastly, it is obvious that the procedures set forth under the relevant articles are in need of reform to function properly.

NOTES

1. The Ankara Agreement of 12.09.1963 (Official Journal L 217, 29.12.1964), www.avrupa.info.tr, (18.12.2010).

2. Tugrul Arat, "Avrupa Birliği ile Türkiye Arasındaki İlişkiler Gümrük Birliği'nin Yeri," *Ankara Üniversitesi Hukuk Fakültesi Dergisi*, 44 (1995): 589-590. Haluk Kabaalioğlu, "The Customs Union: A Final Step Before Turkey's Accession to the European Union," *Marmara Journal of European Studies*, 6 (1998), 1: 117. Süreyya Yiğit, "Turkish Immigration Into Germany: The EU Perspective," *European Community Studies Association*, 1997: 10, aei.pitt.edu/2762/01/002713_1.PDF, (11.12.2010); Hacı Can and Cinar Özen, *Türkiye Avrupa Topluluğu Ortaklık Hukuku*, Gazi Kitabevi, Ankara, 2005: 22; Hacı Can, "Türkiye-Avrupa Topluluğu Ortaklık İlişkisinin Hukuki Çerçevesi," *Ankara Avrupa Çalışmaları Dergisi*, 3 (2003), 1: 21. Arif Köktaş, "Avrupa Toplulukları Adalet Divanı'nın Soysal ve Savatlı Kararı:

Türk Vatandaşları AB Ülkelerine Girişte Vize Almalı mı?," *Uluslararası Hukuk ve Politika*, 5 (2009), 19: 27.

3. Ali Aybey, "Turkey and the European Union Relations:Historical Assesment," *Ankara Avrupa Çalışmaları Dergisi*, 4 (2004), 1: 22. Aslı Sentarhancı and Şeniz Karahan, "The Customs Union between Turkey and the European Union," http://www.deu.edu.tr/userweb/dilek.seymen/dosyalar/Asli-Seniz-Ecomnomic%20Integrations-CU.doc, (29.08.2012). Secretariat General for EU Affairs, "History of Turkey-EU Relations," http://www.abgs.gov.tr/index.php?p=111&l=2 , (05.01.2011); Tugrul Arat, "Avrupa Toplulukları Hukuku," in *Avrupa Birliği El Kitabı*, Ankara: TC Merkez Bankası, 1995: 592. Harun Arıkan, *Turkey and the EU: An awkward candidate for EU membership?*, Ashgate Publishing, 2006: 61.

4. Additional Protocol and Financial Protocol signed on November 23, 1970, annexed to the Agreement establishing the Association between the European Economic Community and Turkey and on measures to be taken for their entry into force, (Official Journal L 293, 29.12.1972), http://eur-lex.europa.eu/smartapi/cgi/sga_doc?smartapi!celexplus!prod!CELEX numdoc&lg=en&numdoc=270A1123%2801%29, (11.12.2010).

5. Decision No. 1/95 of the EC-Turkey Association Council of December 22, 1995 on implementing the final phase of the Customs Union (Official Journal L 035, 13/02/1996), http://eur-lex.europa.eu/LexUriServ/LexUriServ.do?uri=CELEX:21996D0213%2801%29:EN:HTML, (11.12.2010).

6. Kabaalioğlu, 1998: 126; World Trade Organization, *Turkey – Restrictions on Imports of Textile and Clothing Products*, Report of the Panel, 1999: 111, http://www.sice.oas.org/dispute/wto/ds34/1229d18.asp, (11.12.2010).

7. Can, 2003: 40-41.

8. Economic Development Foundation, *Partnership Institutions*, http://www.ikv.org.tr/print_en.asp?id=108&baslik=Partnership%20Institutions, (11.12. 2010).

9. The Ankara Agreement of 12.09.1963 (Official Journal L 217, 29.12.1964), www.avrupa.info.tr, (December 18, 2010).

10. Interpretative Declaration on the definition of the expression "Contracting Parties" used in the Agreement of Association, Official Journal of the European Communities C113/73.

11. Can and Özen, 2005: 123

12. Dominik Lasok, "The Ankara Agreement: Principles and Interpretation," *Marmara Journal of European Studies*, 1 (1991), 1: 47.

13. Douglas A. Irwin, "International Trade Agreements," *The Concise Encyclopedia of Economics*, 2nd Edition, http://www.econlib.org/library/Enc/InternationalTradeAgreements.html, (12.11.2012).

14. Can and Özen, 2005: 127.

15. Consolidated version of Treaty on European Union, (Official Journal C 083, 30.03.2010), http://eur-lex.europa.eu/JOHtml.do?uri=OJ:C:2010:083:SOM:EN:HTML, (January 22, 2010).

16. Case 6/64, Flaminio Costa v ENEL [1964] ECR 585.

17. Case 26/62, Van Gend en Loos, [1963] ECR1; [1963] CMLR 105.

18. For more information see, Alan Dashwood, "The Principle of Direct Effect in European Community," *Journal of Common Market Studies*, 16 (1978), 3: 229-245; Koen Lenaerts and Tim Corthaut, "Of Birds and Hedges: The Role of primacy in Invoking Norms of EU Law," *European Law Review*, 31 (2006), 3: 287-315; Bruno De Witte, "Direct Effect, Supremacy and the Nature of the Legal Order," in Paul Craig and Grainne de Burca (eds), *The Evolution of EU Law*, Oxford University Press; Trevor Hartley, *The Foundations of European Union Law*, Oxford University Press, 7th Edition, 2010: 209-214, 243-245; Paul Craig and Grainne De Burca, *EU Law, Text, Cases and Materials*, 5th Edition, 2011: 180-216, 256-300.

19. For the definition and discussions about judicial activism of the European Court of Justice see, Trevor Hartley, "The European Court, Judicial Objectivity and the Constitution of the European Union," *Law Quarterly Review*, 112, 1996: 95; Joseph Weiler, "The Court of Justice on Trial," *Common Market Law Review*, 24 (1987): 555. Karen Alter, "Who Are the Masters of the Treaty?: European Governments and The European Court of Justice," *International Organization*, 52, 1998; Takis Tridimas, "The Court of Justice and Judicial Activism,"

European Law Review, 21, 1996: 199; Anthony Arnull, "The European Court and Judicial Objectivity: A Reply to Prof. Hartley," *Law Quarterly Review*, 112, 1996: 411.

20. Consolidated version of Treaty on Functioning of the European Union, (Official Journal C 083, 30.03.2010), http://eur-lex.europa.eu/JOHtml.do?uri=OJ:C:2010:083:SOM:EN:HTML, (22.01.2010).

21. Alfred E. Kellermann, "The Rights of Non-Member State Nationals under the EU Association Agreements," *European Journal of Law Reform*, 10 (2008), 3: 341.

22. Can and Özen, 2005: 136.

23. Can and Özen, 2005: 136.

24. For detailed information See Craig and De Burca, 2011: 442-483. Hartley, 1996: 287-320. Jo Steiner et al., *EU Law*, Oxford University Press, Oxford 2006: 192; Damian Chalmers et al., *European Union Law: Text and Materials*, Cambridge University Press, Cambridge, 2008. Elspeth Berry and Sylvia Hargreaves, *European Union Law*, Oxford University Press, Oxford, 2007: 73; Margot Horspool and Matthew Humphreys, *European Union Law* (Core Texts Series) , Oxford University Press, Oxford, 2010: 83.

25. Eglė Rinkeviciute, "Ensuring of the Uniform Interpretation of the EU Law in the Judicial Practice of the Member States," *Jurisprudencija*, 2005: 81–89.

26. Rene Barents, *Directory of EU Case Law on the Preliminary Ruling Procedure*, Kluwer Law International, 2009: 278.

27. Henry G. Schermers and Denis F. Waelbroeck, *Judicial Protection in the European Union*, Kluwer Law International, 2001: 233.

28. Hartley, 2010: 289.

29. Case C-181/73, Haegeman v. Belgium, ECR [1974].

30. Case C-181/73, Haegeman v. Belgium, ECR [1974], paragraphs 2-6.

31. Article 267 of Treaty on Functioning of the European Union.

32. Article 218 of Treaty on Functioning of the European Union.

33. Article 217 of Treaty on Functioning of the European Union.

34. Hartley, 2010: 291.

35. Hartley, 2010: 291-293.

36. Case C-12/86, Meryem Demirel v Stadt Schwäbisch Gmünd [1987] ECR 3719.

37. McGoldrick describes mixed agreement, "an agreement can be regarded as mixed if the European Community and one or more of the Member States are parties to it. An agreement can also be regarded as mixed if the European Community and the Member States share competence in relation to it, even if only Member States can be parties. Finally, an agreement can be in a mixed form because of requirements relating to its financing or relating to its provisions on voting," see Rafael Leal-Arcas, "The European Community and Mixed Agreements," *European Foreign Affairs Review*, 6 (2001): 485. For more information about mixed agreements see, David. O'Keeffe and Henry. Schermers, *Mixed Agreements*, Kluwer Law and Taxation Publishers, 1983; M.J.F.M. Dolmans, *Problems of Mixed Agreements: Division of Powers Within the EEC and the Right of Third States*, Asser Insstituut, 1985; Nanette Neuwahl, "Joint Participation in International Treaties and the Exercise of Powers by the EEC and its Member States: Mixed Agreements," *Common Market Law Review*, 28 (1991): 717–740.

38. The Ankara Agreement is a mixed agreement. See in detail, Craig and De Burca, 2011: 354. Leal-Arcas, 2001: 486; Can, 2003: 37. Tugrul Arat, "Avrupa Toplulukları Hukuku," 1995: 49; Can and Özen, 2005: 292.

39. Case C-12/86, Meryem Demirel v Stadt Schwäbisch Gmünd [1987] ECR 3719, paragraph 7.

40. Case C-12/86, Meryem Demirel v Stadt Schwäbisch Gmünd [1987] ECR 3719, paragraph 8.

41. Case C-12/86, Meryem Demirel v Stadt Schwäbisch Gmünd [1987] ECR 3719, paragraph 9.

42. Armin von Bogdandy and Maja Smrkolj, "European Community and Union Law and International Law," Max Planck Institute for Comparative Public Law and International Law, Heidelberg and Oxford University Press, 2009, http://www.mpepil.com/subscriber_article?script=yes&id=/epil/entries/law-9780199231690-e620&recno=47&subject=Regional%20organizations,%20institutions%20and%20developments, (29.08.2012).

43. Cases C-300 and C-392/98, Parfums Christian Dior [2000] ECR I-11307, paragraph 35; Case C-239/03, Commission v France [2004] ECR I-9325, paragraph 25.
44. Von Bogdandy and Smrkolj, 2009. Hartley, 2011: 293. Craig and De Burca, 2011: 355-356.
45. Von Bogdandy and Smrkolj, 2009.
46. Case C-192/89 Sevince v Staatssecretaris Van Justitie [1990] ECR I-3461.
47. Case C-192/89 Sevince v Staatssecretaris Van Justitie [1990] ECR I-3461, paragraphs 8-11.
48. Craig and de Burca, 2011: 353.
49. The case law of the ECJ will not be examined here. For more information see the cases below: Case C-237/91, Kazım Kuş v. Landehauptstadt Wiesbaden [1992] ECR I-6781 [1993] 2 CMLR 887; Case C-355/93, Hayriye Eroğlu v. Land Baden Württemberg [1994] ECR I-5113; Case C-434/93, Ahmet Bozkurt v. Staatssecretaris van Justıtie [1995] ECR I-1475; Case C-277/94, Z. Taflan-Met and Others v. Bestuur van de Nieuwe A. Bedrijfsvereniging [1996] ECR I-4085; Case C-171/95, Recep Tetik v. Land Berlin [1997] ECR I-329; Case C-351/95, Selma Kadıman v. Freistaat Bayern [1997] ECR I-2133; Case C-386/95, Eker v. Land Baden-Württenberg [1997] ECR I-2697; Case C-285/95, Suat-Kol v. Land Berlin [1997] ECR I-3069; Case C-36/96, Faik Günaydın and Others v. Freistaat Bayern [1997] ECR I-5143; Case C-98/96, Kasım Ertanır v. Land Hessen [1997] ECR I-5179; Case C-210/97, Haydar Akman v. Oberkreisdirektor des Rheinisch-Bergischen-Kreises [1998] ECR I- 7519; Case C-1/97, Mehmet Birden v. Stadtgemeinde Bremen [1998] ECR I-7747; Case C-262/96, Sema Sürül v. Bundesanstalt für Arbeit [1999] ECR I-2685; Case C-340/97, Ömer Nazlı v. Ville de Nurenberg [2000] ECR I-957; Case C-102/98, Ibrahim Kocak v Landesversicherungsanstalt Oberfranken und Mittelfranken [2000] I-1287; Case C-329/97, Sezgin Ergat v. Stadt Ulm. [2000] ECR I-1487; Case C-37/98, The Queen, ex parte: AbdulNasir Savas v. Secretary of State for the Home Department [2000] ECR I-2927; Case C-65/98, Safet Eyüp v. Landesgeschäftsstelle des Arbeitsmarktservice Vorarlberg [2000] ECR I-4747, C-188/00, Bülent Kurz, né Yüce v. Land Baden-Württemberg [2002] ECR I-10691; C-317/01 & C 369/01, Eran Abatay and Others v. Bundesanstalt für Arbeit & Nadi Şahin v. Bundesanstalt für Arbeit, Joined Cases, [2003] ECR I-12301; Case C-16/05, Veli Tüm ve Mehmet Darı v Secretary of State for the Home Department [2007] ECR I-7415; Case C-337/07, İbrahim Altun v. Stadt Böblingen [2008] ECR 00; Case C-453/07, Hakan Er v. Wetteraukreis [2008] ECR 00; Case C-294/06, Ezgi Payir, Burhan Akyuz, Birol Öztürk v. Secretary of State for the Home Department [2008] ECR I-00203; Case C-325/05, İsmail Derin v. Landkreis Darmstadt-Dieburg [2005] ECR I-6181; Case C-4/05, Hasan Güzeli v. Oberbürgermeister der Stadt Aachen [2006] ECR I-10279; Case C-230/03, Mehmet Sedef v. Freie und Hansestadt Hamburg [2006] ECR I-2133; C- 136/03, Georg Dörrv.Sicherheitsdirektion für das Bundesland Kärnten and İbrahim Ünal v. Sicherheitsdirektion für das Bundesland Vorarlberg [2005] ECR I-04759; Case C-374/03, Gaye Gürol v. Bezirksregierung Köln [2005] ECR I-06199; Case C-467/02, Inan Çetinkaya v. Land Baden-Württemberg [2004] ECR I-10895; Case C-275/02, Engin Ayaz v. Land Baden-Württemberg 2004] ECR I-08765.
50. Case C-228/06, Mehmet Soysal and Ibrahim Savatli v. Bundesrepublik Deutschland [2009] ECR I-1031.
51. Summary of the judgment C-228/06, http://ec.europa.eu/dgs/legal_service/arrets/06c228_en.pdf, (12 .11.2012).
52. Case C-228/06, Mehmet Soysal and Ibrahim Savatli v. Bundesrepublik Deutschland [2009] ECR I-1031, para.51-52.
53. Cases C300/09 and C301/09 Toprak and Oguz [2010] ECR I-0000.

REFERENCES

Alter, Karen. "Who Are the Masters of the Treaty?: European Governments and the European Court of Justice." *International Organization*, 52 (1998):121-147.

Arat, Tugrul. "Avrupa Birliği ile Türkiye Arasındaki İlişkiler Gümrük Birliği'nin Yeri." *Ankara Üniversitesi Hukuk Fakültesi Dergisi*, 44 (1995): 589-590.

———. "Avrupa Toplulukları Hukuku," in *Avrupa Birliği El Kitabı*. Ankara: TC Merkez Bankası, 1995: 29-52.

Arıkan, Harun. *Turkey and the EU: An awkward candidate for EU membership?*. 1st Edition. Hampshire: Ashgate Publishing, 2006.

Arnull, Anthony. "The European Court and Judicial Objectivity: A Reply to Prof. Hartley." *Law Quarterly Review*, 112 (1996): 411-423.

Aybey, Ali. "Turkey and the European Union Relations: Historical Assesment." *Ankara Avrupa Çalışmaları Dergisi*, 4 (2004): 19-38.

Barents, Rene. *Directory of EU Case Law on the Preliminary Ruling Procedure*. The Netherlands: Kluwer Law International, 2009.

Berry, Elspeth, and Hargreaves, Sylvia. *European Union Law*, 2nd Edition. Oxford: Oxford University Press, 2007.

Can, Hacı. "Türkiye-Avrupa Topluluğu Ortaklık İlişkisinin Hukuki Çerçevesi." *Ankara Avrupa Çalışmaları Dergisi*, 3 (2003): 19-44.

Can, Hacı, and Özen, Cinar. *Türkiye Avrupa Topluluğu Ortaklık Hukuku*. Ankara: Gazi Kitabevi, 2005.

Chalmers, *EU Law*, 2008 (n24).

Craig, Paul, and De Burca, Grainne. *EU Law, Text, Cases and Materials*, 5th Edition. Oxford: Oxford University Press, 2011.

Dashwood, Alan. "The Principle of Direct Effect in European Community." *Journal of Common Market Studies*, 16 (1978): 229-245.

De Witte, Bruno. "Direct Effect, Supremacy and the Nature of the Legal Order," in the *Evolution of EU Law*, Paul Craig and Grainne de Burca, (eds.). Oxford: Oxford University Press, 1999: 177-208.

Dolmans, M.J.F.M. *Problems of Mixed Agreements : Division of Powers Within the EEC and the Right of Third States*. The Hague: Asser Instituut, 1985.

Economic Development Foundation. "Partnership Institutions," http://www.ikv.org.tr/print_en.asp?id=108&baslik=Partnership%20Institutions , (11.12. 2010).

Hartley, Trevor. *The Foundations of European Union Law*, 7th Edition. Oxford: Oxford University Press, 2010.

———. "The European Court, Judicial Objectivity and the Constitution of the European Union." *Law Quarterly Review*, 112 (1996): 95-109.

Horspool, Margot, and Humphreys, Matthew. *European Union Law* (Core Texts Series), 6th Edition. Oxford: Oxford University Press, 2010.

Irwin, Douglas. "International Trade Agreements," *The Concise Encyclopedia of Economics*, 2nd Edition. http://www.econlib.org/library/Enc/InternationalTradeAgreements.html, (12.11.2012).

Kabaalioglu, Haluk. "The Customs Union: A Final Step Before Turkey's Accession to the European Union." *Marmara Journal of European Studies*, 6 (1998): 113-140.

Kellermann, E. Alfred. "The Rights of Non-Member State Nationals under the EU Association Agreements." *European Journal of Law Reform*, 10 (2008): 339-382.

Koktas, Arif. "Avrupa Toplulukları Adalet Divanı'nın Soysal ve Savatlı Kararı: Türk Vatandaşları AB Ülkelerine Girişte Vize Almalı mı?" *Uluslararası Hukuk ve Politika*, 5 (2009): 23-38.

Lasok, Dominik. "The Ankara Agreement: Principles and Interpretation." *Marmara Journal of European Studies*, 1 (1991): 27-47.

Leal-Arcas, Rafael. "The European Community and Mixed Agreements." *European Foreign Affairs Review*, 6 (2001): 483-513.

Lenaerts, Koen, and Corthaut, Tim. "Of Birds and Hedges: The Role of Primacy in Invoking Norms of EU Law." *European Law Review*, 31 (2006): 287-315.

Neuwahl, Nanette. "Joint Participation in International Treaties and the Exercise of Powers by the EEC and Its Member States: Mixed Agreements." *Common Market Law Review*, 28 (1991): 717–740.

O'Keeffe, David, and Schermers, Henry (eds). *Mixed Agreements*. Leiden: Kluwer Law and Taxation Publishers, 1983.

Rinkeviciute, Eglė. "Ensuring of the Uniform Interpretation of the EU Law in the Judicial Practice of the Member States." *Jurisprudencija*, 72 (2005): 81–89.

Schermers, Henry G., and Waelbroeck, Denis F. *Judicial Protection in the European Union*. 6th Edition. The Netherlands: Kluwer Law International, 2001.

Secretariat General for EU Affairs. "History of Turkey-EU Relations." http://www.abgs.gov.tr/index.php?p=111&l=2, (January 5, 2011).

Sentarhancı, Aslı, and Karahan, Seniz. "The Customs Union between Turkey and the European Union." http://www.deu.edu.tr/userweb/dilek.seymen/dosyalar/Asli-Seniz-Ecomnomic%20Integrations-CU.doc. (29.08.2012).

Steiner, *EU Law*, 2006 (see n24).

Tridimas, Takis. "The Court of Justice and Judicial Activism." *European Law Review*, 21, (1996): 199-210.

Von Bogdandy, Armin, and Smrkolj, Maja. "European Community and Union Law and International Law." Max Planck Institute for Comparative Public Law and International Law, Heidelberg: Oxford University Press, 2009, http://www.mpepil.com/subscriber_article?script=yes&id=/epil/entries/law-9780199231690-e620&recno=47&subject=Regional%20organizations,%20institutions%20and%20developments, (August 29, 2012).

Weiler, Joseph. "The Court of Justice on Trial." *Common Market Law Review*, 24 (1987): 555-589.

World Trade Organization, *Turkey—Restrictions on Imports of Textile and Clothing Products*, Report of the Panel, 1999. http://www.sice.oas.org/dispute/wto/ds34/1229d18.asp, (December 11, 2010).

Yigit, Süreyya. "Turkish Immigration Into Germany: The EU Perspective." *European Community Studies Association*, (1997): 10, aei.pitt.edu/2762/01/002713_1.PDF, (11.12.2010).

Chapter Five

The Principle of Non-Discrimination on Grounds of Nationality with Regard to Turkish Workers in the European Union and Union Workers in Turkey

İlke Göçmen and Orhan Ersun Civan

INTRODUCTION

The principle of equality or non-discrimination on grounds of nationality[1] regarding workers is one of the remarkable aspects of the European Union ("EU")—Turkey association law[2] and accession relationship. On the one hand, the association law which foresees the eventual accession of Turkey to the Union[3] has put the progressive fulfillment of free movement of workers between the parties as one of its objectives.[4] Though the association law falls short of this objective,[5] the legal position of workers who are established legally in the territory of the parties has improved.[6] These improvements include the right to be free from discrimination on grounds of nationality on certain matters, such as working conditions.[7] In this regard, the principle of non-discrimination, which contributes to facilitating the progressive integration of migrant workers,[8] can be deemed as the basic ingredient of the rights devoted to non-national workers.

The accession relationship, on the other hand, requires Turkey to be in line with Union law, *inter alia*, with respect to free movement of workers which embraces the principle of non-discrimination on the grounds of nationality. In this regard, it is noteworthy that in its Progress Report of 2005 the Commission stated that in order to be in line with EU law with respect to free movement of workers' *acquis*, "EU migrant workers must be treated in the same way as national workers in relation to working conditions, social and tax advantages" in Turkey; however, they were not.[9] Nonetheless, the Commission has not yet voiced the same criticism from then onwards. Still, this marks that it is the accession process or membership negotiations which require Turkey to realize the prohibition on discrimination on grounds of nationality with regard to Union workers employed in Turkey.

This paper intends to display the legal armory of Turkish workers in EU and Union workers in Turkey as regards the prohibition of discrimination on grounds of nationality. On the one side, in the EU, it is the association law which serves as a valuable source of rights with specific and general clauses on non-discrimination.[10] Nonetheless, the Directives related to Third-Country Nationals ("TCN") may also be relevant in this regard.[11] On the other side, in Turkey, it is the 1982 Turkish Constitution ("TC") and Turkish Labor Statute No 4857 ("TLS") which is the primary source for non-discrimination of Union workers.[12] However, the international agreements which have been ratified by Turkey and include a non-discrimination clause may also be applicable in this respect.[13] Hence, this paper will focus on these sources of law and try to explain the exact scope of the non-discrimination rights of the mentioned migrant workers. In the end, it will be shown that the principle of non-discrimination on grounds of nationality has been respected and applied almost in the same way in both of the legal orders of the Union and Turkey, since it is a reflection of the general principle of equality which has constitutional value.[14]

PRINCIPLE OF NON-DISCRIMINATION ON GROUNDS OF NATIONALITY WITH REGARD TO TURKISH WORKERS IN THE EU

For Turkish workers, the right to be free from discrimination on grounds of nationality may generally emanate from two sources: the law of the Member States and the Union. Here, we will not deal with the former source (due to reasons of space); instead we will focus on the latter.[15] In Union law, Turkish workers enjoy the said right in the first place owing to the association law. Moreover, the Union legislator grants the same right to particular TCN (so to Turkish workers) by some Directives which might be at times more advantageous than association law. However, it seems that the more beneficial source is mainly the association law. Hence, first, we will analyze the association law in detail and second, consider the relevant Directives briefly. Besides, with regard to each specific provision on prohibition of discrimination on grounds of nationality, we will concentrate on the topics of direct effect, scope of application, restriction and justification, addressees, and consequences of infringement.

Association Law

The provisions relating to non-discrimination concerning Turkish workers are Article ("Art.") 9 Ankara Agreement ("AA"), Art. 37 Additional Protocol ("AP"), Art. 10(1) Association Council Decision ("ACD") 1/80 and Art. 3(1) ACD 3/80. While the latter three Articles are *lex specialis* as regards Art. 9 AA; Art. 10(1) ACD 1/80 is also *lex specialis* with regard to Art. 37 AP. Here, we will explore these Articles from *lex specialis* to *lex generalis*.

ACD 1/80

It is the Art. 10(1) of ACD 1/80 that relates to non-discrimination concerning Turkish workers. Here, we will analyze this Article in this order: Firstly, we will mention that Article and specify its feature of having direct effect. Secondly, we will examine the scope of application of this Article. Thirdly, we will show when there will be an infringement of this Article, *i.e.* the issue of restriction and justification regarding this Article. Fourthly, we will turn to the issue of addressees of this Article. Lastly, we will state briefly the consequences of infringement of this Article.

First of all, it is the Article 10(1) ACD 1/80 which sets the principle of equal treatment:[16]

> The Member States of the Community shall as regards remuneration and other conditions of work grant Turkish workers duly registered as belonging to their labor forces treatment involving no discrimination on the basis of nationality between them and Community workers.

This provision was found to have direct effect,[17] because it "prohibits Member States, in clear, precise and unconditional terms, from discriminating, on the basis of nationality" and the purpose and the nature of the AA do not prevent it from being directly effective.[18] Thus, Turkish workers who are within the scope of application of this Article are entitled to rely on it before the relevant bodies of the Member States and Union, such as the courts.[19]

The next question becomes, therefore, the scope of application of Art. 10(1) ACD 1/80. In this regard, in order to rely on this Article, a situation must be within the scope of application of it and there should not be an abuse of law. The term scope of application gives an answer to three questions: Who can rely on an Article (personal scope), which matters are covered by an Article (material scope), and from when an Article is applicable (temporal scope)? The principle of non-discrimination reveals itself, only when personal, material, and temporal scope are met cumulatively. Besides, there should be no abuse of law. In this respect, Union law recognizes that Member States are entitled to take measures "to prevent individuals from improperly or fraudulently taking advantage of provisions of Union law."[20] Hence, Turkish workers are not allowed to abuse Union law by relying on association law improperly or fraudulently.[21]

We will examine the scope of application of Art. 10(1) ACD 1/80 below in detail. However, before that, we want to mention the rule of interpretation that the Court employs when giving substance to the provisions of ACD 1/80. According to this rule the principles enshrined in Union law regarding the provisions of the free movement of workers will be transposed, as far as possible, to the rights conferred by ACD 1/80.[22] Besides, it should be noted that the Court of Justice of the European Union ("CJEU") has normally taken an expansive view of measures having as their goal the implementation of some aspect of the principle of equality,[23] like the principle of non-discrimination on grounds of nationality. Bearing in mind these rules of interpretation, the personal, material, and temporal scope of Art. 10(1) ACD 1/80 is explained in turn.

As regards the personal scope of Art. 10(1) ACD 1/80, only the Turkish workers who are duly registered as belonging to the labor force can rely on it.[24] Hence, it is necessary to define the terms 'worker' and 'being duly registered as belonging to the labor force.' Firstly, 'worker' has been construed in the same way both for Turkish and Union citizens.[25] Therefore, a person who pursues an effective and genuine activity and performs services for and under the direction of another person for a certain period of time and in return for remuneration is considered to be a worker.[26] Secondly, in order to be regarded as 'being duly registered as belonging to the labor force', a Turkish worker should cumulatively meet two conditions: First, the legal relationship of employment of a Turkish worker must be located within the territory of a Member State or retain a sufficiently close link with that territory. In examining whether there is a sufficiently close link with a territory, the determining criteria are as follows: the place where the Turkish national was hired, the territory on or from which the paid activity is pursued, and the applicable national legislation in the field of labor and social security law.[27] Second, a Turkish worker must have complied with the conditions laid down by law and regulation in the host Member State governing entry into its territory and employment and are thus entitled to pursue an occupation in that State.[28] Therefore, a Turkish worker who is duly registered as belonging to the labor force can invoke Art. 10(1) ACD 1/80, as long as a situation falls within the material and temporal scope of it.

As regards the material scope of Art. 10(1) ACD 1/80, it covers only remuneration and other conditions of work.[29] Hence, in order to reveal the exact scope of this Article, we have to define the term 'conditions of work.' In this respect, we have a guiding principle, *i.e.* "there is no reason to regard [Art. 10(1) ACD] as having a scope other than that given by the Court to [Art. 45(2) TFEU]," since the wording of the former is drafted almost identical to the latter.[30] From this, the Court concluded that the term conditions of work must be construed broadly, given that Art. 10(1) ACD 1/80 lays down the fundamental rule of non-discrimination.[31] This term, therefore, will cover "all matters directly or indirectly related to the exercise of activity as an employee in the host Member State."[32] Hence, this provides Turkish workers with a wide umbrella of protection regarding their economic activities in a Member State.[33]

The case-law of the Court is fruitful with regard to examples of 'conditions of work,' as well as the doctrine. The examples in case-law can be derived from not only the cases related to Turkish workers; but also the ones regarding Union workers on the one hand and Russian, (several) North African, or Central and East European workers on the other, since all of the non-discrimination provisions related to them share the same scope with Art. 45(2) TFEU.[34] With regard to the case-law of the Court on Turkish workers, examples of 'conditions of work' include[35] the right to vote and to stand as candidates in elections of the members of bodies which represent and defend the interests of workers;[36] a rule which authorizes clubs to field only a limited number of players from non-member States in competitions organized at the national level;[37] and the charges required of Turkish nationals when submitting an application for a residence permit.[38] Furthermore, the duration of contract of employments;[39] a rule requiring business managers to be a resident in a Member State;[40] and the length of service requirement,[41] are illustrations of 'working conditions.' Additionally, gaining access to vocational training courses[42] and the termination of employment contracts, such as redundancy and dismissal[43] are potential candidates that are to be deemed within this concept.

One controversial issue remains: Can social and tax advantages be regarded as within the concept of working conditions? For instance, Husmann argues that Art. 10(1) ACD 1/80 does not cover social and tax advantages,[44] because there is no identical provision like Art. 7(2) Regulation ("Reg.") 1612/68[45] in ACD 1/80 and the term working conditions cannot be deemed as including those advantages.[46] One may argue counter to these claims. Firstly, the Court does not limit itself to the Reg. 1612/68 when interpreting Art. 10(1) ACD 1/80; on the contrary it refers to Art. 45(2) TFEU. For example, in the *Wählergruppe* case the Court accepted that the right to vote and to stand as candidates in elections of representative bodies for workers are covered by Art. 10(1) ACD 1/80, although there was no identical provision like Art. 8 Reg. 1612/68 in ACD 1/80.[47] In addition to this Art. 45, TFEU directly affords social and tax advantages to Union workers.[48] Secondly, 'conditions of work' cover "all matters directly or indirectly related to the exercise of activity as an employee in the host Member State,"[49] which is a broad definition capable of involving social and tax advantages. Accordingly, in our view, the Court may likewise choose to or not to bring the said advantages into the material scope of Art. 10(1) ACD 1/80. Besides, one may argue that they fall within the scope of Art. 9 AA.[50]

In regards to the temporal scope of Art. 10(1) ACD 1/80, a Turkish worker may rely on it as from its entry into force, *i.e.* December 1, 1980.[51] Nonetheless, the principle of non-discrimination in this Article applies to all contracts of employment whether they are concluded before or after this date.[52]

Whenever a situation falls within the scope of application of Art. 10(1) ACD 1/80, the next question becomes what will be regarded as an infringement of this Article. In this respect, this Article prohibits discrimination between Turkish and Union (not host Member State)[53] workers within the scope of application of this Article. This comprises directly and indirectly discriminatory measures;[54] unless justified on the basis of permitted grounds, provided that the principles of proportionality and fundamental rights are observed.

To date, the Court has dealt only with cases concerning direct discrimination on grounds of nationality with regard to Art. 10(1) ACD 1/80. One such example can be found in the *Wählergruppe* case.[55] In this case, five Turkish nationals fulfill all criteria except for being Austrian nationals in order to be a candidate for the election of chamber of workers.[56] Hence, the national legislation which subjects such candidature to being a national of Austria is directly discriminatory and incompatible with Art. 10(1) ACD 1/80.[57]

There has been as yet no example of indirect discrimination on grounds of nationality with regard to Art. 10(1) ACD 1/80. However, there is no doubt that this Article embodies a prohibition on indirect discrimination. Firstly, Art. 45(2) TFEU with which Art. 10(1) ACD 1/80 shares the same scope forbids indirect discrimination.[58] Secondly, since it has been settled that Art. 3(1) ACD 3/80 which is the specific expression of the general principle of non-discrimination (Art. 9 AA)[59] rules out indirect discrimination,[60] the same should apply to Art. 10(1) ACD 1/80 which is also *lex specialis* to Art. 9 AA.[61] Thirdly, in the *Pokrzeptowicz-Meyer* case concerning Art. 37 of the EU-Poland Europe Agreement ("EA")—the principle of non-discrimination—the Court adjudicated that "the prohibition of any kind of discrimination against Polish workers based on their nationality applies as much to direct discrimination as to indirect discrimination which might affect their conditions of employment."[62] As both Art. 10(1) ACD 1/80 and Art. 37 of the EU-Poland Europe Agreement share the same scope with Art. 45(2) TFEU,[63] the former also prevents the application of indirectly discriminatory measures. Borrowing the definition of indirect discrimination from internal market case-law:

> a provision of national law must be regarded as indirectly discriminatory if it is intrinsically liable to affect migrant workers more than national workers and if

> there is a consequent risk that it will place the former at a particular disadvantage.[64]

Wherever there is a discriminatory measure, the question of justification arises.[65] First of all, employment in the public service is out of the range of Art. 10(1) ACD 1/80, though this was not mentioned in ACD 1/80.[66] In the *Wählergruppe* case it was argued that the election of foreign workers to a chamber of workers was excluded, as "those chambers are institutions governed by public law which participate in the exercise of public-law powers."[67] According to the Court, this exception which should be interpreted narrowly cannot be applied generally to any participation in a public-law institution, but only permits Member States to restrict the inclusion of foreign workers from "certain specific activities" of the institution which "actually entail direct participation in the exercise of public-law powers conferred."[68]

Secondly, a directly discriminatory measure may be justified only on the grounds of public policy, public security, or public health,[69] given that the principles of proportionality and fundamental rights are observed.[70] In order to define these grounds the Court refers to Art. 45(3) TFEU,[71] therefore, these exceptions are interpreted restrictively and go along with their counterparts in the internal market case-law.[72] For instance the concept of public policy presupposes "the existence of a genuine and sufficiently serious threat to one of the fundamental interests of society" as well as "the disturbance of the social order which any infringement of the law involves."[73] Furthermore, a restrictive measure can only be justified where the personal conduct of a Turkish worker "indicates a specific risk of new and serious prejudice to the requirements of public policy."[74]

Thirdly, an indirectly discriminatory measure may be justified by overriding reasons in the public interest in addition to public policy, public security, or public health,[75] provided that the principles of proportionality and fundamental rights are observed.[76] Until now, the Court has acknowledged lots of reasons as 'overriding reasons in the public interest,' albeit in the context of internal market case-law. The examples include: the coherence of the tax system;[77] the prevention of tax avoidance;[78] the effectiveness of fiscal supervision;[79] the risk of seriously undermining the financial balance of the social security system;[80] the objective of encouraging the recruitment and training of young players;[81] the protection of the recipients of services and consumers;[82] and road safety.[83] These examples may be helpful in some (future) cases regarding Turkish workers.

As regards the addressees of Art. 10(1) ACD 1/80, this Article obliges, in the first place, the Member States and the Union not to discriminate on grounds of nationality in their actions.[84] Secondly, this Article applies to "rules of any other nature aimed at regulating gainful employment in a collective manner,"[85] thus the principle of equal treatment also addresses 'private regulators.'[86] For instance, in the *Kahveci* case the Court decided that this Article precludes a rule laid down by a sports association in a Member State.[87] By contrast, it is not unambiguous as to whether or not private individuals—employers—are bound by this Article.[88] On the one hand, Peers believes that the CJEU will likely be reluctant to grant TCN a remedy which was initially designed to enforce Member States' obligations to one another and to ensure the uniformity of EU law.[89] On the other hand, Can claims that the prohibition of discrimination has direct effects against the state and employer.[90] Moreover, Art. 45(2) TFEU with which Art. 10(1) ACD 1/80 shares the same scope addresses private persons—employers such as banks—even in the case of indirect discrimination.[91] Since the Court has recognized that private regulators are covered by Art. 10(1) ACD 1/80, like Art. 45(2) TFEU, there seems to be no reason to depart from this analogy when it comes to private persons. Besides, this conclusion will be in line with the Court's emphasis on the "fundamental nature" of the principle of equality.[92]

Lastly, regarding the consequences of infringement of Art. 10(1) ACD 1/80, the Member States are precluded from applying the discriminatory provisions of the disputed measure, whenever a measure is contrary to it.[93] For instance, Ehlers notes that where a discriminatory practice excludes individuals from particular benefits, the prohibition of discrimination entails a right to a renewed, non-discriminatory allocation of the benefit in question or even a right to receive the benefit.[94] Besides, it is left to the national law to settle on the remedies to enforce the rights of Turkish workers.[95] However, this is subject to the requirements that whatever remedy is chosen must be not less favorable than those governing similar domestic actions and it must render neither impossible nor excessively difficult the exercise of the particular right concerned.[96]

ACD 3/80

It is Article 3(1) ACD 3/80 that relates to the principle of equal treatment as regards social security. Here, we will analyze this Article in this order: Firstly, we will mention that Article and specify its feature of having direct effect. Secondly, we will examine the scope of application of this Article. Thirdly, we will show when there will be an infringement of this Article, *i.e.* the issue of restriction and justification regarding this Article. Fourthly, we will turn to the issue of addressees of this Article. Lastly, we will state briefly the consequences of infringement of this Article.

First of all, it is the Article 3(1) ACD 3/80 which sets the principle of equal treatment as regards social security:

> Subject to the special provisions of this Decision, persons resident in the territory of one of the Member States to whom this Decision applies shall be

> subject to the same obligations and enjoy the same benefits under the legislation of any Member State as the nationals of that State.[97]

This provision has been found to have direct effect, since it "lays down in clear, precise and unconditional terms a prohibition of discrimination" and the purpose and the nature of the AA do not prevent it from being directly effective.[98] Thus, Turkish workers who are within the scope of application of this Article are entitled to rely on it before the relevant bodies of the Member States and Union, such as the courts.[99]

The next question becomes, therefore, the scope of application of Art. 3(1) ACD 3/80. In this regard, in order to rely on the Art. 3(1) ACD 3/80, a situation must be within the personal, material, and temporal scope of application of this Article and there should be no abuse of law. Here, we will examine thoroughly the scope of application of Art. 3(1) ACD 3/80; however, before that we would like to note the rule of interpretation that relevant Union law will be transposed, as far as possible, to the rights conferred by ACD 3/80.[100]

As regards the personal scope of Art. 3(1) ACD 3/80, Turkish workers who meet certain requirements can rely on it.[101] First of all, the concept of 'worker' regarding ACD 1/80 and ACD 3/80 differs, since the former follows Art. 45 TFEU, while the latter goes along with Reg. 1408/71[102] which has been recently repealed by Reg. 883/2004.[103] In the words of the Court:

> a person has the status of worker where he is covered, even if only in respect of a single risk, on a compulsory or optional basis, by a general or special social security scheme, irrespective of the existence of an employment relationship.[104]

Secondly, a Turkish worker must be or have been subject to the legislation of one or more Member States[105] and lastly, he should be resident in the territory of one of them.[106]

As regards the material scope of Art. 3(1) ACD 3/80, it covers all legislation concerning the following branches of social security: sickness and maternity benefits; invalidity benefits (including those intended for the maintenance or improvement of earning capacity); old-age benefits; survivors' benefits; benefits in respect of accidents at work and occupational diseases; death grants; unemployment benefits; and family benefits.[107] Moreover, in respect of these benefits, all general and special social security schemes, whether contributory or non-contributory and schemes concerning the liability of an employer or ship owner fall within the material scope of this provision.[108] Furthermore, the principle of non-discrimination applies also to the right to elect members of the organs of social security institutions or to participate in their nomination.[109] However, social and medical assistance or benefit schemes for victims of war and its consequences are out of the scope of application of this provision.[110]

As regards the temporal scope of Art. 3(1) ACD 3/80, a Turkish worker may rely on it as from May 4, 1999, though entry into force of ACD 3/80 was September 19, 1980,[111] since the CJEU limited the temporal effect of its first judgment on this Article. In the *Sürül* case, the Court seemed to be concerned with the German, French, and United Kingdom Governments[112] and decided that in order not to "retroactively throw the financing of the social security systems of the Member States into confusion"[113] the general principle of legal certainty requires that:

> [Art. 3(1) ACD 3/80] may not be relied on in support of claims relating to benefits in respect of periods prior to the date of this judgment except as regards those persons who, before that date, initiated proceedings or made an equivalent claim.[114]

Whenever a situation falls within the scope of application of Art. 3(1) ACD 3/80, the next question becomes what will be regarded as an infringement of this Article. In this respect, this Article prohibits both direct and indirect discrimination.[115] However, it is possible to justify the discriminatory measure on the basis of allowed grounds, as long as the principles of proportionality and fundamental rights are respected.

The *Sürül* case is an example of direct discrimination.[116] Here, national legislation required that a lawfully resident Turkish national should hold a certain type of residence document in order to receive family allowances.[117] However, within ACD 3/80:

> A Turkish national . . . must be treated in the same way as nationals of the host Member State, so that the legislation of that Member State cannot impose upon such a Turkish national more or stricter conditions than those applicable to its own nationals.[118]

Therefore, the disputed measure constitutes "unequal treatment on grounds of nationality," given that it demands from non-nationals a special residence permit, while nationals of that State are exempted from such a requirement.[119] Thus, the relevant measure which is directly discriminatory on grounds of nationality is incompatible with ACD 3/80.[120]

An example of indirect discrimination can be found in the *Öztürk* case.[121] In this case in order to qualify for an early old-age pension, a person should have benefited from Austrian unemployment insurance for a certain period of time prior to the qualifying date.[122] In respect of this, according to the settled case-law:

> the rule of equal treatment prohibits not only overt discrimination based on nationality but also all covert forms of discrimination which, by applying other distinguishing criteria, achieve in practice the same result.[123]

Here, the questioned requirement "can be more easily fulfilled by Austrian workers than by Turkish migrant workers who have worked in Austria."[124] Moreover, indirect discrimination occurs when a measure is "liable to have such an effect."[125] Hence, Art. 3(1) ACD 3/80 precludes, in principle, the application of such discriminatory legislation.[126]

Wherever there is a discriminatory measure, the question of justification arises.[127] In this regard, while directly discriminatory measures may be justified only on the grounds of public policy, public security, or public health, indirectly discriminatory measures may be justified by overriding reasons in the public interest as well, as long as the principles of proportionality and fundamental rights are observed.[128] Here, it is sufficient to refer to our explanations with respect to Art. 10(1) ACD 1/80 regarding the justification stage.

As regards the addressees of Art. 3(1) ACD 3/80, it appears to address only Member States, since this Article asserts equality "under the legislation of any Member State."[129]

Lastly, regarding the consequences of infringement of Art. 3(1) ACD 3/80, Union law precludes the application of discriminatory measures to Turkish workers, whenever there is infringement of it.

Additional Protocol

Art. 37 AP lays down the principle of equal treatment:

> As regards conditions of work and remuneration, the rules which each Member State applies to workers of Turkish nationality employed in the Community shall not discriminate on grounds of nationality between such workers and workers who are nationals of other Member States of the Community.[130]

Till now, the Court has not considered the direct effect of Art. 37 AP. However, there are strong arguments in favor of the direct effect of this Article. Following the reasoning of the Court, first of all, the wording of this Article is "clear and precise"[131] or it "contains an obligation which is sufficiently precise and unconditional and the implementation of which is not subject to the adoption of any subsequent measure."[132] In addition to this, it is now settled that the purpose and subject-matter of the AA (and AP) do not invalidate such a conclusion.[133] Besides, the Court has given direct effect to provisions of similar kind, such as Art. 10(1) ACD 1/80[134] or Art. 40 of the EU-Morocco Cooperation Agreement;[135] thus, Art. 37 AP should also have direct effect in a similar vein.[136] As a result, it is very likely that the Court will give direct effect to Art. 37 AP.

In determining the scope of application of Art. 37 AP, it should be borne in mind that this Article is *lex generalis* in comparison with Art. 10(1) ACD 1/80.[137] Hence, the former is only applicable where the latter is not relevant for a particular situation.[138] It looks like there are only two differences between these Articles, which relate to their personal and temporal scope. In respect of personal scope, while Art. 10(1) ACD 1/80 mentions workers who are 'duly registered as belonging to the labor force', Art. 37 AP expresses workers who are 'employed in the Union.' The Court has not ruled on the scope of the latter Article, therefore one may only guess how the latter term might be interpreted. One suggestion might be referring to the concept of 'legal employment' in the meaning of Art. 6(1) ACD 1/80, since being employed in the Union implies an employment which is legal. If this suggestion is appropriate, then Art. 37 AP will be applicable where a Turkish worker's situation is "stable and secure" "as a member of the labor force of a Member State."[139] However, it is not clear how this definition and the one of 'being duly registered as belonging to the labor force' differs in terms of their range of situations covered. Nonetheless, since Art. 37 AP is *lex generalis* to the Art. 10(1) ACD 1/80, the term 'employed' should mean something broader than 'being duly registered as belonging to the labor force.' The term 'employed' might therefore be considered as adding no specification to the concept of 'worker.' Besides, though a Turkish worker may rely on Art. 10(1) ACD 1/80 as from December 1, 1980, he may invoke Art. 37 AP beginning from January 1, 1973.

Bearing in mind the (potential) disparity in personal and temporal scope, Art 37 AP must be applied just like as Art. 10(1) ACD 1/80 in other respects, namely, the material scope, restriction and justification, addressees, and consequences of infringement. Thus, for these matters, it is sufficient to refer to our explanations with regard to Art. 10(1) ACD 1/80.

Ankara Agreement

Art. 9 AA provides the general non-discrimination clause on the grounds of nationality worded as follows:

> The Contracting Parties recognize that within the scope of this Agreement and without prejudice to any special provisions which may be laid down pursuant to Article 8, any discrimination on grounds of nationality shall be prohibited in accordance with the principle laid down in Article 7 of the Treaty establishing the Community.[140]

Till now the Court has not ruled explicitly on the direct effect of Art. 9 AA. However, in one case the Court found a Dutch rule which sets a disproportionate amount for obtaining a residence permit contrary to Art. 9 AA, without apparently discussing its direct effect.[141] According to the Court, such a rule is not only a discriminatory condition of work contrary to Art. 10(1) ACD 1/80 as regards Turkish workers, but also at odds with Art. 9 AA regarding Turkish self-employed and service providers.[142] The Court has, therefore, recognized implicitly the direct effect of Art. 9 AA with this finding.

Besides, there are some indications which are in favor of direct effect of Art. 9 AA. Firstly, the specific non-discrimination clauses, such as Art. 9 and 10(1) ACD 1/80 and 3(1) ACD 3/80 which constitute "nothing other than the application and concrete form"[143] or "merely the implementation and the specific expression"[144] of the general non-discrimination clause—Art. 9 AA—[145] has already been equipped with direct effect. Secondly, the Court stresses at almost all times that Art. 9 AA refers to Art. 18 TFEU[146] and this confirms that the Court in fact ascribes to Art. 9 AA the same role, in the context of the association law as to Art. 18 TFEU[147] which has direct effects in Union law.[148] Thirdly, Art. 9 AA has been regarded as having direct effect not only (cautiously) by some authors in the doctrine, but also (plainly) by the AG (La Pergola), the Commission, and even a national court in a case.[149]

In addition to these indications, Art. 9 AA passes the direct effect test for provisions of international agreements.[150] To begin with, this Article contains "in clear, precise and unconditional terms" an obligation of equal treatment between Turkish and Union nationals.[151] Likewise, this obligation is "not conditional, in its implementation or its effects, upon the adoption of any subsequent measure."[152] Moreover, it is now settled that the purpose and subject-matter of the AA do not preclude the direct effect of its provisions.[153] This means that any person covered by association law can rely on the principle of non-discrimination insofar as the rights at issue fall within the material scope of the association law.[154] In other words, Article 9 AA requires its obligors, "in the absence of adequate and logical justification, not to treat their ... citizens and Turkish citizens ... differently."[155]

Art. 9 AA is *lex generalis* in comparison to specific non-discrimination clauses such as Art. 37 AP, Art. 10(1) ACD 1/80 and Art. 3(1) ACD 3/80 which highlights the fact that the scope of application of these Articles differ.[156] As to the personal scope, it seems that Turkish workers whose position in a Member State is regular may rely on Art. 9 AA.[157] In this regard, workers who are not covered by 3/80 ACD may invoke Art. 9 AA in situations which are falling within the material scope of association law.[158] As to the material scope, neither entry to the Union nor access to the labor market is covered by association law.[159] However, once a Turkish worker is employed legally in a Member State, he may gain benefits like the ones conferred via Art. 45 TFEU to a Union worker who is in a comparable situation.[160] This might include the right to equal access to social advantages and to educational grants.[161] As to the temporal scope, Art. 9 AA has been in force since January 1, 1964.[162]

Bearing in mind the disparity in personal, material, and temporal scope, Art. 9 AA will probably be applied parallel to Art. 10(1) ACD 1/80 with respect to the subjects of restriction and justification, addressees, and consequences of infringement. Thus, for these matters, it is adequate to refer to our explanations regarding Art. 10(1) ACD 1/80.

Union Legislation

The EU adopted some Directives relating to TCN living in the Union which contain a provision of non-discrimination on the grounds of nationality. Accordingly, the non-discrimination provisions of these Directives might be more advantageous for Turkish workers on occasion.[163] Here, presuming that these provisions will have direct effect,[164] we will concisely examine and evaluate the possible favorable effects of them.

Firstly, there is the Directive ("Dir.") 2003/109 which concerns the status of TCN who are long-term residents.[165] The right to equal treatment in this Directive applies generally[166] to TCN who have been a legal resident in a Member State for five years,[167] have stable and regular resources and sickness insurance,[168] and cannot be refused on grounds of public policy or security,[169] once they apply for the 'long-term resident' status.[170] These TCN, including Turkish workers, in principle, benefit from equal treatment with nationals of the host Member State in many fields: access to employment, employment and working conditions, education and vocational training, recognition of qualifications, social security,[171] social assistance and social protection, tax benefits, access to goods and services, housing, freedom of association and affiliation, and membership of an organization representing workers.[172] However, there are (potential) considerable limitations in most of these fields,[173] such as restraining the equal treatment in respect of social assistance and social protection to core benefits.[174] Besides, social advantages are not included in this list.[175] In view of that, it seems that Dir. 2003/109 may surpass the association law in respect of non-discrimination only as regards access to education and vocational training, recognition of qualifications, social assistance and social protection, or tax benefits or access to goods and services or housing.[176] However, it is also arguable that (at least some of) these areas fall within the scope of association law, thus within the general equality clause of Art. 9 AA.[177]

Secondly, there is the Dir. 2009/50 which pertains to highly qualified TCN workers.[178] The right to equal treatment in this Directive applies generally[179] to TCN who have a valid work contract or a binding job offer for highly qualified employment, relevant documents for the regulated or unregulated profession, a valid travel document, sickness insurance, and does not pose a threat to public policy, security, or health,[180] once they are granted the EU Blue Card.[181] These TCN, including Turkish workers, in principle, have the right to equal treatment with nationals of the host Member State in many fields: working conditions, freedom of association and affiliation, membership of an organization representing workers, education and vocational training, recognition of qualifications, social security, access to goods and services and housing.[182] However, certain limitations remain, such as restricting study and maintenance grants and loans.[183] Therefore, keeping in mind that Art. 9 AA might apply to such fields, Dir. 2009/50 may go beyond the provisions of association law as regards education and vocational training or recognition of qualifications or access to goods and services or housing.

Up until now, we have examined the sources of Union law which grant Turkish workers a right not to be discriminated against on grounds of nationality with regard to certain matters. The next section inspects the same right flowing from Turkish law with regard to Union workers.

PRINCIPLE OF NON-DISCRIMINATION ON GROUNDS OF NATIONALITY WITH REGARD TO UNION WORKERS IN TURKEY

For Union workers, the right to be free from discrimination on grounds of nationality may spring from either international agreements to which Turkey is a party or domestic law. Though the association law embodies provisions of equality of treatment, their effect in the legal order of Turkey seems (at least) vague, because till now there has not been any court decision on the basis of them. Nonetheless, due to the 2004 amendments in the TC, the international agreements which concern fundamental rights and freedoms (like the International Convention on the Protection of the Rights of all Migrant Workers and Members of their Families ("ICRMW")) may fill this gap, since their non-discrimination clauses will prevail over conflicting domestic law. Moreover, equality is a principle enshrined in the TC and TLS establishes the principle of equal treatment as regards (all) workers. Here, we will begin with international agreements and then focus on domestic law. For each provision we will try to stick to our scheme in our examination of Union law, *i.e.* the topics of scope of application, restriction and justification, addressees, and consequences of infringement.

International Agreements Binding upon Turkey

Here, we will first demonstrate the relationship of international and national law as regards Turkey. Subsequently, we will move on to explore the international agreements which may affect the position of Union workers in Turkey as regards protection from discrimination on the grounds of nationality, while distinguishing the association law from other agreements.

General Remarks

There are some general remarks which relate to the status and effects of international agreements upon the legal order of Turkey. Firstly, Turkey is a monist country, since a statute approving the ratification is enough for an international agreement to be "duly put into effect" and become part of Turkish law,[184] hence binding on every state organ, including courts.[185] Secondly, regarding the rank of international agreements, since 2004, while the ones related to fundamental rights and freedoms have priority over conflicting statutes,[186] others are at the same level with statutes,[187] which means that the conflicts between them are resolved by the rules of *lex posterior* and *lex specialis*.[188] Thirdly, Turkish courts try usually to solve the conflicts between the international treaties and statutes by way of interpretation at first hand which obviates a conflict most of the time because the national legislation is interpreted in the light of provisions of the international agreements.[189] Fourthly, there are some (exceptional) Turkish court decisions in which a provision of an international agreement applied directly to a case at hand;[190] however, there is no doctrine like "direct effect" or being "self-executing" developed by the case-law.[191] Moreover, even in the doctrine it is hard to find a thorough test for such effects to occur. Nonetheless, generally, a provision of an international agreement may be applied directly to a case when it "introduces very concrete arrangements"[192] or "contains objective rights and obligations"[193] or "draws up rights and obligations which are self-sufficient, definite and concrete and do not need any additional arrangements."[194] Lastly, the term "fundamental rights and freedoms" as regards international agreements has been construed broadly, so as to include not only agreements themselves (for instance the European Convention on Human Rights ("ECHR")) but also the decisions of the judicial organs established by them (for example decisions of the European Court on Human Rights ("ECtHR")).[195]

Association Law

The association law does not have the same legal force in Turkish law as it has in Union law. First of all, an ACD does not have binding effect in Turkish law, because they lack an act of approval[196] which precludes them to be "duly put into effect" and become part of Turkish law. Hence, these Decisions cannot be applied directly in the Turkish legal order, for instance by Turkish courts.[197] On the other hand, it is of course still an international law responsibility of Turkey arising from the AA to obey an ACD.[198] Hence, it is for Turkey to fulfill its duty, maybe by adopting or amending the relevant national legislation.[199] Secondly, the AP and AA are international agreements duly put into effect, thus, they form a part of Turkish legal order.[200] However, Art. 37 AP lays down a prohibition on discrimination only for Turkish nationals in the Union; as a result, this cannot benefit Union workers in Turkey. Alternatively, Art. 9 AA which contains a general ban on discrimination on grounds of nationality might be invoked by Union workers before a Turkish court.[201] However, it should be borne in mind that the AA appears not to be an agreement related to fundamental rights and freedoms, hence, has the same rank with statutes, rather than prevailing over them.[202] In this regard, other international agreements having such status and including non-discrimination clauses may be more useful for Union workers.

Other International Agreements

Here, we will focus on the agreements which, in our view, embody a self-executing or directly applicable provision on non-discrimination, including on grounds of nationality, and can be deemed as related to fundamental rights and freedoms.[203] However, we want to split these agreements into two groups: the ones containing a general clause, not restricting themselves to workers, namely the International Covenant on Civil and Political Rights ("ICCPR"),[204] Revised European Social Charter ("RESC"),[205] ECHR and its Protocols,[206] and the one which relates specifically to workers, that is ICRMW.[207]

There are non-discrimination clauses of different kinds in ICCPR, RESC, and ECHR. While the former sets a general non-discrimination clause, the latter two lay down such clauses with regard only to the rights conferred by those agreements.[208] It is possible to consider these clauses as self-executing or directly applicable in the Turkish legal order, since they comprehend a self-sufficient, definite, and concrete obligation on non-discrimination *inter alia* on grounds of nationality.[209]

To begin with, ICCPR which is an agreement affiliated with the United Nations ("UN") concerns some civil and political rights, and the Human Rights Committee ("HRC"), as the *quasi*-judicial organ of that Convention, monitors the implementation of it.[210] This Convention settles a general non-discrimination clause which forbids discrimination, *inter alia*, on grounds of 'national origin' or 'other status;'[211] thus, either the former or the latter term is capable of being interpreted as including 'nationality.'[212] Besides, there is a decision of the HRC which treats nationality as a quality included in 'other status.'[213] It is up to the Turkish courts to regard the non-discrimination clause of ICCPR as directly applicable; however, in any event, this Convention and the decisions of the HRC should be taken into account when interpreting national legislation (for our purposes) regarding non-discrimination of migrant workers.[214] In this regard, it is essential to note that the HRC construes this prohibition as including not only direct but also indirect discrimination in its decisions. For instance, in one dispute, the Committee decided that a violation of the non-discrimination clause:

> can also result from the discriminatory effect of a rule or measure that is neutral at face value or without intent to discriminate. However, such indirect discrimination can only be said to be based on the grounds (such as of nationality) . . . if the detrimental effects of a rule or decision exclusively or disproportionally affect persons having a particular (nationality).[215]

Secondly, the ECHR and RESC which are both agreements affiliated with the Council of Europe lay down non-discrimination clauses with regard only to the rights conferred by them which are monitored by the ECtHR and the European Committee of Social Rights ("ECSR") in turn.[216] While ECHR forbids discrimination on grounds of 'national origin' and 'other status,' RESC prohibits discrimination on the basis of 'national extraction' and 'other status.'[217] Here, we will draw attention to two developments, both of which concern the ECHR. On the one hand, the non-discrimination clause in the ECHR, in conjunction with the right to property, may be relevant to Union workers, since the ECtHR ruled that entitlement to social benefits such as emergency assistance fall within the scope of their application, and therefore, no discrimination based on nationality is allowed in this regard.[218] Moreover, according to the ECtHR, the principle of equality prevents the treatment of persons who are in different analogous situations[219] and fails to treat people differently whose situations are significantly different,[220] unless there is an 'objective and reasonable justification,' *i.e.* the disputed measure should pursue a 'legitimate aim' and/or there has to be a 'reasonable relationship of proportionality between the means employed and the aim sought to be realized.'[221] Since the Turkish courts are required to take into account the decisions of the ECtHR,[222] these decisions become a valuable legal source, at least with regard to the interpretation of the principle of non-discrimination in Turkish law. On the other hand, there is now the Protocol No 12 to the ECHR which includes a general prohibition on discrimination, on grounds of, *inter alia*, 'national origin' or 'other status.' This Protocol which was signed on November 4, 2000 and entered into force on April 1, 2005 was signed by Turkey on April 18, 2001; however, it has not been ratified yet. Nevertheless, it is very likely that this Protocol will play an influential role in the Turkish legal order, since it will be backed up with the decisions of the ECtHR in the future.

When we turn to the ICRMW, this Convention which is an agreement affiliated with the UN deserves to be emphasised particularly, as it sets the rights of migrant workers in general which are monitored by the 'Committee on Migrant Workers.'[223] Here, we will concentrate on the direct applicability of the non-discrimination clauses in this Convention, as well as their scope of application and addressees.

In the ICRMW, while Art. 25(1) ICRMW sets the principle of non-discrimination in respect of remuneration, other conditions of work and other terms of employment, Art. 27(1) ICRMW settles it as regards social security.[224] According to the former:

> Migrant workers shall enjoy treatment not less favorable than that which applies to nationals of the State of employment...

According to the latter:

> With respect to social security, migrant workers . . . shall enjoy in the State of employment the same treatment granted to nationals in so far as they fulfill the requirements provided for by the applicable legislation of that State and the applicable bilateral and multilateral treaties.

These provisions require the same treatment of migrant workers as for national workers, therefore requiring no discrimination based on nationality.[225] Though Art. 25(1) ICRMW seems to be directly applicable, since it comprehends a self-sufficient, definite, and concrete obligation of non-discrimination, it cannot be unambiguously stated that Art. 27(1) ICRMW is also directly applicable, because it refers not only to applicable legislation of the home State, but also to the applicable bilateral and multilateral treaties.[226] However, the last decision on this point will of course be rendered by Turkish courts.

As regards the scope of application of Art. 25(1) and 27(1) ICRMW, though the personal scope of them does not differ, their material scope does. In this respect, ICRMW applies to all migrant workers[227] and the term "migrant worker" means a person who is to be engaged, is engaged or has been engaged in a remunerated activity in a State of which he or she is not a national.[228]

Art. 25(1) and 27(1) ICRMW, on the other hand, differ in material scope. The latter covers only 'social security.' However, the former covers remuneration, other conditions of work, and other terms of employment. In this regard, 'other conditions of work' connotes overtime, hours of work, weekly rest, holidays with pay, safety, health, termination of the employment relationship, and any other conditions of work which according to national law and practice are covered by these terms.[229] In addition to this, 'other terms of employment' refers to minimum age of employment, restriction on work, and any other matters which according to national law and practice are considered a term of employment.[230] Hence, it is apparent that this Convention aims to cover areas in the broadest way, since in addition to specifically stating the conditions of work and terms of employment, it also refers to national law and practices regarding the other matters which may be covered by these terms.

Regarding the addressees of Art. 25(1) and 27(1) ICRMW, there seems to be a difference. While the former explicitly mentions that it is also not allowed to derogate from the principle of equal treatment in private employment contracts,[231] the latter refers to 'states' at several times which implies that it is binding only upon them.[232]

To sum up, all of these international agreements may become significant instruments for Union workers, since they form part of the Turkish legal order and as agreements related to fundamental rights and freedoms, prevail over conflicting national legislation. Though it is for the Turkish courts to settle the question of the direct applicability of their non-discrimination clauses, in any event, they must be deemed as guiding principles, since national legislation is interpreted in the light of provisions of the international agreements. However, Turkish courts will hardly refer to international law when there are comprehensible provisions of domestic law on a point, like the principle of equality or non-discrimination.

Domestic Law

The principle of equality is, first of all, a constitutional principle. Besides, it is taken under protection in various Statutes, one of which is the TLS. However, there is not any such clause in the social security legislation of Turkey, namely in the Social Insurance and Universal Health Insurance Statute No 5510 ("SIUHIS"). Here, these arrangements will be scrutinized in turn.

1982 Turkish Constitution

Art. 10 TC lays down the principle of equality under the heading of "Equality before the Law" as follows:

> All individuals are equal without any discrimination before the law, irrespective of language, race, color, sex, political opinion, philosophical belief, religion and sect, or any such considerations. . . . State organs and administrative authorities shall act in compliance with the principle of equality before the law in all their proceedings.[233]

Though there is no explicit reference to nationality, the term 'any such considerations' applies to it.[234]

Doctrine and courts have clarified the meaning of Art. 10 TC. According to the doctrine this Article regulates, on the one hand, the 'prohibition on discrimination' which provides protection for persons who receive negative treatment or are deprived of certain benefits due to their particular characteristics or choices; and on the other hand the 'principle of equal treatment' which requires that persons who are in the same or similar situation are not to be treated differently, in other words there should be no differentiation between persons, unless there are legitimate and objective reasons.[235] With regard to Turkish courts, for instance, according to the Constitutional Court:

> The aim of the principle of equality is to assure that persons in the same situation are treated alike and to prevent discriminatory treatment of them by the Statutes. . . . The principle of equality will not be violated, if same legal situations are subject to same rules and different legal situations are subject to different rules.[236]

Moreover, according to the Court of Appeals, Art. 10(1) TC "recognises equality between equals. The obligation of equal treatment cannot be deployed, whenever there are objective reasons."[237] Furthermore, the principle of non-discrimination of Art. 10(1) TC is considered as a fundamental right.[238]

Additionally, the provisions of the TC may be relied on under certain circumstances. This is stated in Art. 11 TC as follows:

> The provisions of the Constitution are fundamental legal rules binding upon legislative, executive and judicial organs, and administrative authorities and other institutions and individuals.

In accordance with this Article, the provisions of the TC apply to situations which occur not only between persons and the state (the so-called vertical ones), but also between persons (the so-called horizontal ones). Hence, the constitutional principle of equality has the characteristics of a general principle which is applicable in the whole legal system, and thus in employment relationships.[239] For example, if there is an infringement of the principle of equality laid down in Art. 10(1) TC in an employment contract, the relevant clause will be deemed void.[240] Therefore, this constitutional principle will serve as a safety net, in addition to the non-discrimination clauses regulated in Turkish Statutes, like Art. 5(1) TLS.

Turkish Labor Statute No 4857

It is Art. 5(1) TLS that sets the principle of non-discrimination. Here, we will analyze this Article in this order: Firstly, we will mention that Article and some of its features. Secondly, we will examine the scope of application of this Article. Thirdly, we will show when there will be an infringement of this Article, *i.e.* the issue of restriction and justification regarding this Article. Fourthly, we will turn to the issue of addressees of this Article. Lastly, we will state briefly the consequences of infringement of this Article.

First of all, Art. 5(1) TLS sets the principle of non-discrimination, under the heading of "the Principle of Equal Treatment"[241] as follows:

> There shall be no discrimination based on language, race, color, political opinion, philosophical belief, religion and sect, or any such considerations, regarding employment relationship.

This Article does not arrange the discrimination grounds *numerus clausus*[242] and though it is not overtly mentioned in this Article, non-discrimination on the grounds of nationality should be considered under the term 'any such considerations' for two reasons. Firstly, nationality is a distinguishing feature just like language or race and accordingly covered by 'any such considerations.'[243] Secondly, Art. 5(1) TLS should be interpreted in the light of the international agreements, especially the ones which are related to fundamental rights and freedoms and they contain provisions prohibiting discrimination on the basis of national origin,[244] national extraction,[245] or nationality.[246] Hence, Art. 5(1) TLS forbids discrimination on the grounds of nationality during the employment relationship,[247] similarly to Art. 10(1) ACD 1/80 and Art. 37 AP.

As regards the scope of application of Art. 5 TLS, a person who is within the personal and material scope of this Article may invoke it. In order to fall within the personal scope of this Article, a foreign—thus Union—worker[248] has to cumulatively satisfy the following conditions: Firstly, as a worker, he/she must work on the basis of an employment contract.[249] Secondly, he/she is obliged to hold a visa for work, a work permit, and a residence permit.[250] While the visa for work can and should be obtained beforehand from Turkish delegations where the foreigner stays,[251] the work permit is given and extended by the Ministry of Labor and Social Security.[252] However, in this regard, there is a special arrangement for Union workers: They may be granted a work permit without a time limit, since they form a part of a special group because of the obligations of Turkey arising from association law.[253] Hence, in this regard, Turkish law is similar to association law which also requires a Turkish worker to be 'duly registered as belonging to the labor force.'

In order to fall within the material scope of Article 5(1) TLS, a situation should be deemed within the 'employment relationship.' This term is construed broadly, and accordingly the said Article applies not only during the employment relationship, but also to the recruitment process and in the termination of the employment contract.[254] On the other hand, access to the labor market is out of range of the said Article and in this respect some professions such as pharmacist or lawyer are reserved to Turkish nationals,[255] mostly on the grounds of public policy, security, or health as well as public interest.[256] Turkish law also seems to be in line with association law on this point. Moreover, just as the potential function of Art. 9 AA with regard to Union law, Art. 10(1) TC may function as a gap-filler in Turkish law, for instance regarding social and tax advantages.

Whenever a situation falls within the scope of application of Art. 5(1) TLS, the next question becomes what will be regarded as an infringement of this Article. In this respect, in terms of Turkish doctrine Art. 5(1) TLS imposes a prohibition of discrimination and a principle of equal treatment, in accordance with Art. 10(1) TC,[257] which in the terminology of Union law corresponds nearly to direct and indirect discrimination.[258] Moreover, there are special rules on the burden of proof, *i.e.* though it is for the worker to prove that the employer acted or has been acting in a discriminatory manner, when "a worker reveals a case which strongly discloses the *possibility* of the presence of the breach," then it is up to the employer to show that there has not been such a breach.[259]

The Court of Appeals has a settled case-law regarding the principle of equal treatment laid down in Art. 5(1) TLS. It is, therefore, constructive to highlight some significant remarks of that Court about this Article:

> The principle of equality of treatment imposes on the employer the obligation not to treat differently between employees working in the workplace, unless there is a legitimate and objective reason. . . . In other words the prohibition on discrimination forbids differentiation between workers arbitrarily. . . . The said principle aims to prevent workers who are in an identical situation from being treated differently.
> [The principle of equality can be found in the TC and relevant international agreements, like the ECHR or TFEU.]
> There is no obligation to equal treatment where "there are substantial reasons" and "biologic reasons or reasons of the nature of the work require so."[260]

Hence, it seems that both direct (overt) and indirect (covert) forms of discrimination are covered by the prohibition in Art. 5(1) TLS.[261] In this regard, direct discrimination occurs where individuals or groups are expressly treated less favorably because of a particular characteristic, such as nationality.[262] On the other hand indirect discrimination arises where a measure, even though it is equally applicable notwithstanding nationality, in its application is more disadvantageous for nationals of other Member States than for those of the state taking the measure.[263] For instance if an employer sets the criteria of having ten years working experience in Turkey for an appointment to a higher post, this would produce indirect discrimination, given that this condition is harder to fulfill by and more disadvantageous to non-national workers, including Union workers. Lastly, in determining discrimination, the decisive factor is not the intent of the employer, but the effects of the relevant measure.[264]

As regards justification of a discriminatory measure, there seems to be no compact criteria. It appears that both direct and indirect discrimination may be justified by an objective reason which can be considered as legitimate, or in the other words of the Court of Appeals 'substantial reasons.'[265] However, it is hard to give examples of such reasons, especially with regard to discrimination on grounds of nationality, since there has not been any case that has reached this court of last instance on this matter, at least to our knowledge. Nonetheless, it is common ground that public policy, security, or health may be considered as such reasons.[266] Moreover, it is to be expected that the principle of proportionality will also take its place in such a justification process.[267]

As regards the addressees of Art. 5(1) TLS, since it is a 'Statute' which lays down the principle of non-discrimination, it can be invoked against any person, including the state and private persons, such as employers.

Lastly, regarding the consequences of infringement of Art. 5(1) TLS, various Turkish Statutes foresee different kinds of remedies in case of a breach of the non-discrimination principle laid down in this Article. Firstly, a provision of a contract which violates the principle of equal treatment is void, in accordance with Art. 20 of the Statute of Obligations, when read in conjunction with Art. 5(1) TLS.[268] Moreover, "this gap which arises because of such invalidity should be fulfilled pursuant to the requirements of the principle of equal treatment."[269] Secondly, there is the 'compensation of discrimination' set out in Art. 5(6) TLS:

> In the case of infringement of [the non-discrimination principle] during the employment relationship or in its termination a worker may demand an appropriate compensation the upper limit of which is the remuneration up to four months, as well as his/her rights that he/she is deprived of.[270]

This compensation is only for the situations which fall within the scope of TLS and it also does not cover the recruitment process. Hence, for these matters which are out of the range of TLS, it is possible to rely on the general provisions, like the ones in the Statute of Obligations and recover the relevant damages.[271] In addition to this, the infringement of not only prohibition on discrimination (*i.e.* direct discrimination), but also equality of treatment (*i.e.* indirect discrimination) will give rise to the compensation for discrimination.[272] Moreover, neither the existence of damages nor the fault of the employer is necessary in order to take this compensation.[273] Also, the term 'rights deprived of' represents for instance the remuneration which has not been paid or paid incompletely or premiums or other welfare benefits.[274]

Thirdly, in addition to the compensation for discrimination, a worker is entitled to terminate the employment contract on valid grounds. This right may be based either on non-payment of his/her remuneration or non-application of the working conditions.[275] Accordingly, under these circumstances a worker will have the right to demand 'severance pay' when he/she has worked for at least one year and 'notice pay,' because of the substantial changes made to the employment contract contrary to the principle of equal treatment.[276]

Lastly, there is a sanction against discrimination in the Turkish Penal Statute. According to Art. 122(1) of the said Statute:

> Any person who makes discrimination between individuals on the grounds of their language, race, color, sex, political opinion, philosophical belief, religion and sect, or any such considerations and therefore;
> a) binds the recruitment of a person to above listed grounds,
> c) prevents a person to perform an ordinary economical activity . . . is sentenced to imprisonment from six months to one year or imposed punitive fine.

Though this sanction is limited in scope compared to Art. 5(1) TLS, it still has a deterrent effect on all forms of discrimination in general which will probably include discrimination on grounds of nationality, though there has not been any conclusive court decision on this point, since this will be in line with Art. 5(1) TLS and the related provisions of relevant international agreements, such as Art. 25(1) ICRMW.

Social Insurance and Universal Health Insurance Statute No 5510

SIUHIS controls the social security of individuals,[277] but it does not include an apparent non-discrimination clause. However, any Union worker with a work permit will benefit from this legislation in the same way as Turkish workers. Hence, they will not be subject to discrimination on grounds of nationality in this respect. On the other hand, in general, the social security legislation of Turkey is quite complex and it includes several exceptions which may put Union workers out of the scope of application of that legislation. Nonetheless, general non-discrimination clauses of relevant international treaties or TC might benefit Union workers at this juncture.[278] However, here, we will briefly explain SIUHIS, since it is the major legislation regarding social security.

Firstly, SIUHIS covers both short and long term insurance branches and universal health insurance.[279] The former term indicates the following: sickness and maternity benefits; invalidity benefits; old-age benefits; survivors' benefits; benefits in respect of accidents at work; and occupational diseases and death grants. Universal health insurance, on the other hand, refers to the maintenance of health statuses of individuals, and the financing of costs that arise in case the individuals experience health risks. In addition to these, though unemployment insurance is settled in another Statute, this Statute refers to the SIUHIS concerning the personal scope of this insurance branch.[280] Hence, family benefits are the only disparity between Turkish legislation and Art. 3(1) ACD 3/80.

Secondly, SIUHIS applies to Turkish and foreign or Union workers. In this regard, first of all, the foreign workers who have a work permit and work upon employment contract are insured compulsorily as regard the above-mentioned short and long term insurance branches, except the workers who are citizens of the states with which Turkey has concluded an international social security agreement on the basis of the principle of reciprocity.[281]

Moreover, with regard to universal health insurance, a foreign worker who has a residence permit and is not insured in accordance with the legislation of another state can enjoy the said insurance in Turkey.[282] On the other hand, if Turkey and a state, for instance a Member State of the EU, concluded an international social security agreement, that agreement will primarily be applied and a worker of that State will be regarded as insured on the terms of that agreement.[283] However, if that agreement does not have explicit provisions on a social security matter or refers to Turkish legislation, then the provisions of the SIUHIS will become applicable.[284] Accordingly, it seems that Turkish legislation which applies to Turkish and foreign or Union workers alike would not give arise to situations of discrimination on grounds of nationality.

CONCLUSION

The EU and Turkey are still in the negotiation process for the future accession of the latter to the former. In the Negotiating Framework of October 3, 2005 it was written that "long transitional periods, derogations, specific arrangements or permanent safeguard clauses may be considered," *inter alia*, as regards freedom of movement of persons.[285] Though it is common to agree on long transitional periods, especially with regard to free movement of workers, the legality or the rationale of permanent safeguard clauses is disputable.[286] Nonetheless, prohibiting discrimination on grounds of nationality is, to some extent, separate from this accession process, since it is a requirement of the constitutional or general principle of equality observed by the legal order of the EU and Turkey.[287]

This paper illustrates that the protection of the principle of equality or non-discrimination on grounds of nationality is almost identical in Union and Turkish law. In this regard, both legal orders comprise more than one instrument in the protection of migrant workers as regards such discrimination, which complement each other. Hence, the specific circumstances of each case must be taken into account when relying on one of these instruments. Even in the case of uncertainty with regard to the exact scope of a non-discrimination clause, general clauses should be invoked side by side with the special ones. For instance, although the social and tax advantages seem not to be covered by Art. 10(1) ACD 1/80, they might be included in Art. 9 AA, or though the same advantages appear not to be covered by Art. 5(1) TSL, they may be considered as within the scope of Art. 10(1) TC or Art. 25(1) ICRMW. However, in both cases, these questions are still waiting for an answer.

This paper confirms also that Turkey (almost) aligns with Union law as regards its responsibilities arising from association law and the accession relationship. It was the remark of the Commission in 2005 that Turkey did not treat Union workers in the same way as Turkish workers regarding working conditions, social and tax advantages.[288] In addition to the fact that the Commission has not reiterated this view in subsequent Progress Reports, this paper makes clear that Union workers have the necessary legal sources to claim equal treatment regarding such matters and more. Nonetheless, we are still in need of clearance from Turkish courts to prove this conclusion or else from legislative or executive actions to adopt clearer legislation mentioning this point. However, it must be stated that more convergence is on its way, since Turkey is a country which carries on accession talks with the EU.

In any event, bearing in mind the fundamental right nature of the principle of non-discrimination on grounds of nationality, this principle should be construed as broadly as possible in order to align it with the important function of facilitating the progressive integration of migrant workers to the host State.

NOTES

1. We will use these terms interchangeably. In this regard see Dagmar Schiek *et al.*, "A Comparative Perspective on Non-Discrimination Law," in *Cases, Materials and Text on National, Supranational and International Non-discrimination Law*, ed. Dagmar Schiek *et al.* (Portland: Hart Publishing, 2007, 2; Opinion of AG Sharpston in Case C–578/08 *Rhimou Chakroun v Minister van Buitenlandse Zaken*, judgment of March 4, 2010, *nyr*, pt. 40.

2. The "association law" refers to the AA and other acts such as the AP and the ACD which form an integral part of that AA.

3. Art. 28 AA.

4. Art. 12 AA and Art. 36 AP.

5. See Art. 12 AA and Art. 36 AP, where its call upon the Association Council to take the necessary decisions to achieve the free movement of workers between the parties between 1976 and 1986. However, this objective cannot be reached, because of lack of such a decision.

6. See note 16.

7. Art. 10(1) ACD 1/80; Art. 37 AP.

8. Case C-92/07 *European Commission v Kingdom of the Netherlands*, judgment of April 29, 2010, *nyr*, para. 68.

9. European Commission (SEC (2005) 1426), *2005 Turkey Progress Report*, Brussels, November 9, 2005, p. 59.

10. See respectively, Art. 10 ACD 1/80; Art. 3 ACD 3/80; Art. 37 AP; Art. 9 AA.

11. Art. 11 of Directive ("Dir.") 2003/109/EC; Art. 14 of Dir. 2009/50/EC. Council Directive 2003/109/EC of November 25, 2003 concerning the status of third-country nationals who are long-term residents [2004] Official Journal ("OJ") L 16/44. Council Directive 2009/50/EC of May 25, 2009 on the conditions of entry and residence of third-country nationals for the purposes of highly qualified employment [2009] OJ L 155/17.

12. Art. 10 TC; Art. 5 TLS.

13. See Art. 25 ICRMW.

14. Art. 2 Treaty on European Union (as amended by Lisbon Treaty) ("TEU"); Art. 8 Treaty on the Functioning of the European Union ("TFEU"); Art. 10 TC.

15. It should be borne in mind that the law of the Member States might be more advantageous than Union law in some cases. For an analysis of the law of the Member States see Kees Groenendijk *et al.*, *The Legal Status of Third Country Nationals Who Are Long-Term Residents in a Member State of the European Union* (Strasbourg: Council of Europe, 2000), 12–98.

16. In addition to this Article, Art. 6 and 7 ACD 1/80 regulates, respectively, the residence and employment rights of Turkish workers and their family members under certain conditions. Further, Art. 10(2) ACD 1/80 settles that Turkish workers are entitled to be free from discrimination in relation to assistance from the employment services in their search for employment in the application of Art. 6 and 7 ACD 1/80. Besides, Art. 9 ACD 1/80 lays down the right to equal treatment as regards education in respect of children of Turkish workers. Furthermore, Art. 13 ACD 1/80 introduces a standstill clause with regard to access to the employment of workers legally resident and employed in one of the Member States.

17. The doctrine of state liability may also be a relevant remedy with regard to this Article. See Gavin Barrett, "Re-examining the Concept and Principle of Equality in EC Law," *Yearbook of European Law* 22 (2003): 143; Martin Hedemann-Robinson, "An Overview of Recent Legal Developments at Community Level in Relation to Third Country Nationals within the EU," *Common Market Law Review* 38 (2001): 537.

18. Case C-171/01 *Wählergruppe v Gemeinsam Zajedno/Birlikte Alternative und Grüne GewerkschafterInnen/UG and Others* [2003] ECR I-4301 paras. 57, 61, 67.

19. See *Wählergruppe*, (note 18), para. 58; Alfred E. Kellermann, "The Rights of Non-Member State Nationals under the EU Association Agreements," *European Journal of Law Reform* X (2008): 380; Norbert Reich, "The Constitutional Relevance of Citizenship and Free Movement in an Enlarged Union," *European Law Journal* 11 (2005): 684.

20. Case C-212/97 *Centros Ltd v Erhvervs- og Selskabsstyrelsen* [1999] ECR I-1459 para. 24.

21. See Case C-285/95 *Suat Kol v Land Berlin* [1997] ECR I-3069 para. 29.

22. Case C-434/93 *Ahmet Bozkurt v Staatssecretaris van Justitie* [1995] ECR I-1475 paras. 19–20; *Wählergruppe*, (note 18), para. 72. There are authors who seem to be for and against such a principle of interpretation. Respectively see Nicola Rogers and Rick Scannel, *Free Movement of Persons in the Enlarged European Union* (London: Sweet & Maxwell, 2005), 327–9; Kail Hailbronner, *Immigration and Asylum Law and Policy of the European Union* (The Netherlands: Kluwer Law International, 2000), 229–31. Besides, according to Tezcan/Idriz, in practice Member States have the same obligations regarding both Union and Turkish workers, and the Court uses the phrase "as far as possible," since this equips itself with some flexibility and underlines the different context of association law, namely its bilateral agreement character. Narin Tezcan/Idriz, "Free Movement of Persons between Turkey and the EU: To Move or Not to Move–The Response of the Judiciary," *Common Market Law Review* 46 (2009): 1647–8.

23. Barrett, "Principle of Equality," 139.

24. As an example see *Wählergruppe*, (note 18), pr. 68–69.

25. Then, the difference between association and Union law rests in the material scope. Elspeth Guild, *Immigration Law in the European Community* (The Netherlands: Kluwer Law International, 2001), 154.

26. Case C-1/97 *Mehmet Birden v Stadtgemeinde Bremen* [1998] ECR I-7747 para. 25. For more on the definition of the term 'worker' see Case C-188/00 *Bülent Kurz, né Yüce v Land Baden-Württemberg* [2002] ECR I-10691 paras. 30–35; Case C-294/06 *The Queen, on the application of Ezgi Payir, Burhan Akyuz and Birol Ozturk v Secretary of State for the Home Department* [2008] ECR I-203 paras. 28, 31; Case C-14/09 *Hava Genc v Land Berlin*, judgment of February 4, 2010, *nyr*, paras. 27–28.

27. *Kurz*, (note 26), para. 37; Case C-98/96 *Kasim Ertanir v Land Hessen* [1997] ECR I-5179 para. 39.

28. *Kurz*, (note 26), para. 39; Case C-337/07 *Ibrahim Altun v Stadt Böblingen* [2008] ECR I-10323 para. 23.

29. As an example see *Wählergruppe*, (note 18), paras. 71–78.

30. *Wählergruppe*, (note 18), paras. 74, 88.

31. See *Wählergruppe*, (note 18), paras. 85, 88; Rogers and Scannel, *Free Movement of Persons*, 351.

32. See *Wählergruppe*, (note 18), paras. 85, 88; Rogers and Scannel, *Free Movement of Persons*, 351.

33. Tezcan/Idriz, "Free Movement," 1647.

34. In respect of Union workers see *Wählergruppe*, (note 18), para. 88. In respect of Polish workers see Case C-162/00 *Land Nordrhein-Westfalen v Beata Pokrzeptowicz-Meyer* [2002] ECR I-1049 para. 39. In respect of Russian workers see Case C-265/03 *Igor Simutenkov v Ministerio de Educación y Cultura and Real Federación Española de Fútbol* [2005] ECR I-2579, para. 57. See also Kellermann, "Association Agreements," 351.

35. Besides, the issue of refusal of a residence permit comes before the Court in the *Güzeli* case. There seems to be a collision between the AG Geelhoed and the First Chamber of the Court in this case. According to the AG this issue cannot be regarded as discrimination as regards conditions of work, since residence is dealt with separately in ACD 1/80. (Opinion of AG Geelhoed in Case C-4/05 *Hasan Güzeli v Oberbürgermeister der Stadt Aachen* [2006] ECR I-10279 pt. 50–56.) On the other hand, the Court seems to have accepted this issue within the 'conditions of work,' albeit only where the duration of the residence permit is shorter than that of the work permit. (Case C-4/05 *Hasan Güzeli v Oberbürgermeister der Stadt Aachen* [2006] ECR I-10279 paras. 47–55.)

36. *Wählergruppe*, (note 18), paras. 83, 85. In the context of the European Economic Agreement see Case C-465/01 *Commission of the European Communities v Republic of Austria* [2004] ECR I-8291 paras. 37–41.

37. Case C-152/08 *Real Sociedad de Fútbol SAD and Nihat Kahveci v Consejo Superior de Deportes and Real Federación Española de Fútbol* [2008] ECR I-6291 para. 32. In the context of the EU-Slovakia Europe Agreement see Case C-438/00 *Deutscher Handballbund e.V. v Maros Kolpak* [2003] ECR I-4135 para. 46.

38. *Commission v Netherlands*, (note 8), paras. 26, 75.

39. Case 33/88 *Pilar Allué and Carmel Mary Coonan v Università degli studi di Venezia* [1989] ECR 1591 para. 19; *Pokrzeptowicz-Meyer*, (note 34), para. 45.

40. Case C-350/96 *Clean Car Autoservice GesmbH v Landeshauptmann von Wien* [1998] ECR I-2521 para. 30.

41. Case C-15/96 *Kalliope Schöning-Kougebetopoulou v Freie und Hansestadt Hamburg* [1998] ECR I-47 para. 23.

42. Pieter A. van der Mei, *Free Movement of Persons within the European Community: Cross-Border Access to Public Benefits* (Great Britain: Hart Publishing, 2003), 398.

43. Hedemann-Robinson, "Third Country Nationals," 563, 555.

44. For a similar view see Hedemann-Robinson, "Third Country Nationals," 555.

45. Regulation (EEC) No 1612/68 of the Council of October 15, 1968 on freedom of movement for workers within the Community [1968] OJ L 257/2.

46. Manfred Husmann, "Arbeitnehmerfreizügigkeitsregeln in Assoziationsabkommen der EG," *Zeitschrift für Ausländerrecht und Ausländerpolitik* 9 (2009): 307.

47. *Wählergruppe*, (note 18), paras. 83, 85. See also *Commission v Austria*, (note 36), paras. 37–41, where the Court extends this ruling to the EEA context.

48. See Case C-185/04 *Ulf Öberg v Försäkringskassan, länskontoret Stockholm* [2006] ECR I-1453 para. 13.

49. See note 32.

50. See below "Ankara Agreement" at p. 110.

51. Art. 16(1) ACD 1/80.

52. Compare with *Pokrzeptowicz-Meyer*, (note 34), para. 56.

53. See Steve Peers, "Towards Equality: Actual and Potential Rights of Third-country Nationals in the European Union," *Common Market Law Review* 33 (1996): 27.

54. See Tezcan/Idriz, "Free Movement," 1645–6. In the (similar) context of Art. 37 EU-Latvia EA see Reich, "Citizenship," 685. For the indirect discrimination and Member States see Sacha Prechal, "Equality of Treatment, Non-Discrimination and Social Policy: Achievements in Three Themes," *Common Market Law Review* 41 (2004): 535–7.

55. *Wählergruppe*, (note 18).

56. *Wählergruppe*, (note 18), para. 70.

57. *Wählergruppe*, (note 18), para. 78.

58. See Reich, "Citizenship," 685. He comes to this conclusion in the context of the EU-Poland Europe Agreement and this argument can be fully transposed to the association law sphere.

59. Case C-373/02 *Sakir Öztürk v Pensionsversicherungsanstalt der Arbeiter* [2004] ECR I-3605 para. 49.

60. Joined cases C-102/98 and C-211/98 *Ibrahim Kocak v Landesversicherungsanstalt Oberfranken und Mittelfranken and Ramazan Örs v Bundesknappschaft* [2000] ECR I-1287 para. 39.

61. *Wählergruppe*, (note 18), para. 59.

62. *Pokrzeptowicz-Meyer*, (note 34), para. 42.

63. Respectively see *Wählergruppe*, (note 18), para. 88; *Pokrzeptowicz-Meyer*, (note 34), para. 39.

64. Case C-237/94 *John O'Flynn v Adjudication Officer* [1996] ECR I-2617 para. 20. AG Ruiz-Jarabo Colomer referred also to the *O'Flynn* judgment in the context of Art. 3(1) ACD 3/80 when determining the test for indirect discrimination. Opinion of AG Ruiz-Jarabo Colomer in *Öztürk*, (note 59), pt. 34. The Court also quoted from its *O'Flynn* judgment in this case, albeit not as regards the test for indirect discrimination, but with respect to one characteristic of this test, namely, to indicate the emphasis on the 'effects' regarding this test. *Öztürk*, (note 59), para. 57.

65. For the justification of direct and indirect discrimination in the Member States see Mark Bell, "Direct Discrimination," in *Cases, Materials and Text on National, Supranational and International Non-discrimination Law*, ed. Dagmar Schiek *et al.* (Portland: Hart Publishing, 2007), 269.

66. Compare with Art. 45(4) TFEU. See Peers, "Equality," 30, 46.

67. *Wählergruppe*, (note 18), para. 90. On the other hand, the national court thought the opposite. (para. 91.)

68. *Wählergruppe*, (note 18), para. 92.

69. Art. 14(1) ACD 1/80.

70. See Hacı Can, *Türkiye–Avrupa Topluluğu Ortaklık Hukukunda Kişilerin Serbest Dolaşımı* (Ankara: Türkiye Odalar ve Borsalar Birliği, 2006), 62; Tezcan/Idriz, "Free Movement," 1649. Compare with Case C-60/00 *Mary Carpenter v Secretary of State for the Home Department* [2002] ECR I-6279 para. 40.

71. Case C-340/97 *Ömer Nazli, Caglar Nazli and Melike Nazli v Stadt Nürnberg* [2000] ECR I-957 paras. 55–56.

72. See Can, *Kişilerin Serbest Dolaşımı*, 62.

73. *Nazli*, (note 71), para. 57. See Case 30/77 *Régina v Pierre Bouchereau* [1977] ECR 1999 para. 35.

74. *Nazli*, (note 71), paras. 58–61. See Case C-348/96 *Criminal proceedings against Donatella Calfa* [1999] ECR I-11 paras. 22–24.

75. Art. 14(1) ACD 1/80 and in comparison to Case C-325/08 *Olympique Lyonnais SASP v Olivier Bernard and Newcastle UFC*, judgment of March 16, 2010, *nyr*, para. 38; *Carpenter*, (note 70), para. 40.

76. See Can, *Kişilerin Serbest Dolaşımı*, 62; Tezcan/Idriz, "Free Movement," 1649. See also (in comparison to) *Olympique Lyonnais*, (note 75), para. 38.

77. Case C-269/07 *Commission of the European Communities v Federal Republic of Germany* [2009] ECR I-7811 para. 113.

78. Case C-150/04 *Commission of the European Communities v Kingdom of Denmark* [2007] ECR I-1163 para. 51.

79. *Commission v Denmark*, (note 78), para. 51.

80. *Commission v Germany*, (note 77), para. 84.

81. *Olympique Lyonnais*, (note 75), para. 39.

82. Case C-330/03 *Colegio de Ingenieros de Caminos, Canales y Puertos v Administración del Estado* [2006] ECR I-801 para. 32.

83. Joined cases C-151/04 and C-152/04 *Criminal proceedings against Claude Nadin, Nadin-Lux SA and Jean-Pascal Durré* [2005] ECR I-11203 paras. 47, 49.

84. See Peers, "Equality," 30. See *Wählergruppe*, (note 18), para. 78.

85. Compare with Case C-415/93 *Union royale belge des sociétés de football association ASBL v Jean-Marc Bosman, Royal club liégeois SA v Jean-Marc Bosman and others and*

Union des associations européennes de football (UEFA) v Jean-Marc Bosman [1995] ECR I-4921 para. 82.

86. Bernard Ryan, "The European Union and labor Migration: Regulating Admission or Treatment?," in *Whose Freedom, Security and Justice?*, ed. Anneliese Baldaccini *et al.* (Portland: Hart Publishing, 2007), 513.

87. *Kahveci*, (note 37), para. 32.

88. Ryan, "labor Migration," 513. Similarly, in the context of EAs Cremona notes that it is perhaps more debatable whether the non-discrimination principle would be enforceable against a private employer. Marise Cremona, "Movement of Persons, Establishment and Services," in *Enlarging the European Union: Relations between the EU and Central and Eastern Europe*, ed. Marc Maresceau (United States of America: Longman, 1997), 198.

89. Peers, "Equality," 30.

90. Can, *Kişilerin Serbest Dolaşımı*, 60. In a similar context of Art. 37 EU-Latvia EA see Reich, "Citizenship," 685.

91. Case C-281/98 *Roman Angonese v Cassa di Risparmio di Bolzano SpA* [2000] ECR I-4139 para. 45.

92. See Case C-262/96 *Sema Sürül v Bundesanstalt für Arbeit* [1999] ECR I-2685 para. 68.

93. See *Wählergruppe*, (note 18), para. 58.

94. Dirk Ehlers, "General Principles," in *European Fundamental Rights and Freedoms*, ed. Dirk Ehlers (Germany: De Gruyter, 2007), 186.

95. Case 33/76 *Rewe-Zentralfinanz eG and Rewe-Zentral AG v Landwirtschaftskammer für das Saarland* [1976] ECR 1989 para. 5.

96. Barrett, "Principle of Equality," 142. See *Rewe-Zentralfinanz*, (note 95), para. 5.

97. This provision is almost identical to Art. 3(1) Reg. 1408/71 and Art. 4 Reg. 883/2004 which has been recently replaced the former. Regulation (EEC) No 1408/71 of the Council of June 14, 1971 on the application of social security schemes to employed persons and their families moving within the Community [1971] OJ L 149/2. Regulation (EC) No 883/2004 of the European Parliament and of the Council on the coordination of social security systems [2004] OJ L 166/1. See note 103.

98. *Sürül*, (note 92), paras. 62, 69, 74. See Bülent Çiçekli, "The Rights of Turkish Migrants in Europe under International Law and EU Law," *International Migration Review* 33 (1999): 343; Peers, "Equality," 34. Compare with Case C-277/94 *Z. Taflan-Met, S. Altun-Baser, E. Andal-Bugdayci v Bestuur van de Sociale Verzekeringsbank and O. Akol v Bestuur van de Nieuwe Algemene Bedrijfsvereniging* [1996] ECR I-4085 para. 38 Arif Köktaş, *Avrupa Birliğinde İşçilerin Serbest Dolaşım Hakkı ve Türk Vatandaşlarının Durumu* (Ankara: Nobel, 1999), 208–14.

99. See *Sürül*, (note 92), para. 74. See also note 19.

100. Compare with *Bozkurt*, (note 22), paras. 19–20.

101. As an example see *Sürül*, (note 92), paras. 86, 93.

102. *Sürül*, (note 92), paras. 82, 84.

103. The Reg. 883/2004 (note 97) entered into force in May 1, 2010.

104. *Sürül*, (note 92), para. 86. See also Steve Peers, "Social Security Equality for Turkish Nationals," *European Law Review* 24 (1999): 634.

105. Art. 2 ACD 3/80.

106. Art. 3(1) ACD 3/80.

107. Art. 4(1) ACD 3/80. This provision is almost identical to Art. 4(1) Reg. 1408/71 (note 97) and Art. 3(1) Reg. 883/2004 (note 97). As an example see *Sürül*, (note 92), para. 75.

108. Art. 4(2) ACD 3/80.

109. Art. 3(2) ACD 3/80. However, according to the same provision, this will not affect the legislative provisions of any Member State relating to eligibility or methods of nomination of persons concerned to those organs.

110. Art. 4(4) ACD 3/80.

111. Rogers and Scannel, *Free Movement of Persons*, 331.

112. *Sürül*, (note 92), para. 106.

113. *Sürül*, (note 92), para. 111.

114. *Sürül*, (note 92), para. 113. The Court's reasoning on this point has been criticised. See Peers, "Social Security," 632–633.

115. *Kocak and Örs*, (note 60), para. 39. See Herwig Verschueren, "The *Sürül* Judgment: Equal Treatment for Turkish Workers in Matters of Social Security," *European Journal of Migration and Law* 1 (1999): 380; Tezcan/Idriz, "Free Movement," 1646.

116. *Sürül*, (note 92).

117. *Sürül*, (note 92), para. 96.

118. *Sürül*, (note 92), para. 97.

119. *Sürül*, (note 92), paras. 101–102.

120. *Sürül*, (note 92), paras. 104–105.

121. *Öztürk*, (note 59).

122. *Öztürk*, (note 59), para. 56.

123. *Öztürk*, (note 59), para. 54.

124. *Öztürk*, (note 59), para. 56.

125. *Öztürk*, (note 59), paras. 57–58.

126. *Öztürk*, (note 59), para. 68.

127. See *Sürül*, (note 92), para. 104. Also see Verschueren, "*Sürül* Judgment," 380.

128. See *Kocak and Örs*, (note 60), para. 52. As an example see *Öztürk*, (note 59), paras. 66–68.

129. Art. 3(1) ACD 3/80. See Peers, "Equality," 30.

130. Compare with Art. 15(3) Charter of Fundamental Rights of the European Union ("CFREU"): "Nationals of third countries who are authorized to work in the territories of the Member States are entitled to working conditions equivalent to those of citizens of the Union." This principle which is not evident in the Treaties is an element of the fundamental right to equality. Christophe Vigneau, "Freedom to Choose an Occupation and Right to Engage in Work (Article 15)," in *European labor Law and the EU Charter of Fundamental Rights*, ed. Brian Bercusson (Baden-Baden: Nomos, 2006), 189, 192. Compare also with Art. 153(1/g, 2) TFEU where the Council may adopt measures unanimously with respect to conditions of employment for TCN legally residing in Union territory.

131. Friedl Weiss and Frank Wooldridge, *Free Movement of Persons within the European Community* (2nd Edition, The Netherlands: Kluwer Law International, 2007), 209.

132. Jean-Philippe Dubey, "C-438/00, *Deutscher Handballbund eV v. Maros Kolpak*, judgment of the Court of Justice (First Chamber) of May 8, 2003, [2003] ECR I-4135," *Common Market Law Review* 42 (2005): 514.

133. Case C-37/98 *The Queen v Secretary of State for the Home Department, ex parte Abdulnasir Savas* [2000] ECR I-2927 para. 51.

134. *Wählergruppe*, (note 18), paras. 57, 61, 67.

135. Case C-416/96 *Nour Eddline El-Yassini v Secretary of State for Home Department* [1999] ECR I-1209 para. 27.

136. See Hedemann-Robinson, "Third Country Nationals," 543; Nicola Rogers, "Comments on *Nour Eddline El-Yassini v. Secretary of State for the Home Department*, March 2, 1999 (Case C-416/96)," *European Journal of Migration and Law* 1 (1999): 370.

137. *Kocak and Örs*, (note 60), para. 38.

138. See Can, *Kişilerin Serbest Dolaşımı*, 59.

139. *Bozkurt*, (note 22), para. 26.

140. The counterpart of this Article in the context of Union law is Art. 18 TFEU (and Art. 21(2) CFREU). Art. 18 TFEU, however, cannot be invoked by TCN. See Joined cases C-22/08 and C-23/08 *Athanasios Vatsouras and Josif Koupatantze v Arbeitsgemeinschaft (ARGE) Nürnberg 900* [2009] ECR I-4585 para. 52. See Pieter Boeles *et al.*, *European Migration Law* (Antwerp: Intersentia, 2009), 70. Some authors challenge the Court's settled view on the personal scope of Art. 18 TFEU and claim that a TCN may invoke this Article, for instance when they fall within the scope of a Directive. See Sonja Boelaert-Suominen, "Non-EU Nationals and Council Directive 2003/109/EC on the Status of Third Country Nationals Who Are Long-Term Residents: Five Paces Forward and Possibly Three Paces Back," *Common Market Law Review* 42 (2005): 1028; Astrid Epiney, "The Scope of Article 12 EC: Some Remarks on the Influence of European Citizenship," *European Law Journal* 13 (2007): 614. On the other

hand, for instance, Veneziani argues that TCN workers could benefit from the application of an expansive approach to Art. 21(2) CFREU. Bruno Veneziani, "Non-discrimination (Article 21)," in *European labor Law and the EU Charter of Fundamental Rights*, ed. Brian Bercusson (Baden-Baden: Nomos, 2006), 215.

141. *Commission v Netherlands*, (note 8), para. 75.

142. *Commission v Netherlands*, (note 8), para. 75, 76.

143. With respect to Art. 9 ACD 1/80 see Case C-374/03 *Gaye Gürol v Bezirksregierung Köln* [2005] ECR I-6199 para. 24.

144. With respect to Art. 10(1) ACD 1/80 see *Wählergruppe*, (note 18), para. 59.

145. With respect to Art. 3(1) ACD 3/80 see *Öztürk*, (note 59), para. 49.

146. See *Gürol*, (note 143), para. 24; *Wählergruppe*, (note 18), para. 59; *Öztürk*, (note 59), para. 49. See also Hedemann-Robinson, "Third Country Nationals," 542.

147. Verschueren, "*Sürül* Judgment," 378. See (Second) Opinion of AG La Pergola in *Sürül*, (note 92), pt. 7–8.

148. Case C-43/95 *Data Delecta Aktiebolag and Ronny Forsberg v MSL Dynamics Ltd* [1996] ECR I-4661 paras. 16, 22.

149. See Hedemann-Robinson, "Third Country Nationals," 542; Peers, "Equality," 18–19; Peers, "Social Security," 635. For the Commission and national court respectively see *Commission v Netherlands*, (note 8), para. 26; *Öztürk*, (note 59), paras. 46, 33.

150. See Case 12/86 *Meryem Demirel v Stadt Schwäbisch Gmünd* [1987] ECR 3719 para. 14.

151. (Second) Opinion of AG La Pergola in *Sürül*, (note 92), pt. 7.

152. (Second) Opinion of AG La Pergola in *Sürül*, (note 92), pt. 7.

153. See (Second) Opinion of AG La Pergola in *Sürül*, (note 92), pt. 9; *Savas*, (note 133), para. 51.

154. Verschueren, "*Sürül* Judgment," 378–9.

155. Opinion of Advocate General La Pergola in *Savas*, (note 133), pt. 18.

156. See *Commission v Netherlands*, (note 8), para. 26; *Öztürk*, (note 59), para. 47.

157. Compare with *Savas*, (note 133), para. 65.

158. See Verschueren, "*Sürül* Judgment," 379. According to Peers, in this case the Court should develop *de novo* interpretations of the concept of worker, social security, etc. and while social security may be borrowed from Reg. No 1408/71 (note 97), other terms may be imitated from ACD 1/80. Peers, "Social Security," 635.

159. See Case C-36/96 *Faik Günaydin, Hatice Günaydin, Günes Günaydin and Seda Günaydin v Freistaat Bayern* [1997] ECR I-5143 para. 23. In addition to this there is no right to move freely within the Union. (para. 22.)

160. See Peers, "Social Security," 635.

161. Peers, "Social Security," 635. Moreover, according to the author, even family reunions might be covered by Art. 9 AA. (p. 635.)

162. According to Peers, for instance, the temporal scope of Art. 9 AA and Art. 3(1) ACD 3/80 might be distinct. Peers, "Social Security," 635.

163. In this regard, Turkish workers enjoy "an intermediate position between that of Union citizens and that of nationals of third countries." Opinion of AG Bot in Case C325/05 *Ismail Derin v Landkreis Darmstadt-Dieburg* [2007] ECR I-6495 pt. 137. Moreover, the provisions of those Directives, generally, complement and supplement the provisions of association law. See Catherine Barnard, *The Substantive Law of the EU: The Four Freedoms* (3rd Edition, Great Britain: Oxford University Press, 2010), 552.

164. See Kees Groenendijk, "The Long-Term Residents Directive, Denizenship and Integration," in *Whose Freedom, Security and Justice?*, ed. Anneliese Baldaccini *et al.* (Portland: Hart Publishing, 2007), 440; Ryan, "labor Migration," 512.

165. [2004] OJ L 16/1.

166. This Directive is not applicable to persons such as students or refugees. See Art. 2 Dir. 2003/109 (note 11).

167. Art. 4(1) Dir. 2003/109 (note 11).

168. Art. 5(1) Dir. 2003/109 (note 11).

169. Art. 6(1) Dir. 2003/109 (note 11).

170. Art. 8 Dir. 2003/109 (note 11). See Boelaert-Suominen, "Long-Term Residents," 1021; Groenendijk, "Long-Term Residents," 436.

171. See also Reg. 859/03 which extends the scope of Reg. 1408/71 (note 97) to TCN moving within the Union. Art. 1 Reg. 859/03. [2003] OJ L 124/1. See Boelaert-Suominen, "Long-Term Residents," 1033.

172. Art. 11(1) Dir. 2003/109 (note 11). Hence, this Directive could become a major instrument in combating discrimination of immigrants from countries outside the EU. Kees Groenendijk, "Legal Concepts of Integration in EU Migration Law," *European Journal of Migration and Law* 6 (2004): 122.

173. See Art. 11(2, 3) Dir. 2003/109 (note 11). See Boelaert-Suominen, "Long-Term Residents," 1026–7.

174. Art. 11(4) Dir. 2003/109 (note 11). See Louise Halleskov, "The Long-Term Residence Directive: A fulfillment of the Tampere Objective of Near Equality?," *European Journal of Migration and Law* 7 (2005): 198; Achilles Skordas, "Immigration and Market: The Long-Term Residents Directive," *Columbia Journal of European Law* 13 (2007): 209–11.

175. See Halleskov, "Long-Term Residence Directive," 198.

176. See Barnard, *Substantive Law*, 552; Boelaert-Suominen, "Long-Term Residents," 1040; Groenendijk, "Long-Term Residents," 441. On the other hand, in other areas association law offers more positive treatment. For instance, regarding access to employment Art. 6(1) and 7 ACD 1/80 are more generous than Art. 11 Dir. 2003/109 (note 11). Moreover, working conditions, worker representation, or social security have already been protected respectively by Art. 10(1) ACD 1/80 and Art. 3(1) ACD 3/80 which do not require conditions similar to being long-term resident. In addition to this Turkish workers avail themselves of a more favorable regime as regards protection from expulsion. See Barnard, *Substantive Law*, 552; Boelaert-Suominen, "Long-Term Residents," 1038–40; Groenendijk, "Long-Term Residents," 441; Halleskov, "Long-Term Residence Directive," 192, 199.

177. See "Ankara Agreement" at p. 110.

178. [2009] OJ L 155/17.

179. This Directive is not applicable to lots of groups of people. See Art. 3(2) Dir. 2009/50 (note 11). Moreover, there are various restraints on several grounds, such as it is for the Member States to determine the volume of admission of highly qualified TCN workers. See Art. 6, 7, 8, 9 Dir. 2009/50 (note 11).

180. Art. 5(1) Dir. 2009/50 (note 11).

181. Art. 7(1) Dir. 2009/50 (note 11).

182. Art. 14(1) Dir. 2009/50 (note 11).

183. Art. 14(2) Dir. 2009/50 (note 11).

184. Art. 90(1) TC. See Kemal Başlar and Erdoğan İshakoğlu, "Turkey," in *The Impact of EU Accession on the Legal Orders of New EU Member States and (Pre-) Candidate Countries: Hopes and Fears*, ed. Alfred E. Kellermann *et al.* (Cambridge: Cambridge University Press, 2006), 195; Kellermann, "Association Agreements," 376; Melda Sur, "Sosyal Haklara İlişkin Andlaşmaların İç Hukukta Yeri," in *Prof. Dr. Devrim Ulucan'a Armağan* (İstanbul: Legal Yayıncılık, 2008) 49; Rıza Türmen, "Avrupa İnsan Hakları Sözlesmesi'nin İç Hukukumuza Etkileri," *Anayasa Yargısı* 17 (2000): 33.

185. See Sur, "Sosyal Haklar," 49; Melek Onaran Yüksel, *Karşılaştırmalı Hukuk Işığında Türk İş Hukukunda Kadın-Erkek Eşitliği* (İstanbul: Beta, 2000), 64.

186. See Decision of Civil General Council of the Court of Appeals, Registry Number ("RN"): 2005/9–320, Decision Number ("DN"): 2005/355, Decision Day ("DD"): May 25, 2005; Decision of Consolidation of Case-Law Council of the Council of State, RN: 2005/1, DN: 2006/1, DD: March 3, 2006. See also Başlar and İshakoğlu, "Turkey," 201–2; Levent Gönenç and Selin Esen, "The Problem of the Application of Less Protective International Agreements in Domestic Legal Systems: Article 90 of the Turkish Constitution," *European Journal of Law Reform* VIII (2007): 490; Sur, "Sosyal Haklar," 60–61.

187. See Servet Armağan, "1982 Anayasası'nda Uluslararası Andlaşmaların İmzalanması ve Onaylanması Sistemi," *Anayasa Yargısı* 17 (2000): 358; Hüseyin Pazarcı, *Uluslararası Hukuk* (9. Bası, Ankara: Turhan Kitabevi, 2010), 27.

188. See Decision of the Constitutional Court, RN: 1996/55, DN: 1997/33, DD: February 27, 1997; Decision of 21th Civil Chamber of the Court of Appeals, RN: 1996/2261, DN: 1996/5790, DD: November 8, 1996. See also Başlar and İshakoğlu, "Turkey," 221; Hacı Can and Çınar Özen, *Türkiye–Avrupa Topluluğu Ortaklık Hukuku* (Ankara: Gazi Kitabevi, 2005), 333; Pazarcı, *Uluslararası Hukuk*, 27.

189. Constitutional Court, RN: 1996/55, (note 188).

190. See Decision of Criminal General Council of the Court of Appeals, RN: 1996/6–2, DN: 1996/33, DD: March 12, 1996, where the Court ruled that a provision of ECHR will be applied to the case at hand, since it is *lex specialis*. (It should be noted that this decision was given before the amendments to the TC in 2004.) See also Decision of Criminal General Council of the Court of Appeals, RN: 2005/7–24, DN: 2005/56, DD: May 24, 2005. However, these decisions can be contrasted with Decision of Civil General Council of the Court of Appeals, RN: 1995/4–367, DN: 1995/550, DD: May 24, 1995, where the Court adjudicated that the unions formed by civil servants cannot be regarded as having legal personality, since there has not been any domestic arrangement on this matter; although the relevant International labor Organization ("ILO") convention which has been duly put into effect provides otherwise. See Sur, "Sosyal Haklar," 57.

191. See Pazarcı, *Uluslararası Hukuk*, 25.

192. Serap Akipek, "Türk Mevzuatının Onaylanan Uluslararası Antlaşmalar ile Uyumlaştırılması Sorunu," *Ankara Üniversitesi Hukuk Fakültesi Dergisi* 48 (1999): 21.

193. Başlar and İshakoğlu, "Turkey," 200.

194. Can and Özen, *Ortaklık Hukuku*, 371. On the other hand, when a provision of an international agreement is of programmatic nature, it cannot be applied directly to a case by Turkish courts. See Süleyman Başterzi, "Uluslararası Sözleşmeler ve İç Hukuk Kuralları Çerçevesinde Kamu Görevlilerinin Toplu Pazarlık ve Toplu Sözleşme Sorunu," *Tisk Akademi* 1 (2006): 35.

195. See Decision of the Constitutional Court, RN: 2008/1, DN: 2008/2, DD: July 30, 2008; Decision of Criminal General Council of the Court of Appeals, RN: 2004/8–201, DN: 2005/30, DD: March 15, 2005.

196. See Tuğrul Arat, "Avrupa Birliği ile Türkiye Arasındaki İlişkiler ve Gümrük Birliğinin Yeri," *Ankara Üniversitesi Hukuk Fakültesi Dergisi* 44 (1995): 597; Can, *Kişilerin Serbest Dolaşımı*, 25; Can and Özen, *Ortaklık Hukuku*, 296. On the contrary see Hacı Can, "Türkiye–Avrupa Topluluğu Ortaklık İlişkisinin Hukuki Çerçevesi," *Ankara Avrupa Çalışmaları Dergisi* 3 (2003): 40.

197. See Arat, "Gümrük Birliği," 597; Can, *Kişilerin Serbest Dolaşımı*, 25.

198. See Arat, "Gümrük Birliği," 597.

199. See Art. 11 ACD 1/80. In this regard, an example is the Law on the Work Permit for Foreigners and the by-law to implement it. See Art. 2 and 8(e) Statute on Work Permit of Foreigners No 4817 ("SWPF"); Art. 50 of the By-Law on the Implementation of the Law on the Work Permit for Foreigners. (See respectively OJ March 6, 2003, No: 25040 and OJ August 29, 2003, No: 25214.)

200. See Başlar and İshakoğlu, "Turkey," 217.

201. On the contrary see Başlar and İshakoğlu, "Turkey," 217. (They deem both the AA and AP as agreements which cannot be directly applicable in Turkish municipal law.)

202. See Başlar and İshakoğlu, "Turkey," 198.

203. In addition to these agreements, other agreements which may be used by the Turkish courts as interpretative tools, especially since they are prior to Statutes as agreements related to fundamental rights and freedoms, are as follows: Discrimination (Employment and Occupation) Convention (C111) of ILO which was adopted on June 25, 1958 and entered into force on June 15, 1960. It was approved by Turkey with the Statute No 811 on December 13, 1996 (OJ No 12484, at December 22, 1996). See Art. (1) of that Convention. Social Security (Minimum Standards) Convention (C102) of ILO which was adopted on June 28, 1952 and entered into force on April 27, 1955. It was approved by Turkey with the Statute No 1451 on July 29, 1971 (OJ No 13922, at August 10, 1971) with some reservations, albeit they do not affect the non-discrimination clause. See Art. 68 of that Convention. Equality of Treatment (Social Security) Convention (C118) which was adopted on June 28, 1962 and entered into force on April 25,

1964. It was approved by Turkey with the Statute No 1453 on July 29, 1971 (OJ No 13922, at August 10, 1971). See Art. 3, 4 of that Convention.

204. ICCPR was adopted on December 16, 1966 and entered into force on March 23, 1976 in accordance with its Art. 49. Turkey signed it on August 15, 2000 and approved it on September 23, 2003 with the Statute No 4867 (OJ No 25142, of June 18, 2003) with some reservations, albeit they do not affect the non-discrimination clause.

205. RESC was adopted on May 3, 1996 and entered into force on July 1, 1999. Turkey signed it on October 6, 2004 and approved on September 27, 2006 with the Statute No 5547 (OJ No 26308, of October 3, 2006) with some reservations, albeit they do not affect the non-discrimination clause.

206. ECHR was adopted on November 4, 1950 and entered into force on September 3, 1953. Turkey signed it on November 4, 1950 and approved it on May 18, 1954 and published it in OJ No 8662 of March 19, 1954. Moreover, this Convention has been amended several times and most important of which are Protocol No 11 and 14 which entered into force respectively on November 1, 1998 and June 1, 2010. Turkey approved and published them respectively in OJ No 23025 of June 10, 1997 and OJ No 26253 of August 8, 2006.

207. ICRMW was adopted on December 18, 1990 and entered into force on July 1, 2003 in accordance with its Art. 87(1). Turkey signed it on January 13, 1999 and approved it on April 26, 2001 with the Statute No 4662 (OJ No 24397, of May 9, 2001) with some reservations, albeit they do not affect the non-discrimination clause. As regard the fundamental rights character of ICRMW see Bülent Çiçekli, "Uluslararası Hukukta Yabancıların Hak ve Özgürlükleri," *Uluslararası Hukuk ve Politika* 3 (2007): 4; Ockert Dupper, "Migrant Workers and the Right to Social Security: An International Perspective," *Stellenbosch Law Review* 18 (2007): 226; Sandesh Sivakumaran, "The Rights of Migrant Workers One Year on: Transformation or Consolidation," *Georgetown Journal of International Law* 36 (2004-2005): 140.

208. Respectively see Art. 26 ICCPR; Art. 14 ECHR; Art. E (Part V) RESC.

209. Namely, 'national origin' and 'other status' (Art. 26 ICCPR; Art. 14 ECHR) and 'national extraction' and 'other status' (Art. E (Part V) RESC). These can be regarded as a prohibition on the grounds of nationality. See Çiçekli, "Yabancılar," 13; Sara Iglesias Sánchez, "Free Movement of Third Country Nationals in the European Union? Main Features, Deficiencies and Challenges of the New Mobility Rights in the Area of Freedom, Security and Justice," *European Law Journal* 15 (2009): 794; Sivakumaran, "Migrant Workers," 128; Veneziani, "Non-discrimination," 214.

210. See Optional Protocol to the ICCPR was adopted on December 16, 1966 and entered into force on March 23, 1976 in accordance with its Art. 9. Turkey signed it on February 3, 2004 and approved it on November 24, 2006 and published in OJ No 26250, of August 5, 2006 with some reservations, albeit they do not affect the non-discrimination clause.

211. Art. 26 ICCPR.

212. See Iglesias Sánchez, "Third Country Nationals," 794; Veneziani, "Non-discrimination," 214. These Articles mention also 'other status' which probably include 'nationality.' See HRC, Communication No 196/1985 *Ibrahima Gueye et al. v France*, Decision of April 6, 1989, pt. 9.4.

213. *Gueye et al.*, (note 212), pt. 9.4.

214. Compare with Constitutional Court, RN: 1996/55, (note 188); Constitutional Court, RN: 2008/1, (note 195); Court of Appeals, RN: 2004/8–201, (note 195).

215. HRC, Communication No 998/2001 *Althammer v Austria*, decision of August 8, 2003, pt. 10.2.

216. For instance see ECtHR, Applications Nos. 25088/94, 28331/95 and 28443/95, *Case of Chassagnou and Others v. France*, judgment of April 29, 1999, para. 89.

217. See Art. 14 ECHR; Art. E (Part V) RESC.

218. Art. 14 ECHR; Art. 1 of the Protocol No 1 of the ECHR. See ECtHR, Application No 17371/90, *Gaygusuz v Austria*, judgment of September 16, 1996, paras. 36–41. Protocol No 1 was adopted on March 20, 1952 and entered into force on May 18, 1954. Turkey signed it on March 20, 1952 and approved it on May 18, 1954 and published it in OJ No 8662 of March 19, 1954.

219. *Chassagnou and Others*, (note 216), para. 91.

220. ECtHR, Application No 34369/97, *Thlimmenos v. Greece*, judgment of April 6, 2000, para. 44.

221. *Chassagnou and Others*, (note 216), para. 91.

222. See Constitutional Court, RN: 2008/1, (note 195); Court of Appeals, RN: 2004/8–201, (note 195).

223. Art. 72–78 ICRMW. It is important to record that this Committee is not able to consider individual complaints as yet which are a valuable source for clarification at most times. Art. 77 ICRMW. For more on the Committee see Dupper, "Migrant Workers," 242–3.

224. See Sivakumaran, "Migrant Workers," 139.

225. See Art. 1 and 2(1) ICRMW.

226. Regarding Art. 27(1) ICRMW see Dupper, "Migrant Workers," 233.

227. Art. 1 ICRMW.

228. Art. 2(1) ICRMW.

229. Art. 25(1/a) ICRMW.

230. Art. 25(1/b) ICRMW.

231. Art. 25(2) ICRMW.

232. Art. 27 ICRMW.

233. Art. 10(1, 5) TC.

234. Moreover many national constitutions do not refer specifically to nationality (Italy, Sweden); some refer to "any other grounds" (The Netherlands), "personal conditions or circumstances" (Spain), or "territory of origin" (Portugal). Veneziani, "Non-discrimination," 215.

235. See Ulaş Baysal, "İşverenin Eşit Davranma Borcu ve İş Sözleşmesinin Feshinde Uygulanması," *Legal İş Hukuku ve Sosyal Güvenlik Hukuku Dergisi* 25 (2010): 71; Sibel İnceoğlu, "Türk Anayasa Mahkemesi ve İnsan Hakları Avrupa Mahkemesi Kararlarında Eşitlik ve Ayrımcılık Yasağı," *Çalışma ve Toplum* 4 (2006): 48–49; Onaran Yüksel, *Kadın-Erkek Eşitliği*, 81; Sarper Süzek, *İş Hukuku* (4. Bası, İstanbul: Beta, 2008), 396–398; Sarper Süzek, "İşverenin Eşit Davranma Borcu," *Sicil* 3 (2008): 24–25; Vahap Ünlü, "İşe Alımda Cinsiyet Ayrımcılığı," *Sicil* 5 (2010): 249; Gaye Burcu Yıldız, *İşverenin Eşit İşlem Yapma Borcu* (Ankara: Yetkin Basımevi, 2008), 56.

236. Decision of the Constitutional Court, RN: 1999/10, DN: 1999/22, DD: June 7, 1999. For identical observations see Decision 21st Chamber of the Council of State, RN: 2004/4382, DN: 2006/539, DD: February 22, 2006. Also see Süzek, "Eşit Davranma," 24; İnceoğlu, "Eşitlik," 53–54.

237. Decision of 9th Civil Chamber of the Court of Appeals, RN: 2008/33837, DN: 2009/32939, DD: December 2, 2009. See Ünlü, "Cinsiyet Ayrımcılığı," 250.

238. See Can Tuncay, "İş Hukukunda Eşit Davranma İlkesi," in *İş ve Sosyal Güvenlik Hukuku Sorunlar ve Çözüm Önerileri* (İstanbul: İstanbul Barosu Yayınları, 2007), 24; Ünlü, "Cinsiyet Ayrımcılığı," 250; Kübra Doğan Yenisey, "İşyerinde Psikolojik Taciz (Mobbing), Cinsel Taciz, Eşitlik İlkesi ve Ayrım Yasağı," *Çalışma ve Toplum* 4 (2006): 65.

239. See Onaran Yüksel, *Kadın-Erkek Eşitliği*, 83; Süzek, *İş Hukuku*, 400; Süzek, "Eşit Davranma," 26; Yıldız, *Eşit İşlem*, 65.

240. In this regard, Art. 10(1) TC will apply in conjunction with Art. 20 of the Statute of Obligations. See Onaran Yüksel, *Kadın-Erkek Eşitliği*, 84.

241. See Süzek, "Eşit Davranma," 25; Yıldız, *Eşit İşlem*, 63.

242. See Decision of 9th Civil Chamber of the Court of Appeals, RN: 2009/25544, DN: 2009/20096, DD: July 7, 2009.

243. Similarly see Yıldız, *Eşit İşlem*, 151.

244. Art. 26 ICCPR.

245. Art. E (Part V) RESC.

246. Art. 1, 25 ICRMW.

247. See İştar Cengiz (Urhanoğlu), "Türk Hukukunda Yabancıların İş Sözleşmesi Ehliyeti," *Çalışma ve Toplum* 4 (2008): 191.

248. According to Turkish Statutes a person who does not hold Turkish nationality is a foreigner. See Art. 3(1/ç, d) of the Turkish Citizenship Statute No 5901 and Art. 3 SWPF.

249. Art. 2 TLS. In addition to this, according to Art. 48(1) TC, "everyone has the freedom to work and conclude contracts in the field of his/her choice." In this regard see Mustafa Cin, "Yabancıların Kendilerine Yasak İşlerde veya Çalışma İzni Almadan Çalışmasının İş Sözleşmesine Etkisi," *Kamu-İş İş Hukuku ve İktisat Dergisi* 8 (2005): 24; Hakan Keser, "Yabancıların Çalışma İzinleri Hakkında Kanun Tasarısı Işığında Türkiye'de Yabancıların Çalışma Hakkı ve Yabancı Kaçak İşçilik," *Kamu-İş İş Hukuku ve İktisat Dergisi* 7 (2003): 327; Cengiz (Urhanoğlu), "İş Sözleşmesi Ehliyeti," 191.

250. See Cin, "Yabancılar," 24; Bülent Çiçekli, *Yabancıların Çalışma İzinleri* (Ankara: Türkiye İşveren Sendikaları Konfederasyonu, 2004), 36, 43; Bülent Çiçekli, *Yabancılar Hukuku* (Ankara: Seçkin Yayıncılık, 2007), 118; Ömer Ekmekçi, "Genel Hatlarıyla 4817 Sayılı Yabancıların Çalışma İzinleri Hakkında Kanun," *Mercek* 8 (2003): 30–31; Süzek, *İş Hukuku*, 275; Gülören Tekinalp, *Türk Yabancılar Hukuku* (8. Bası, İstanbul: Vedat Kitapçılık, 2003), 121; This is in accordance with the Art. 16 TC, where it is settled that "the fundamental rights and freedoms of aliens may be restricted by law in a manner consistent with international law." See also Cin, "Yabancılar," 24; Cengiz (Urhanoğlu), "İş Sözleşmesi Ehliyeti," 191.

251. Art. 12(1) SWPF.

252. See Levent Akın, "Die Arbeitserlaubnis für Ausländer in der Türkei," *Zeitschrift für Ausländisches und Internationales Arbeits und Sozialrecht* 4 (2006): 332–40.

253. Art. 2 and 8(e) SWPF.

254. See Tuncay, "Eşit Davranma İlkesi," 24; Yıldız, *Eşit İşlem*, 150–1. In this regard, Art. 25(1) ICRMW may also be relevant when interpreting the term 'employment relationship.'

255. Art. 2 of the Statute concerning Pharmacist and Pharmacies and Art. 3 of the Statute on Lawyers.

256. See Cengiz (Urhanoğlu), "İş Sözleşmesi Ehliyeti," 192; Keser, "Yabancılar," 327.

257. See Süzek, *İş Hukuku*, 400; Süzek, "Eşit Davranma," 26; Yıldız, *Eşit İşlem*, 65.

258. This has been explicitly acknowledged with regard to discrimination on the grounds of sex in Art. 5(3) TLS; however, this should not be seen as limiting indirect discrimination only to the grounds of sex; on the contrary this has to be perceived as a sign that both direct and indirect discrimination are prohibited regarding all such grounds, because the prohibition of discrimination on all grounds is of absolute nature.

259. Art. 5(7) TLS. (*Emphasis* added.) See Hakan Keser, "4857 Sayılı İK'na Göre İşverenin İş Sözleşmesi Yapma ve İş İlişkilerinde Eşit İşlem Yapma Yükümlülükleri ve Bunlara Aykırı Davranması Durumunda Karşılaşacağı Yaptırımlar," *Kamu-İş İş Hukuku ve İktisat Dergisi* 7 (2004): 70; Süzek, *İş Hukuku*, 418. This is in accordance with various European legal systems, where attempts have been made to preserve the vitality of non-discrimination by introducing specific rules relating to evidence and proof. See Bell, "Direct Discrimination," 185.

260. Court of Appeals, RN: 2009/25544, (note 242). See also Decision of 9th Civil Chamber of the Court of Appeals, RN: 2008/27310, DN: 2008/ 22095, DD: July 25, 2008; Decision of 9th Civil Chamber of the Court of Appeals, RN: 2008/27309, DN: 2008/22094, DD: July 25, 2008. Compare with the case mentioned in note 221.

261. This is in line with the decisions of the (*quasi*-)judicial organs established by international agreements which relate to fundamental rights and freedoms. See *Althammer*, (note 215), pt. 10.2; *Thlimmenos*, (note 220), para. 44.

262. See Bell, "Direct Discrimination," 185; Ünlü, "Cinsiyet Ayrımcılığı," 251–2; Yıldız, *Eşit İşlem*, 73.

263. P.J.G. Kapteyn *et al.*, *The Law of the European Union and the European Communities* (4th Edition, The Netherlands: Kluwer Law International, 2008), 160. Similarly and specifically with regard to Art. 5 TLS see Ünlü, "Cinsiyet Ayrımcılığı," 252; Yıldız, *Eşit İşlem*, 75.

264. See Onaran Yüksel, *Kadın-Erkek Eşitliği*, 354–355.

265. See Court of Appeals, RN: 2009/25544, (note 242). These criteria are in line with case-law of ECtHR, since the Court also holds that "the principle of equality of treatment is violated if the distinction has no objective and reasonable justification." *Thlimmenos*, (note 220), para. 44. For indirect discrimination see also Manuela Tomei, "Discrimination and Equality at Work: A Review of the Concepts," *International labor Review* 142 (2003): 402; Ünlü, "Cinsiyet Ayrımcılığı," 252; Yıldız, *Eşit İşlem*, 75.

266. This is in analogy with the restrictions on access to certain professions. In that regard see Cengiz (Urhanoğlu), "İş Sözleşmesi Ehliyeti," 192; Keser, "Yabancılar," 327.

267. This would align the justification of discriminatory measures with the case-law of ECtHR. See *Chassagnou and Others*, (note 216), para. 91.

268. As mentioned above, the same effect occurs with the concurrent application of Art. 10(1) TC and Art. 20 of the Statute of Obligations. See note 240.

269. Court of Appeals, RN: 2009/25544, (note 242).

270. See Court of Appeals, RN: 2009/25544, (note 242).

271. See Baysal, "Eşit Davranma Borcu," 75; Süzek, *İş Hukuku*, 414; Süzek, "Eşit Davranma," 34; Tuncay, "Eşit Davranma İlkesi," 36; Yıldız, *Eşit İşlem*, 204.

272. See Decision of 9th Civil Chamber of the Court of Appeals, RN: 2006/28933, DN: 2007/26947, DD: September 18, 2007. See also Baysal, "Eşit Davranma Borcu," 76; Onaran Yüksel, *Kadın-Erkek Eşitliği*, 354; Kübra Doğan Yenisey, "Eşit Davranma İlkesinin Uygulanmasında Metodoloji ve Orantılılık İlkesi," *Legal İş Hukuku ve Sosyal Güvenlik Hukuku Dergisi* 7 (2005): 984; Yıldız, *Eşit İşlem*, 320, 329.

273. See Tuncay, "Eşit Davranma İlkesi," 36.

274. See Keser, "Eşit İşlem," 69; Süzek, *İş Hukuku*, 413.

275. Respectively see Art. 24(2/e, f) TLS. See also Baysal, "Eşit Davranma Borcu," 74–75; Onaran Yüksel, *Kadın-Erkek Eşitliği*, 351–2; Süzek, "Eşit Davranma," 34; Tuncay, "Eşit Davranma İlkesi," 37; Yenisey, "İşyeri," 76.

276. Art. 22 TLS.

277. In this regard, according to the Art. 60(1) TC, "everyone has the right to social security"; hence, there is not any distinction between nationals and foreigners, such as between Turkish and Union workers.

278. See Art. 10 TC; Art. 3 of the Equality of Treatment (Social Security) Convention (C118) (note 203); Art. 68 of the Social Security (Minimum Standards) Convention (C102) (note 203); Art. 27(1) ICRMW.

279. Art. 4, 60 SIUHIS.

280. Unemployment Insurance Statute No 4447.

281. Art. 4(2/c) SIUHIS. See also Can Tuncay and Ömer Ekmekçi, *Yeni Mevzuat Açısından Sosyal Güvenlik Hukukunun Esasları* (2. Bası, İstanbul: Legal Yayınevi, 2009), 218. Ali Güzel *et al.*, *Sosyal Güvenlik Hukuku* (13. Bası, İstanbul: Beta Basım Yayın, 2010), 107.

282. Art. 60(1/d) SIUHIS. Nonetheless, foreign workers who are residing in Turkey for a period of less than one year are not in the scope of application of universal health insurance. Art. 60(3) SIUHIS.

283. In this regard, it should be stated that equality of treatment is one of the principles underpinning such bilateral and multilateral agreements. Dupper, "Migrant Workers," 235, 236. For example see Art. 3 of the Equality of Treatment (Social Security) Convention (C118) (note 203).

284. Resul Aslanköylü, *Sosyal Sigortalar ve Genel Sağlık Sigortası Kanunu Şerhi (SSK. İle karşılaştırmalı)* (Ankara: Yetkin Yayınevi, 2009), 285; Güzel *et al.*, *Sosyal Güvenlik Hukuku*, 107. However, there is another exception: A foreign worker, who is posted by a firm established in a foreign country and documents that he/she is subject to social security in that country, is not covered by this arrangement. Art. 6(1/e) SIUHIS.

285. Negotiating Framework, October 3, 2005, pt. 12.

286. See Sergio Carrera, "What Does Free Movement Mean in Theory and Practice in an Enlarged EU?," *European Law Journal* 11 (2005): 708; Christophe Hillion, "Negotiating Turkey's Membership to the European Union: Can the Member States Do as They Please?," *European Constitutional Law Review* 3 (2007): 269–84; Neill Nugent, "The EU's Response to Turkey's Membership Application: Not Just a Weighing of Costs and Benefits," *Journal of European Integration* 29 (2007): 495.

287. Art. 2 TEU; Art. 8 TFEU; Art. 10 TC.

288. European Commission (SEC (2005) 1426), Turkey Progress Report, Brussels, November 9, 2005, p. 59.

REFERENCES

Akın, Levent. "Die Arbeitserlaubnis für Ausländer in der Türkei." *Zeitschrift für Ausländisches und Internationales Arbeits und Sozialrecht* 4 (2006): 332–40.

Akipek, Serap. "Türk Mevzuatının Onaylanan Uluslararası Antlaşmalar ile Uyumlaştırılması Sorunu." *Ankara Üniversitesi Hukuk Fakültesi Dergisi* 48 (1999): 15–22.

Arat, Tuğrul. "Avrupa Birliği ile Türkiye Arasındaki İlişkiler ve Gümrük Birliğinin Yeri." *Ankara Üniversitesi Hukuk Fakültesi Dergisi* 44 (1995): 587–606.

Armağan, Servet. "1982 Anayasası'nda Uluslararası Andlaşmaların İmzalanması ve Onaylanması Sistemi." *Anayasa Yargısı* 17 (2000): 340–61.

Aslanköylü, Resul. *Sosyal Sigortalar ve Genel Sağlık Sigortası Kanunu Şerhi (SSK. İle karşılaştırmalı)*. Ankara: Yetkin Yayınevi, 2009.

Barnard, Catherine. *The Substantive Law of the EU: The Four Freedoms*. 3rd Edition. Great Britain: Oxford University Press, 2010.

Barrett, Gavin. "Re-examining the Concept and Principle of Equality in EC Law." *Yearbook of European Law* 22 (2003): 117–53.

Başlar, Kemal, and İshakoğlu, Erdoğan. "Turkey." In *The Impact of EU Accession on the Legal Orders of New EU Member States and (Pre-) Candidate Countries: Hopes and Fears*, edited by Alfred E. Kellermann *et. al.*, 195–238. Cambridge: Cambridge University Press, 2006.

Başterzi, Süleyman. "Uluslararası Sözleşmeler ve İç Hukuk Kuralları Çerçevesinde Kamu Görevlilerinin Toplu Pazarlık ve Toplu Sözleşme Sorunu." *Tisk Akademi* 1 (2006): 15–49.

Baysal, Ulaş. "İşverenin Eşit Davranma Borcu ve İş Sözleşmesinin Feshinde Uygulanması." *Legal İş Hukuku ve Sosyal Güvenlik Hukuku Dergisi* 25 (2010): 59–99.

Bell, Mark. "Direct Discrimination." In *Cases, Materials and Text on National, Supranational and International Non-discrimination Law*, edited by Dagmar Schiek *et al.*, 185–322. Portland: Hart Publishing, 2007.

Boelaert-Suominen, Sonja. "Non-EU Nationals and Council Directive 2003/109/EC on the Status of Third Country Nationals Who Are Long-Term Residents: Five Paces Forward and Possibly Three Paces Back." *Common Market Law Review* 42 (2005): 1011–52.

Boeles, Pieter et al. *European Migration Law*. Antwerp: Intersentia, 2009.

Can, Hacı. *Türkiye–Avrupa Topluluğu Ortaklık Hukukunda Kişilerin Serbest Dolaşımı*. Ankara: Türkiye Odalar ve Borsalar Birliği, 2006.

———. "Türkiye–Avrupa Topluluğu Ortaklık İlişkisinin Hukuki Çerçevesi." *Ankara Avrupa Çalışmaları Dergisi* 3 (2003): 19–43.

Can, Hacı, and Özen, Çınar. *Türkiye–Avrupa Topluluğu Ortaklık Hukuku*. Ankara: Gazi Kitabevi, 2005.

Carrera, Sergio. "What Does Free Movement Mean in Theory and Practice in an Enlarged EU?" *European Law Journal* 11 (2005): 699–721.

Cengiz (Urhanoğlu), İştar. "Türk Hukukunda Yabancıların İş Sözleşmesi Ehliyeti." *Çalışma ve Toplum* 4 (2008): 187–211.

Çiçekli, Bülent. "Uluslararası Hukukta Yabancıların Hak ve Özgürlükleri." *Uluslararası Hukuk ve Politika* 3 (2007): 1–14.

———. *Yabancılar Hukuku*. Ankara: Seçkin Yayıncılık, 2007.

———. *Yabancıların Çalışma İzinleri*. Ankara: Türkiye İşveren Sendikaları Konfederasyonu, 2004.

———. "The Rights of Turkish Migrants in Europe under International Law and EU Law." *International Migration Review* 33 (1999): 300–53.

Cin, Mustafa. "Yabancıların Kendilerine Yasak İşlerde veya Çalışma İzni Almadan Çalışmasının İş Sözleşmesine Etkisi." *Kamu-İş İş Hukuku ve İktisat Dergisi* 8 (2005): 23–45.

Cremona, Marise. "Movement of Persons, Establishment and Services." In *Enlarging the European Union: Relations between the EU and Central and Eastern Europe*, edited by Marc Maresceau, 195–208. United States of America: Longman, 1997.

Dubey, Jean-Philippe. "C-438/00, *Deutscher Handballbund eV v. Maros Kolpak*, judgment of the Court of Justice (First Chamber) of May 8, 2003, [2003] ECR I-4135." *Common Market Law Review* 42 (2005): 499–522.

Dupper, Ockert. "Migrant Workers and the Right to Social Security: An International Perspective." *Stellenbosch Law Review* 18 (2007): 217–54.

Ehlers, Dirk. "General Principles." In *European Fundamental Rights and Freedoms*, edited by Dirk Ehlers, 175–225. Germany: De Gruyter, 2007.

Ekmekçi, Ömer. "Genel Hatlarıyla 4817 Sayılı Yabancıların Çalışma İzinleri Hakkında Kanun." *Mercek* 8 (2003): 29–35.

Epiney, Astrid. "The Scope of Article 12 EC: Some Remarks on the Influence of European Citizenship." *European Law Journal* 13 (2007): 611–22.

Gönenç, Levent, and Esen, Selin. "The Problem of the Application of Less Protective International Agreements in Domestic Legal Systems: Article 90 of the Turkish Constitution." *European Journal of Law Reform* VIII (2007): 485–500.

Groenendijk, Kees. "Legal Concepts of Integration in EU Migration Law." *European Journal of Migration and Law* 6 (2004): 111–26.

———. "The Long-Term Residents Directive, Denizenship and Integration." In *Whose Freedom, Security and Justice?*, edited by Anneliese Baldaccini *et al.*, 429–50. Portland: Hart Publishing, 2007.

Groenendijk, Kees et al. *The Legal Status of Third Country Nationals Who Are Long-Term Residents in a Member State of the European Union*. Strasbourg: Council of Europe, 2000.

Guild, Elspeth. *Immigration Law in the European Community*. The Netherlands: Kluwer Law International, 2001.

Güzel, Ali et al.. *Sosyal Güvenlik Hukuku*. 13. Bası, İstanbul: Beta Basım Yayın, 2010.

Hailbronner, Kail. *Immigration and Asylum Law and Policy of the European Union*. The Netherlands: Kluwer Law International, 2000.

Halleskov, Louise. "The Long-Term Residence Directive: A fulfillment of the Tampere Objective of Near Equality?" *European Journal of Migration and Law* 7 (2005): 181–201.

Hedemann-Robinson, Martin. "An Overview of Recent Legal Developments at Community Level in Relation to Third Country Nationals Within the EU." *Common Market Law Review* 38 (2001): 525–86.

Hillion, Christophe. "Negotiating Turkey's Membership to the European Union: Can the Member States Do as They Please?" *European Constitutional Law Review* 3 (2007): 269–84.

Husmann, Manfred. "Arbeitnehmerfreizügigkeitsregeln in Assoziationsabkommen der EG." *Zeitschrift für Ausländerrecht und Ausländerpolitik* 9 (2009): 305–14.

Iglesias Sánchez, Sara. "Free Movement of Third Country Nationals in the European Union? Main Features, Deficiencies and Challenges of the New Mobility Rights in the Area of Freedom, Security and Justice." *European Law Journal* 15 (2009): 791–805.

İnceoğlu, Sibel. "Türk Anayasa Mahkemesi ve İnsan Hakları Avrupa Mahkemesi Kararlarında Eşitlik ve Ayrımcılık Yasağı." *Çalışma ve Toplum* 4 (2006): 45–61.

Kapteyn, P.J.G. et al. *The Law of the European Union and the European Communities*. 4th Edition, the Netherlands: Kluwer Law International, 2008.

Kellermann, Alfred E. "The Rights of Non-Member State Nationals under the EU Association Agreements." *European Journal of Law Reform* X (2008): 339–82.

Keser, Hakan. "4857 Sayılı İK'na Göre İşverenin İş Sözleşmesi Yapma ve İş İlişkilerinde Eşit İşlem Yapma Yükümlülükleri ve Bunlara Aykırı Davranması Durumunda Karşılaşacağı Yaptırımlar." *Kamu-İş İş Hukuku ve İktisat Dergisi* 7 (2004): 37–73.

———. "Yabancıların Çalışma İzinleri Hakkında Kanun Tasarısı Işığında Türkiye'de Yabancıların Çalışma Hakkı ve Yabancı Kaçak İşçilik." *Kamu-İş İş Hukuku ve İktisat Dergisi* 7 (2003): 323–69.

Köktaş, Arif. *Avrupa Birliğinde İşçilerin Serbest Dolaşım Hakkı ve Türk Vatandaşlarının Durumu*. Ankara: Nobel, 1999.

Nugent, Neill. "The EU's Response to Turkey's Membership Application: Not Just a Weighing of Costs and Benefits." *Journal of European Integration* 29 (2007): 481–502.

Onaran Yüksel, Melek. *Karşılaştırmalı Hukuk Işığında Türk İş Hukukunda Kadın-Erkek Eşitliği*. İstanbul: Beta, 2000.

Pazarcı, Hüseyin. *Uluslararası Hukuk*. 9. Bası, Ankara: Turhan Kitabevi, 2010.

Peers, Steve. "Social Security Equality for Turkish Nationals." *European Law Review* 24 (1999): 627–37.

———. "Towards Equality: Actual and Potential Rights of Third-country Nationals in the European Union." *Common Market Law Review* 33 (1996): 7–50.
Prechal, Sacha. "Equality of Treatment, Non-Discrimination and Social Policy: Achievements in Three Themes." *Common Market Law Review* 41 (2004): 533–51.
Reich, Norbert. "The Constitutional Relevance of Citizenship and Free Movement in an Enlarged Union." *European Law Journal* 11 (2005): 675–98.
Rogers, Nicola. "Comments on *Nour Eddline El-Yassini v. Secretary of State for the Home Department*, March 2, 1999 (Case C-416/96)." *European Journal of Migration and Law* 1 (1999): 365–70.
Rogers, Nicola, and Scannel, Rick. *Free Movement of Persons in the Enlarged European Union*. London: Sweet & Maxwell, 2005.
Ryan, Bernard. "The European Union and labor Migration: Regulating Admission or Treatment?" In *Whose Freedom, Security and Justice?*, edited by Anneliese Baldaccini *et al.*, 489–515. Portland: Hart Publishing, 2007.
Schiek, Dagmar *et al.* "A Comparative Perspective on Non-Discrimination Law." In *Cases, Materials and Text on National, Supranational and International Non-discrimination Law*, edited by Dagmar Schiek *et al.*, 1–32. Portland: Hart Publishing, 2007.
Sivakumaran, Sandesh. "The Rights of Migrant Workers One Year on: Transformation or Consolidation." *Georgetown Journal of International Law* 36 (2004-2005): 113–54.
Skordas, Achilles. "Immigration and Market: The Long-Term Residents Directive." *Columbia Journal of European Law* 13 (2007): 201–29.
Sur, Melda. "Sosyal Haklara İlişkin Andlaşmaların İç Hukukta Yeri." In *Prof. Dr. Devrim Ulucan'a Armağan*, 47–62. İstanbul: Legal Yayıncılık, 2008.
Süzek, Sarper. "İşverenin Eşit Davranma Borcu." *Sicil* 3 (2008): 24–38.
———. *İş Hukuku*. 4. Bası, İstanbul: Beta, 2008.
Tekinalp, Gülören. *Türk Yabancılar Hukuku*. 8. Bası, İstanbul: Vedat Kitapçılık, 2003.
Tezcan/Idriz, Narin. "Free Movement of Persons between Turkey and the EU: To Move or Not to Move–The Response of the Judiciary." *Common Market Law Review* 46 (2009): 1621–66.
Tomei, Manuela. "Discrimination and Equality at Work: A Review of the Concepts." *International labor Review* 142 (2003): 401–18.
Tuncay, Can, "İş Hukukunda Eşit Davranma İlkesi." In *İş ve Sosyal Güvenlik Hukuku Sorunlar ve Çözüm Önerileri*, 21–38. İstanbul: İstanbul Barosu Yayınları, 2007.
Tuncay, Can, and Ekmekçi, Ömer. *Yeni Mevzuat Açısından Sosyal Güvenlik Hukukunun Esasları*. 2. Bası, İstanbul: Legal Yayınevi, 2009.
Türmen, Rıza. "Avrupa İnsan Hakları Sözlesmesi'nin İç Hukukumuza Etkileri." *Anayasa Yargısı* 17 (2000): 32–42.
Ünlü, Vahap. "İşe Alımda Cinsiyet Ayrımcılığı." *Sicil* 5 (2010): 247–55.
Van Der Mei, Pieter A.. *Free Movement of Persons within the European Community: Cross-Border Access to Public Benefits*. Great Britain: Hart Publishing, 2003.
Veneziani, Bruno, "Non-discrimination (Article 21)." In *European labor Law and the EU Charter of Fundamental Rights*, edited by Brian Bercusson, 193–216. Baden-Baden: Nomos, 2006.
Verschueren, Herwig. "The *Sürül* Judgment: Equal Treatment for Turkish Workers in Matters of Social Security." *European Journal of Migration and Law* 1 (1999): 371–84.
Vigneau, Christophe. "Freedom to Choose an Occupation and Right to Engage in Work (Article 15)." In *European labor Law and the EU Charter of Fundamental Rights*, edited by Brian Bercusson, 171–92. Baden-Baden: Nomos, 2006.
Weiss, Friedl, and Wooldridge, Frank. *Free Movement of Persons Within the European Community*. 2nd Edition. The Netherlands: Kluwer Law International, 2007.
Yenisey, Kübra Doğan. "Eşit Davranma İlkesinin Uygulanmasında Metodoloji ve Orantılılık İlkesi." *Legal İş Hukuku ve Sosyal Güvenlik Hukuku Dergisi* 7 (2005): 973–1003.
———"İşyerinde Psikolojik Taciz (Mobbing), Cinsel Taciz, Eşitlik İlkesi ve Ayrım Yasağı." *Çalışma ve Toplum* 4 (2006): 63–81.
Yıldız, Gaye Burcu. *İşverenin Eşit İşlem Yapma Borcu*. Ankara: Yetkin Basımevi, 2008.

Conclusion

When the relations of Turkey and the EU are considered there are certain important milestones. The first one is the Ankara Agreement in 1963. The second one is that Turkey applied for membership in 1987, but in 1989 the Commission refused to proceed with the application due to economic and political problems including human rights. Following certain ups and downs in the relations the European Council decided to begin accession negotiations with Turkey in 2004 and the negotiations started on 3 October 2005. The negotiation process is still going on with some suspensions or opening of new chapters.

During the course of this relation Turkey initiated many reforms in order to meet the Copenhagen criteria. Most of these reforms have been realized in the legal field, including many important amendments in the Turkish Constitution, major Codes such as the Criminal Code, the Civil Code, and very recently the Code of Obligations and the Commercial Code. Also there have been many new laws on certain specific fields of law such as consumer protection and competition. The only reason of the amendments and the new laws is not only the relations with the EU, but it played one of the major roles together with some other igniting factors.

Especially the period of 1999-2004 can easily be considered as a very important period and as stated by some authors those days were the honeymoon days between Turkey and the EU. But unfortunately after the negotiation process started this momentum lost its speed. Now both sides need a new wave of optimism.

When the legal dimension of these relations is examined, this could be a new wave that may bring optimism. Since from the legal aspects Turkey is very close to being a member, that point should be shown to both sides, so that a new spark will emerge and help the relations blossom again.

With this book and the collection of articles we tried to clarify the legal situation in Turkey and to create public awareness to the relations between both sides. We hope that this awareness will work as a tool to deepen and develop the relations and help the negotiation process to go further.

Index

About the Contributors

Belgin Akçay is a professor in the Faculty of Law and Faculty of Political Sciences at Ankara University. In addition to her academic experience, she has worked in different positions in government. She holds the Jean Monnet Chair of the EU economic integration at Ankara University. E-mail: akcay@law.ankara.edu.tr

Şebnem Akipek is a professor in the Department of Civil Law in the Law School at Ankara University. She has been working as a Chief Legal Advisor at Middle East Technical University since 2001. She is also the director of Vocational School of Justice. E-mail: sakipek@law.ankara.edu.tr

Derya Büyüktanır is a PhD candidate in the Department of European Union and International Economic Relations at Ankara University. She has been actively participating in civil society and has worked in different projects with civil society as a coordinator, trainer, or participant at national and international level for ten years. E-mail: buyuktanir@gmail.com

A. Aslı Bilgin is an assistant professor in the Department of International Relations Law School at Çukurova University. She worked as a legal advisor in some private companies from 2000 to 2003. She got the research scholarship from The Scientific and Technological Research Council of Turkey and studied with Prof. Paul Craig at Oxford University for ten months in 2009. E-mail: aabilgin@cu.edu.tr

Orhan Ersun Civan is a PhD candidate in labor and Social Security Law at Ankara University. He has been working as a research assistant in the same university since 2008. Also, he worked as a lawyer in the Serezli Law Office in 2007. E-mail: ersunc06@yahoo.com

Gamze Aşcıoğlu Öz is an assistant professor in the Department of International Relations at the Middle East Technical University, Ankara. She has also served as the Counsel to the Chairman of the Turkish Competition Authority from 1990–1992 during its foundation. E-mail: agamze@metu.edu.tr

İlke Göçmen is an assistant professor in the Department of EU Law in the Law School at Ankara University. He has been working in the Law School since 2007. He worked as a public prosecutor in the Ministry of Justice from 2005 to 2007. E-mail: igocmen@ankara.edu.tr

Lightning Source UK Ltd.
Milton Keynes UK
UKOW02n1016020616

275448UK00006B/118/P

9 780739 181744